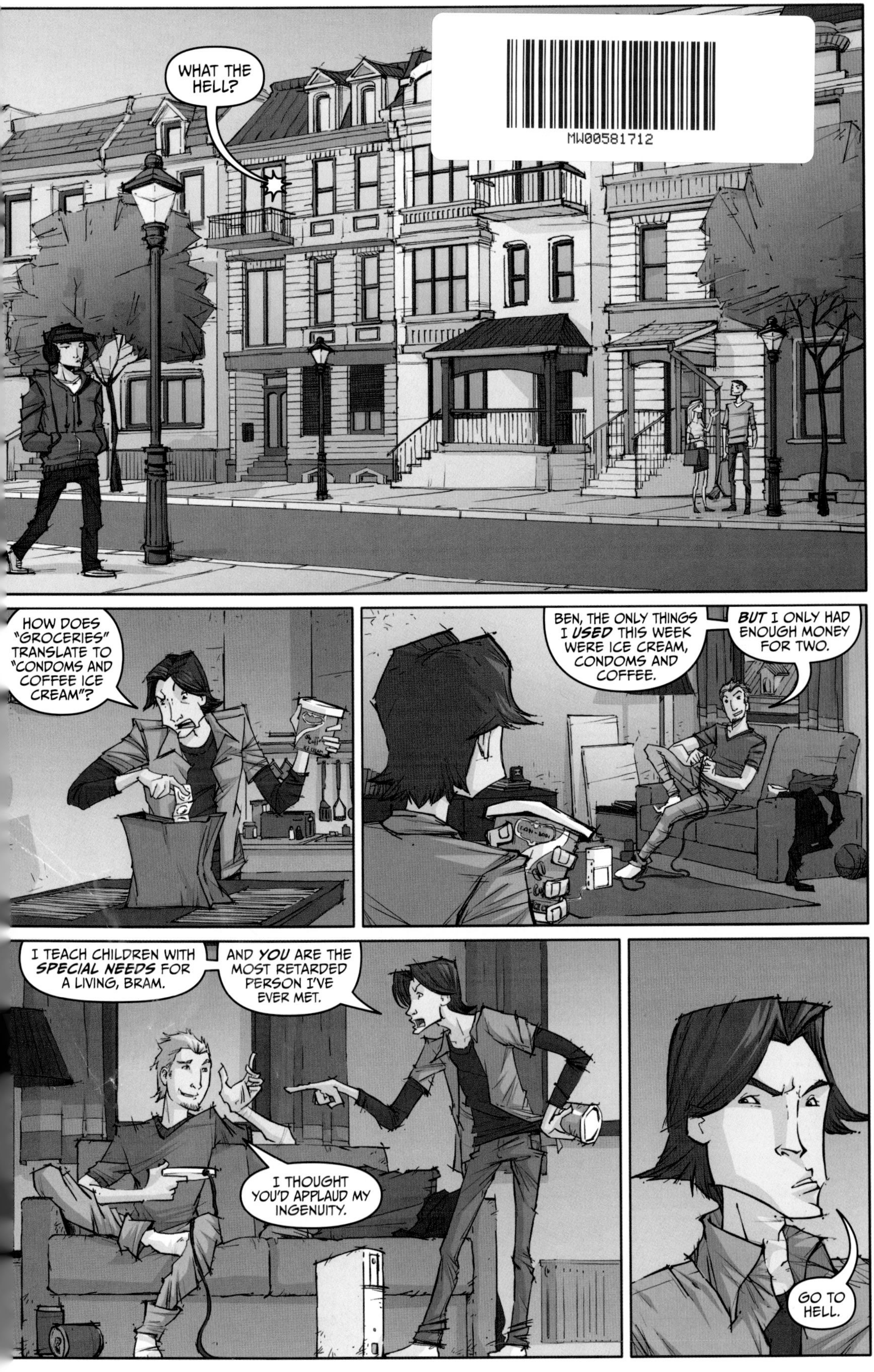
WHAT THE HELL?
HOW DOES "GROCERIES" TRANSLATE TO "CONDOMS AND COFFEE ICE CREAM"?
BEN, THE ONLY THINGS I *USED* THIS WEEK WERE ICE CREAM, CONDOMS AND COFFEE.
*BUT* I ONLY HAD ENOUGH MONEY FOR TWO.
I TEACH CHILDREN WITH *SPECIAL NEEDS* FOR A LIVING, BRAM.
AND *YOU* ARE THE MOST RETARDED PERSON I'VE EVER MET.
I THOUGHT YOU'D APPLAUD MY INGENUITY.
GO TO HELL.

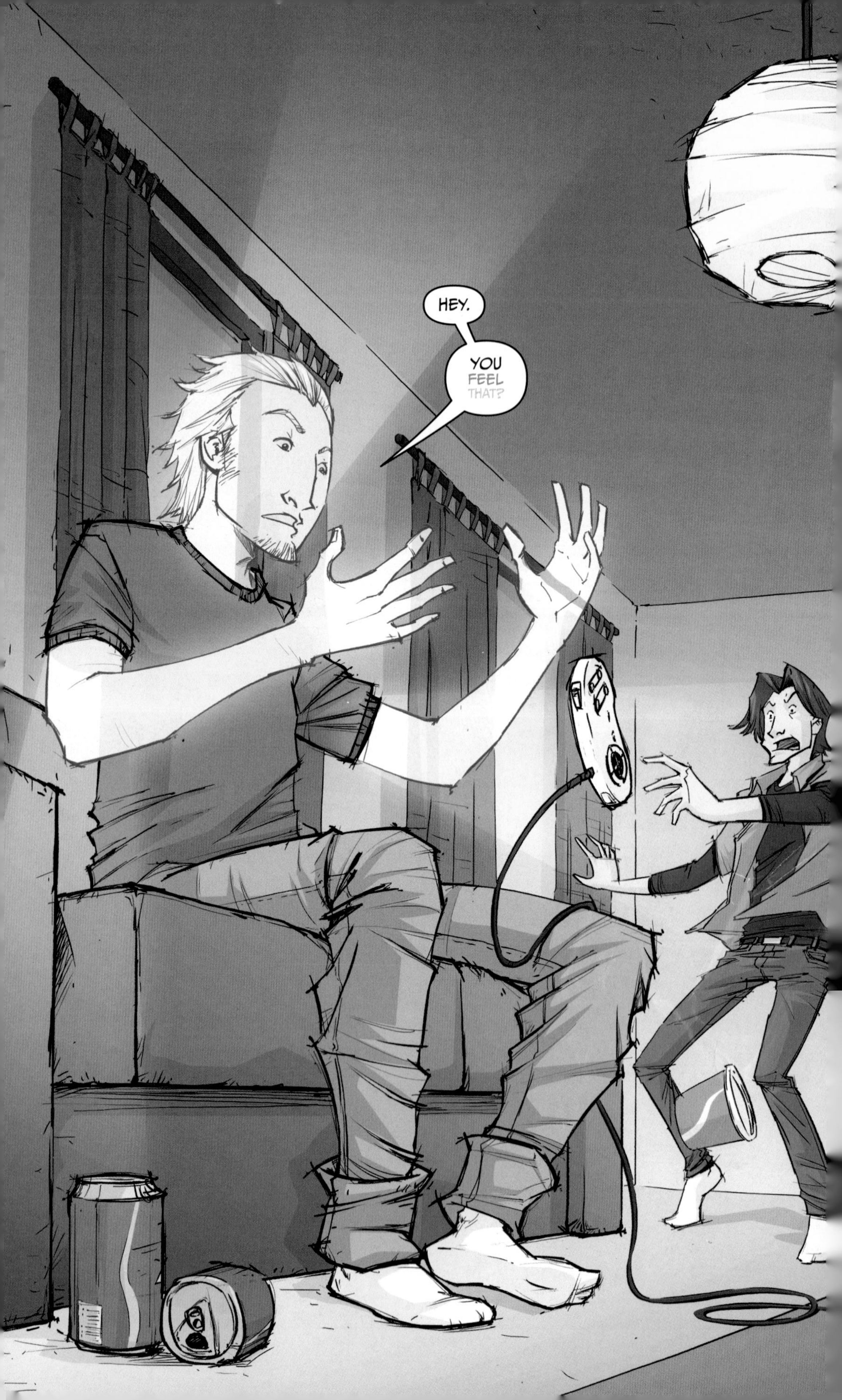
HEY.
YOU FEEL THAT?

the
# END TIMES
## of Bram and Ben

CO-CREATED & WRITTEN BY James Asmus & Jim Festante    CO-CREATED & PENCILED BY Rem Broo

COLORS BY Overdrive Studio    LETTERS BY crank!    CONSULTING EDITOR Sebastian Girner

COVERS BY Rem Broo, Jim Mahfood, J.A.W. Cooper, Juan Doe, AND Ben Templesmith

BRAM POSTER BY Rob Donnelly

IMAGE COMICS, INC.
Robert Kirkman - Chief Operating Officer
Erik Larsen - Chief Financial Officer
Todd McFarlane - President
Marc Silvestri - Chief Executive Officer
Jim Valentino - Vice-President

Eric Stephenson - Publisher
Ron Richards - Director of Business Development
Jennifer de Guzman - Director of Trade Book Sales
Kat Salazar - Director of PR & Marketing
Jeremy Sullivan - Director of Digital Sales
Emilio Bautista - Sales Assistant
Branwyn Bigglestone - Senior Accounts Manager
Emily Miller - Accounts Manager
Jessica Ambriz - Administrative Assistant
Tyler Shainline - Events Coordinator
David Brothers - Content Manager
Jonathan Chan - Production Manager
Drew Gill - Art Director
Meredith Wallace - Print Manager
Monica Garcia - Senior Production Artist
Jenna Savage - Production Artist
Addison Duke - Production Artist
IMAGECOMICS.COM

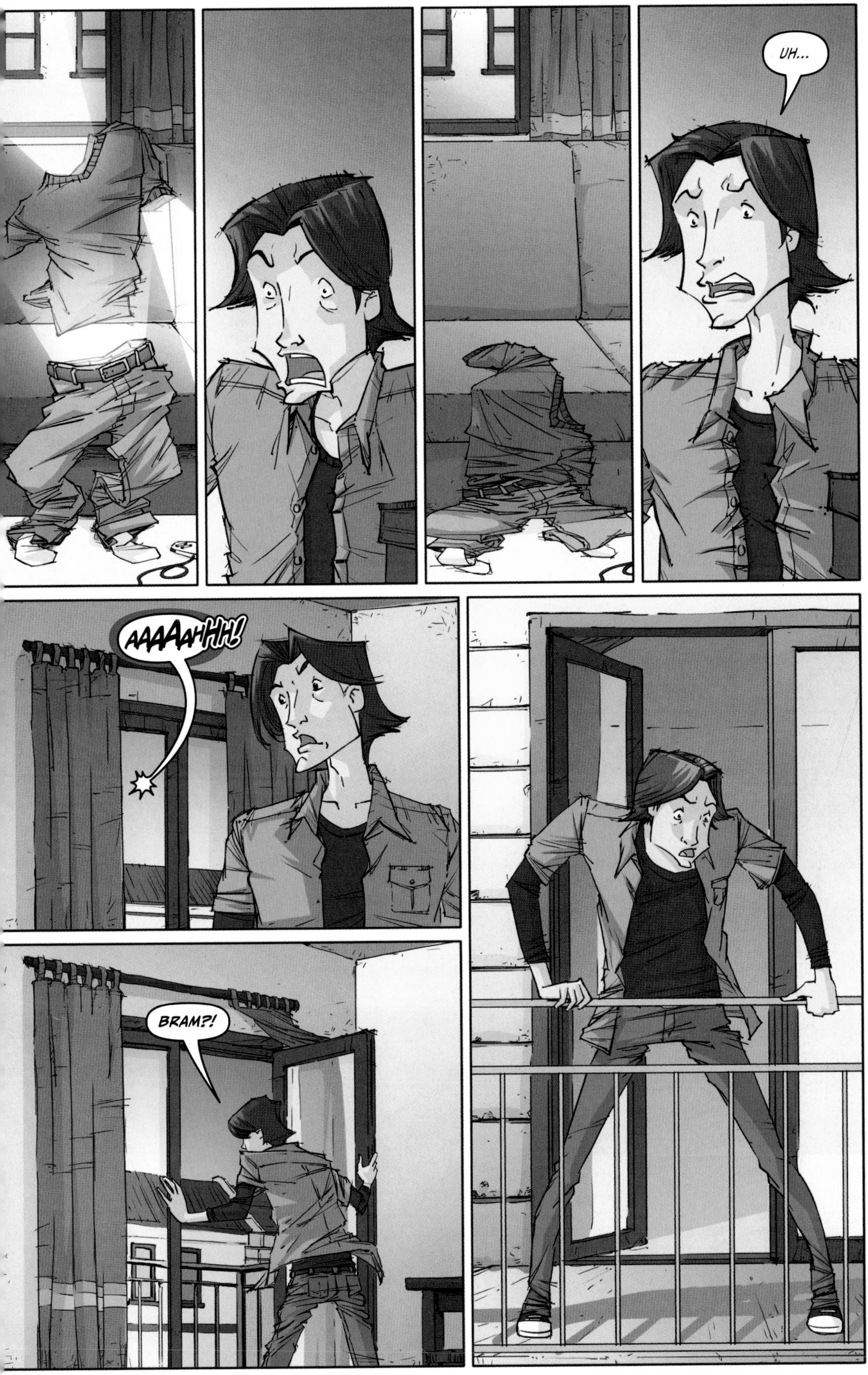
UH...
AAAAAHHH!
BRAM?!

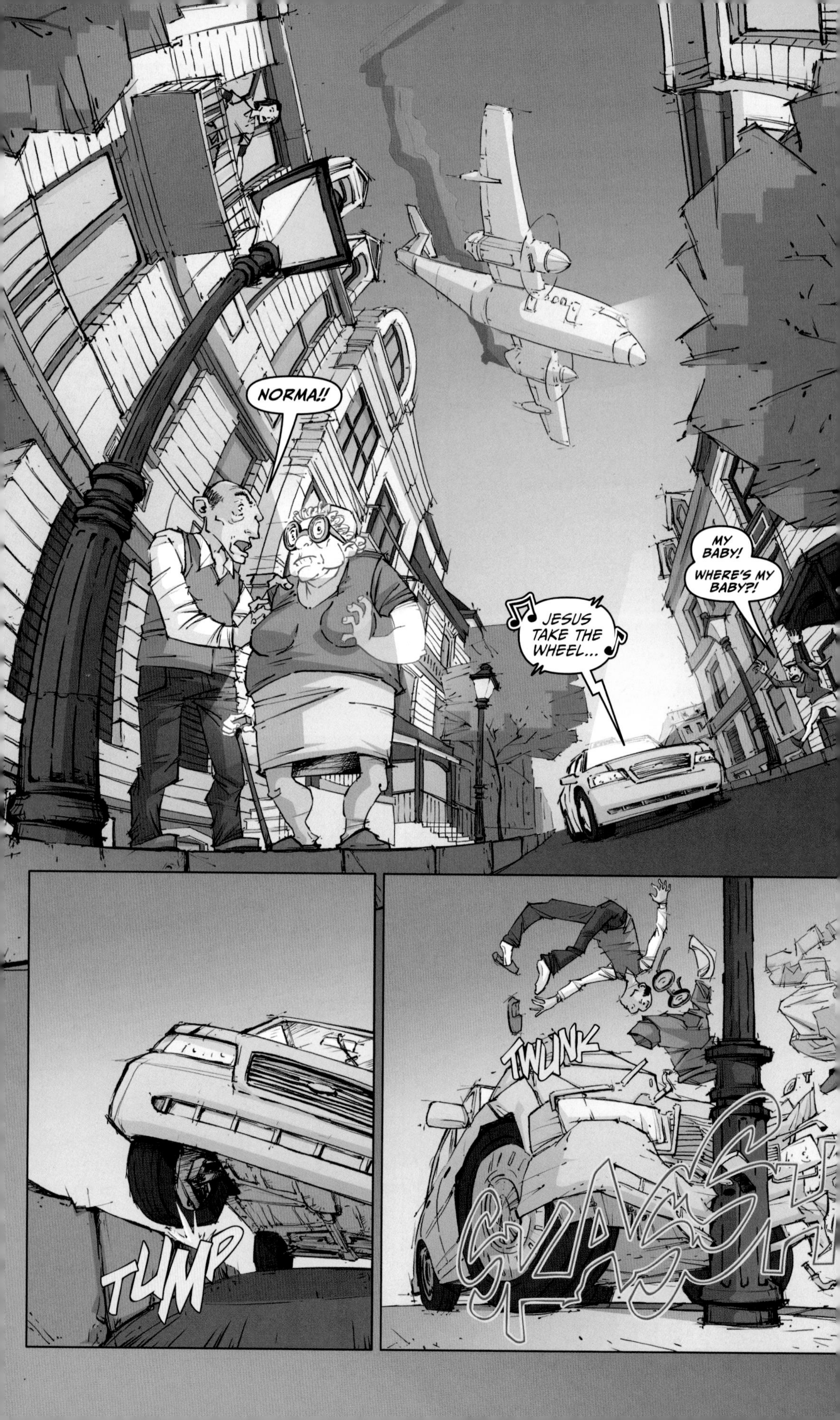
NORMA!!
JESUS TAKE THE WHEEL...
MY BABY! WHERE'S MY BABY?!
TUMP
TWUNK
CLASSH

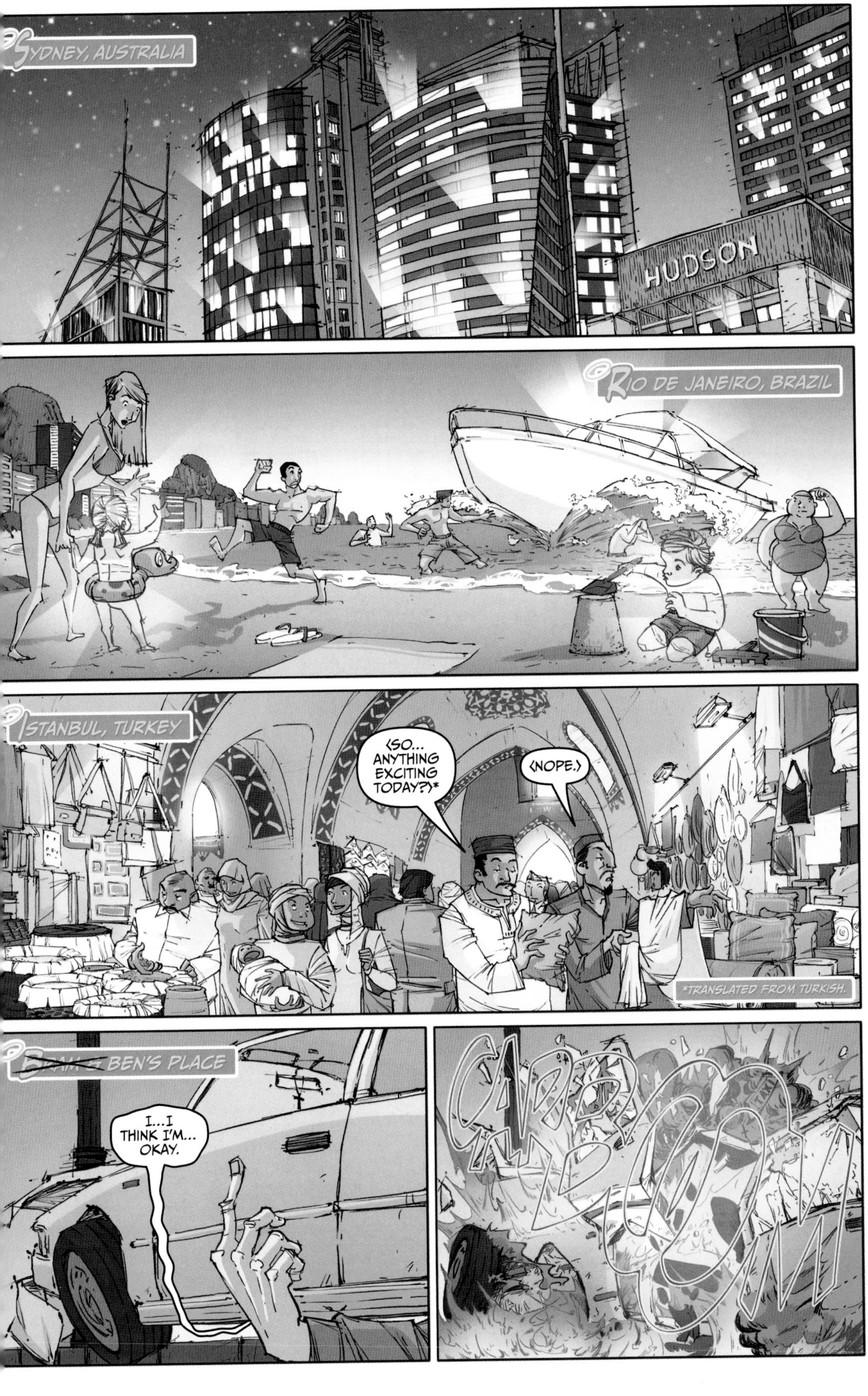
SYDNEY, AUSTRALIA
HUDSON
RIO DE JANEIRO, BRAZIL
ISTANBUL, TURKEY
‹SO... ANYTHING EXCITING TODAY?›*
‹NOPE.›
*TRANSLATED FROM TURKISH.
~~BRAM &~~ BEN'S PLACE
I... I THINK I'M... OKAY.

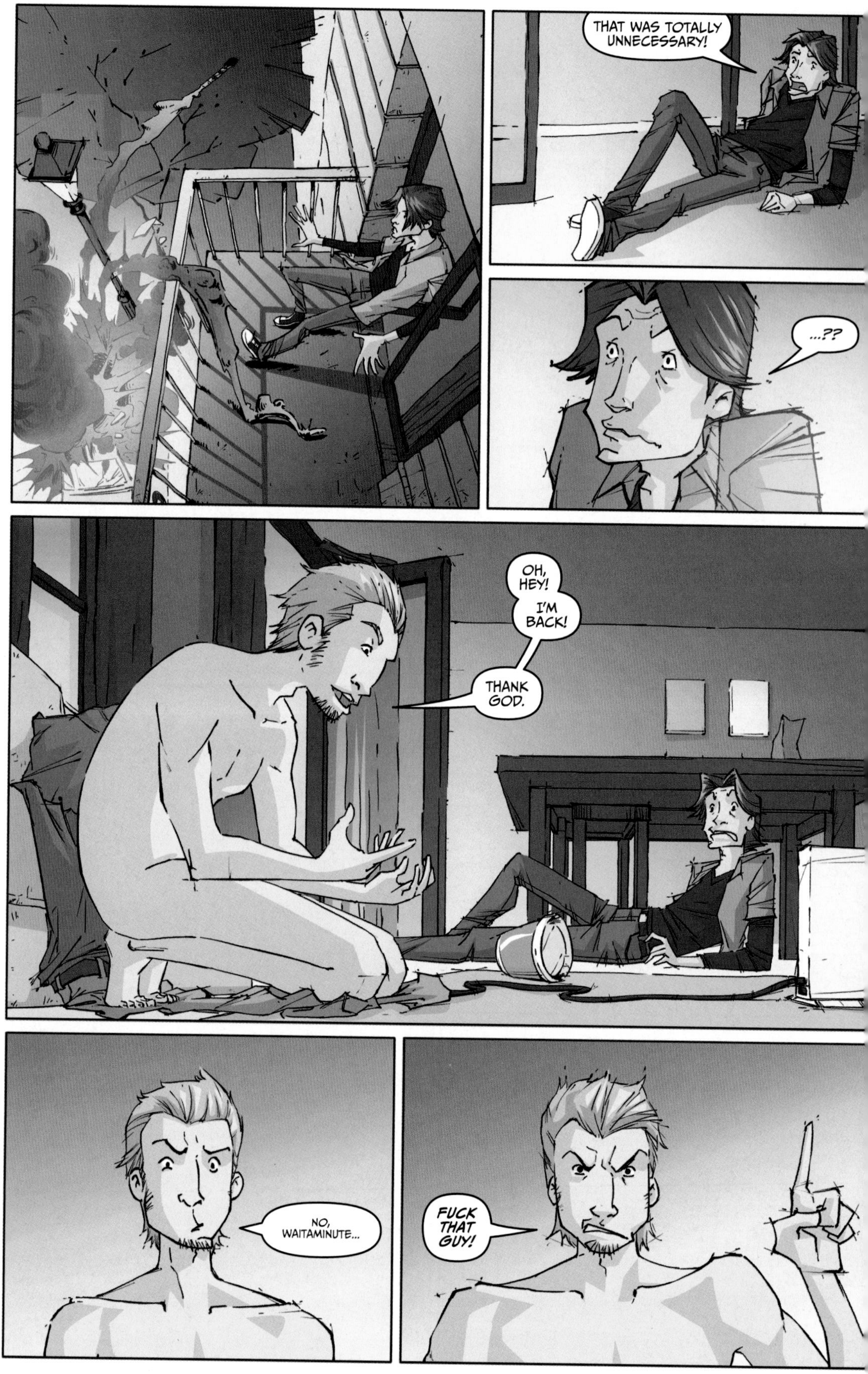
THAT WAS TOTALLY UNNECESSARY!
...??
OH, HEY!
I'M BACK!
THANK GOD.
NO, WAITAMINUTE...
FUCK THAT GUY!

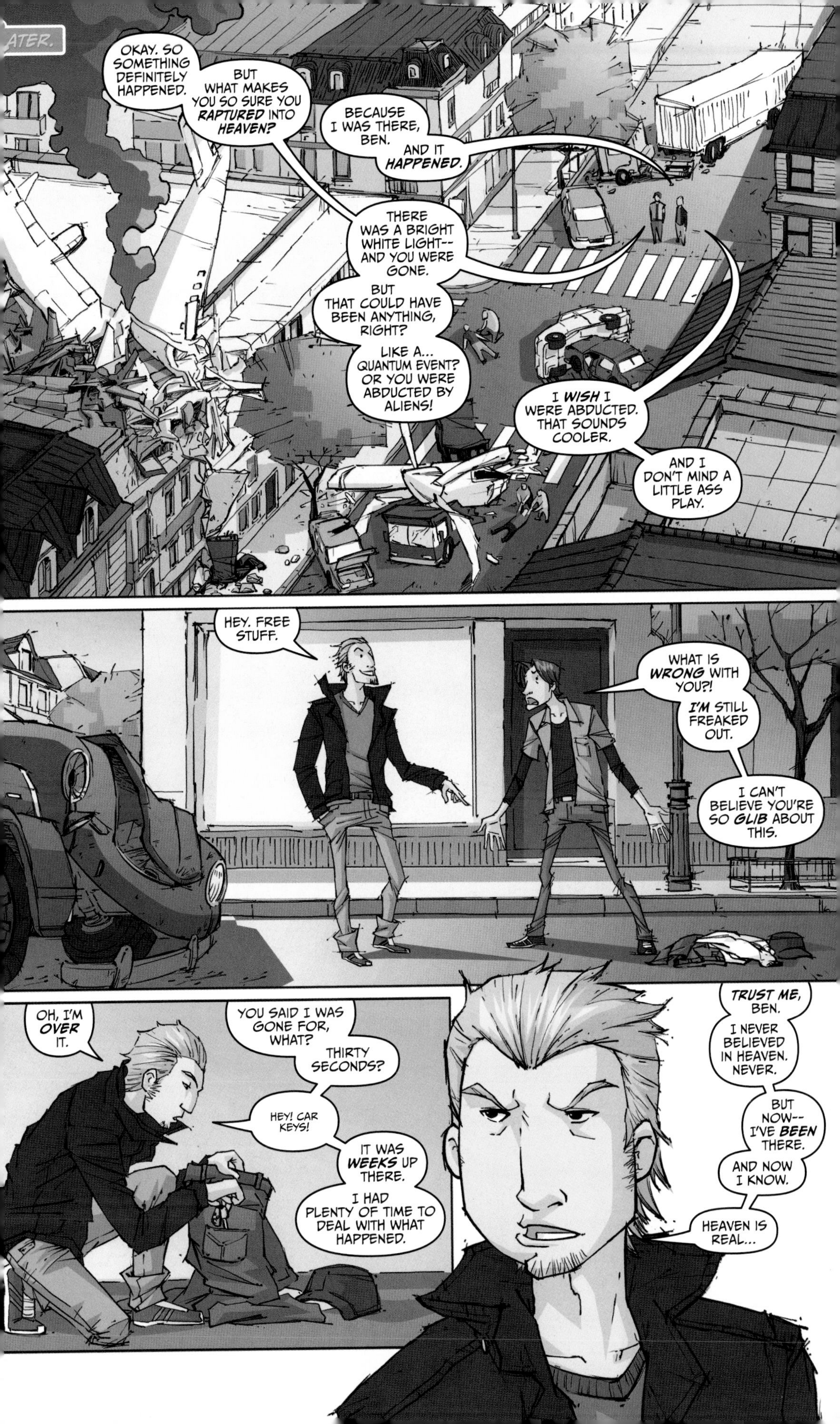
ATER.
OKAY. SO SOMETHING DEFINITELY HAPPENED.
BUT WHAT MAKES YOU SO SURE YOU RAPTURED INTO HEAVEN?
BECAUSE I WAS THERE, BEN.
AND IT HAPPENED.
THERE WAS A BRIGHT WHITE LIGHT-- AND YOU WERE GONE.
BUT THAT COULD HAVE BEEN ANYTHING, RIGHT?
LIKE A... QUANTUM EVENT? OR YOU WERE ABDUCTED BY ALIENS!
I WISH I WERE ABDUCTED. THAT SOUNDS COOLER.
AND I DON'T MIND A LITTLE ASS PLAY.
HEY. FREE STUFF.
WHAT IS WRONG WITH YOU?!
I'M STILL FREAKED OUT.
I CAN'T BELIEVE YOU'RE SO GLIB ABOUT THIS.
OH, I'M OVER IT.
YOU SAID I WAS GONE FOR, WHAT?
THIRTY SECONDS?
HEY! CAR KEYS!
IT WAS WEEKS UP THERE.
I HAD PLENTY OF TIME TO DEAL WITH WHAT HAPPENED.
TRUST ME, BEN.
I NEVER BELIEVED IN HEAVEN. NEVER.
BUT NOW-- I'VE BEEN THERE.
AND NOW I KNOW.
HEAVEN IS REAL...

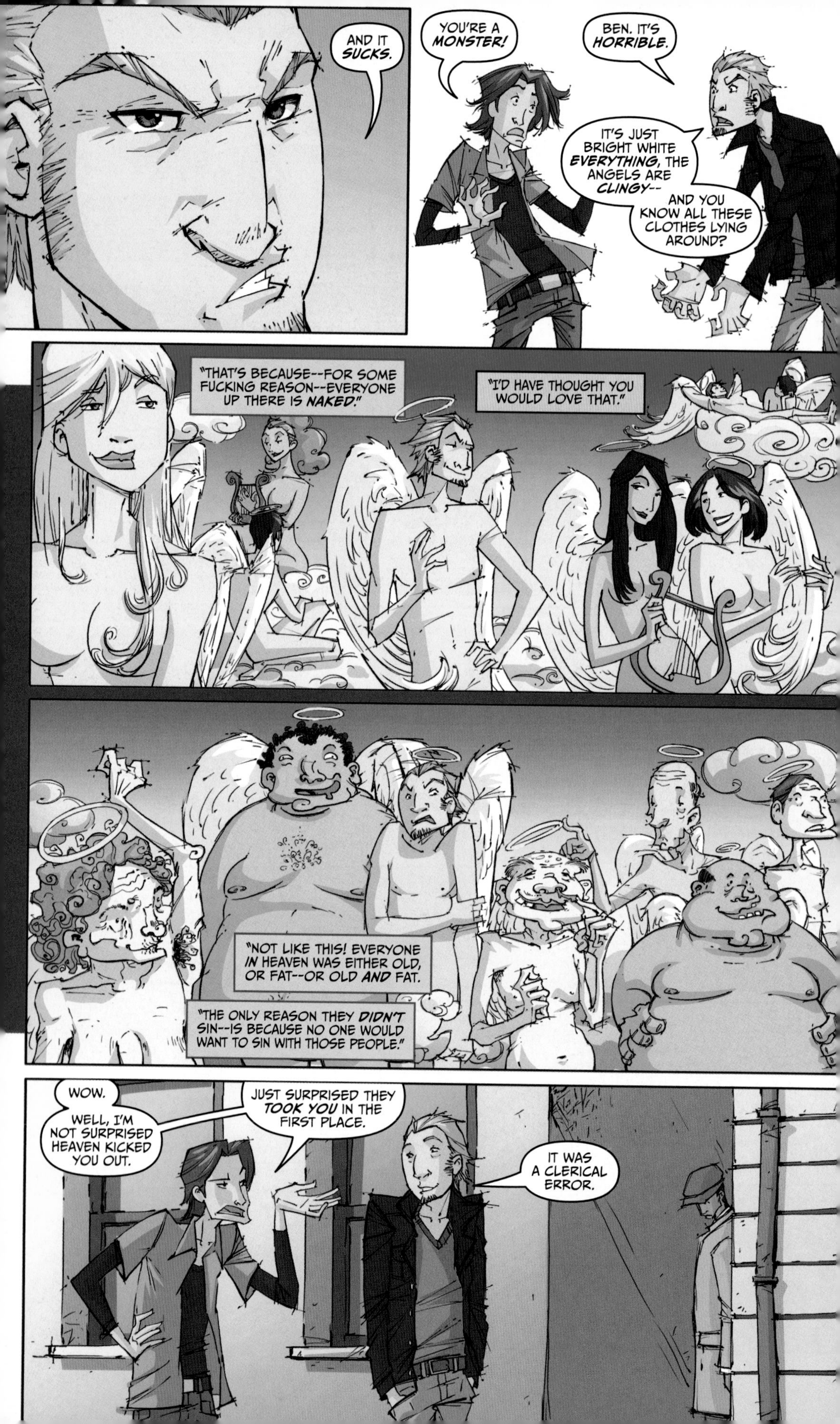

AND IT SUCKS.
YOU'RE A MONSTER!
BEN. IT'S HORRIBLE.
IT'S JUST BRIGHT WHITE EVERYTHING, THE ANGELS ARE CLINGY--
AND YOU KNOW ALL THESE CLOTHES LYING AROUND?
"THAT'S BECAUSE--FOR SOME FUCKING REASON--EVERYONE UP THERE IS NAKED."
"I'D HAVE THOUGHT YOU WOULD LOVE THAT."
"NOT LIKE THIS! EVERYONE IN HEAVEN WAS EITHER OLD, OR FAT--OR OLD AND FAT.
"THE ONLY REASON THEY DIDN'T SIN--IS BECAUSE NO ONE WOULD WANT TO SIN WITH THOSE PEOPLE."
WOW.
WELL, I'M NOT SURPRISED HEAVEN KICKED YOU OUT.
JUST SURPRISED THEY TOOK YOU IN THE FIRST PLACE.
IT WAS A CLERICAL ERROR.

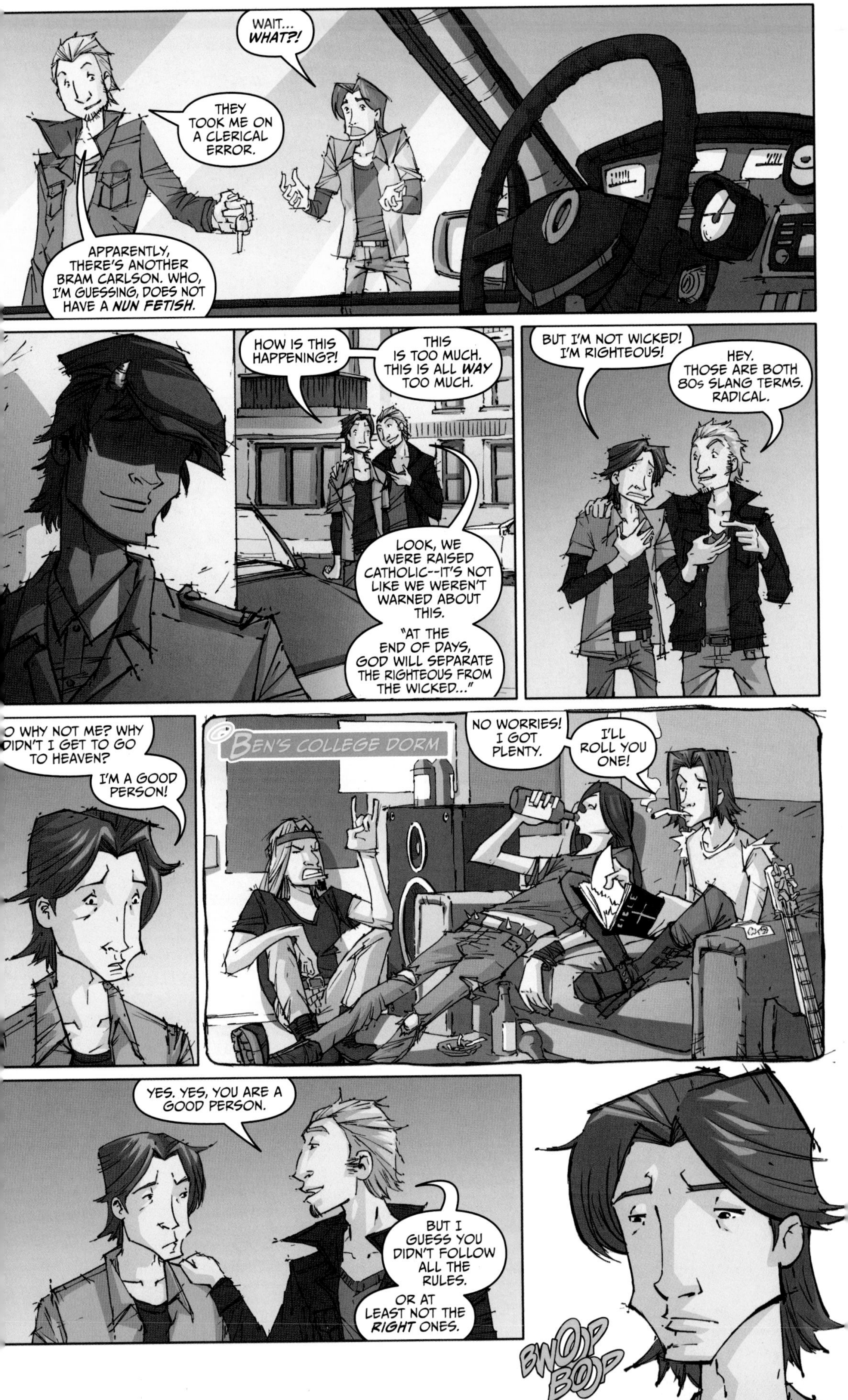
WAIT... *WHAT?!*
THEY TOOK ME ON A CLERICAL ERROR.
APPARENTLY, THERE'S ANOTHER BRAM CARLSON. WHO, I'M GUESSING, DOES NOT HAVE A *NUN FETISH*.
HOW IS THIS HAPPENING?!
THIS IS TOO MUCH. THIS IS ALL *WAY* TOO MUCH.
LOOK, WE WERE RAISED CATHOLIC--IT'S NOT LIKE WE WEREN'T WARNED ABOUT THIS.
"AT THE END OF DAYS, GOD WILL SEPARATE THE RIGHTEOUS FROM THE WICKED..."
BUT I'M NOT WICKED! I'M RIGHTEOUS!
HEY. THOSE ARE BOTH 80s SLANG TERMS. RADICAL.
O WHY NOT ME? WHY DIDN'T I GET TO GO TO HEAVEN?
I'M A GOOD PERSON!
BEN'S COLLEGE DORM
NO WORRIES! I GOT PLENTY.
I'LL ROLL YOU ONE!
YES. YES, YOU ARE A GOOD PERSON.
BUT I GUESS YOU DIDN'T FOLLOW ALL THE RULES.
OR AT LEAST NOT THE *RIGHT* ONES.
BWOOP BOOP

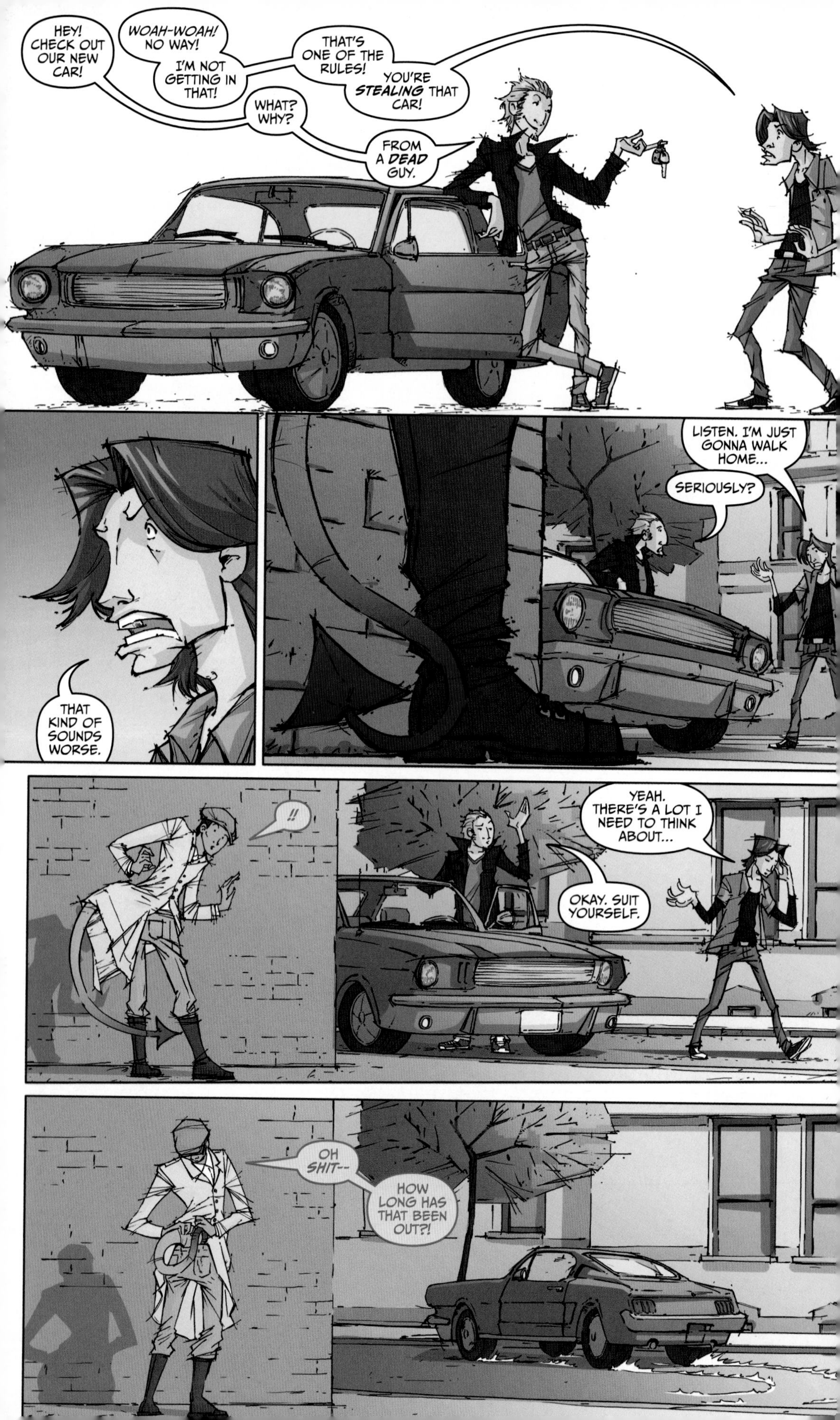
HEY! CHECK OUT OUR NEW CAR!
WOAH-WOAH! NO WAY!
I'M NOT GETTING IN THAT!
THAT'S ONE OF THE RULES!
YOU'RE STEALING THAT CAR!
WHAT? WHY?
FROM A DEAD GUY.
THAT KIND OF SOUNDS WORSE.
LISTEN. I'M JUST GONNA WALK HOME...
SERIOUSLY?
!!
YEAH. THERE'S A LOT I NEED TO THINK ABOUT...
OKAY. SUIT YOURSELF.
OH SHIT--
HOW LONG HAS THAT BEEN OUT?!

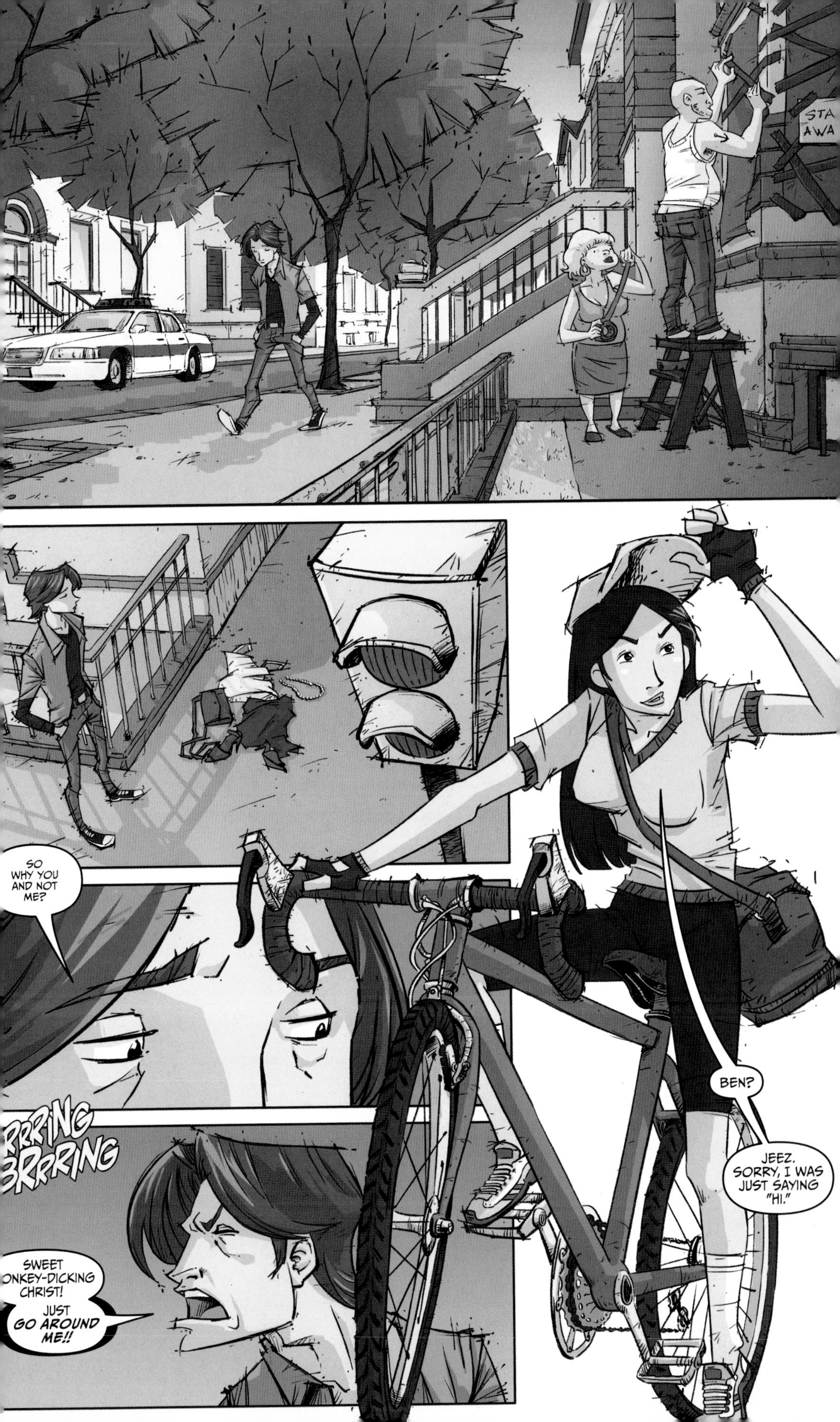
STA
AWA
SO WHY YOU AND NOT ME?
RRRING
BRRRING
SWEET ONKEY-DICKING CHRIST!
JUST GO AROUND ME!!
BEN?
JEEZ. SORRY, I WAS JUST SAYING "HI."

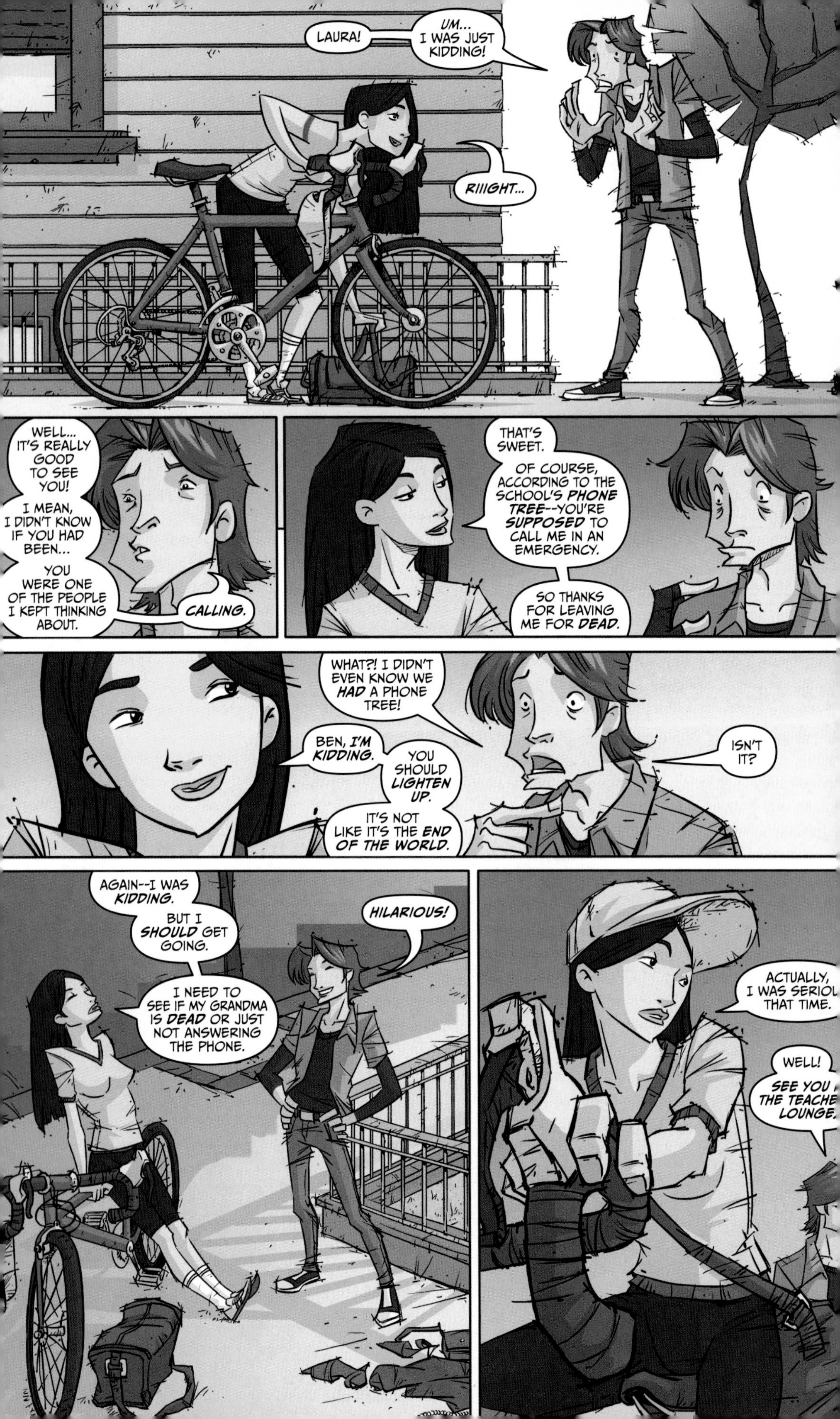
LAURA!
UM... I WAS JUST KIDDING!
RIIIGHT...
WELL... IT'S REALLY GOOD TO SEE YOU!
I MEAN, I DIDN'T KNOW IF YOU HAD BEEN...
CALLING.
YOU WERE ONE OF THE PEOPLE I KEPT THINKING ABOUT.
THAT'S SWEET.
OF COURSE, ACCORDING TO THE SCHOOL'S PHONE TREE--YOU'RE SUPPOSED TO CALL ME IN AN EMERGENCY.
SO THANKS FOR LEAVING ME FOR DEAD.
WHAT?! I DIDN'T EVEN KNOW WE HAD A PHONE TREE!
ISN'T IT?
BEN, I'M KIDDING.
YOU SHOULD LIGHTEN UP.
IT'S NOT LIKE IT'S THE END OF THE WORLD.
AGAIN--I WAS KIDDING.
BUT I SHOULD GET GOING.
I NEED TO SEE IF MY GRANDMA IS DEAD OR JUST NOT ANSWERING THE PHONE.
HILARIOUS!
ACTUALLY, I WAS SERIOU THAT TIME.
WELL!
SEE YOU THE TEACHE LOUNGE.

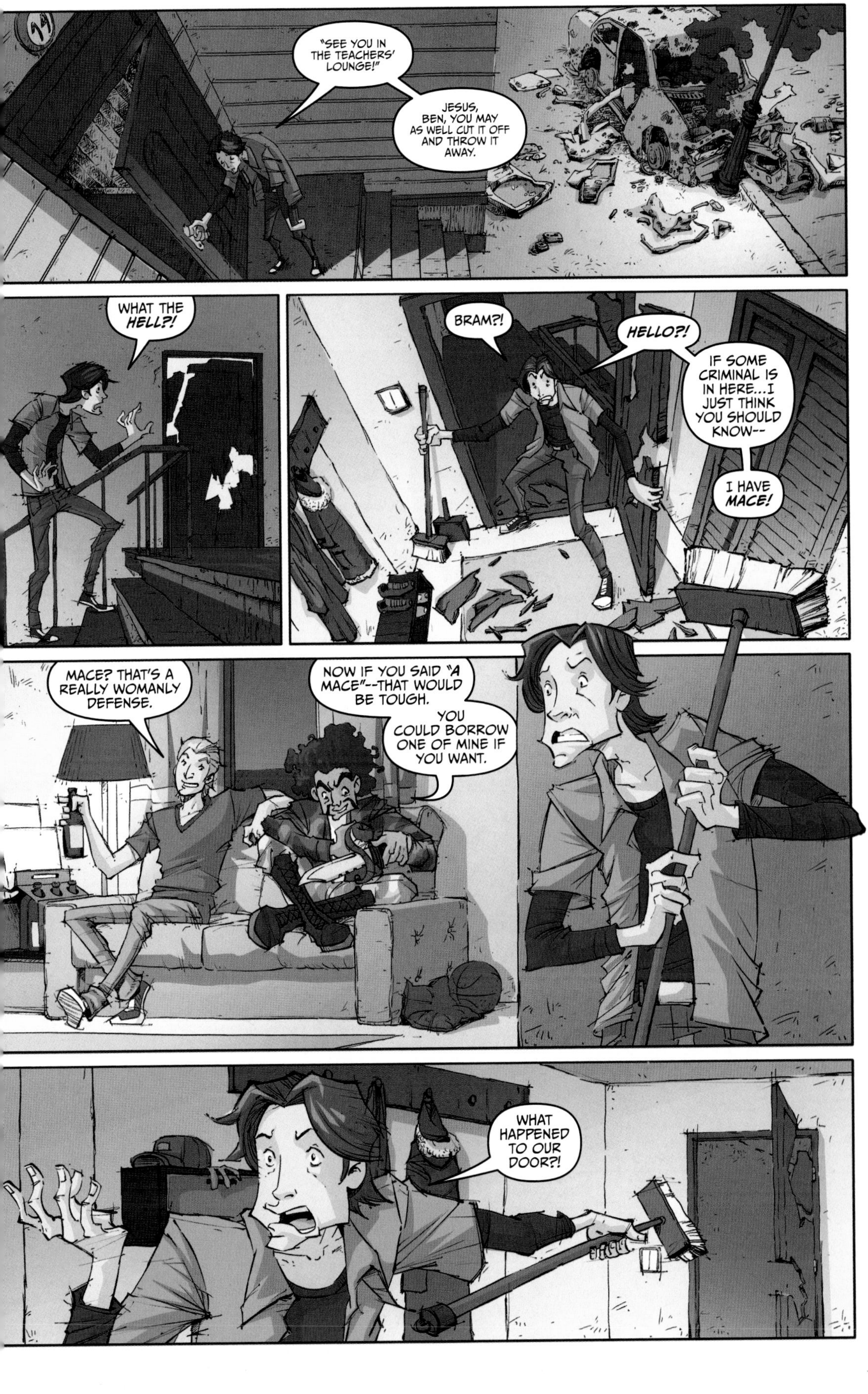
"SEE YOU IN THE TEACHERS' LOUNGE!"
JESUS, BEN, YOU MAY AS WELL CUT IT OFF AND THROW IT AWAY.
WHAT THE *HELL?!*
BRAM?!
*HELLO?!*
IF SOME CRIMINAL IS IN HERE...I JUST THINK YOU SHOULD KNOW--
I HAVE *MACE!*
MACE? THAT'S A REALLY WOMANLY DEFENSE.
NOW IF YOU SAID "*A* MACE"--THAT WOULD BE TOUGH.
YOU COULD BORROW ONE OF MINE IF YOU WANT.
WHAT HAPPENED TO OUR DOOR?!

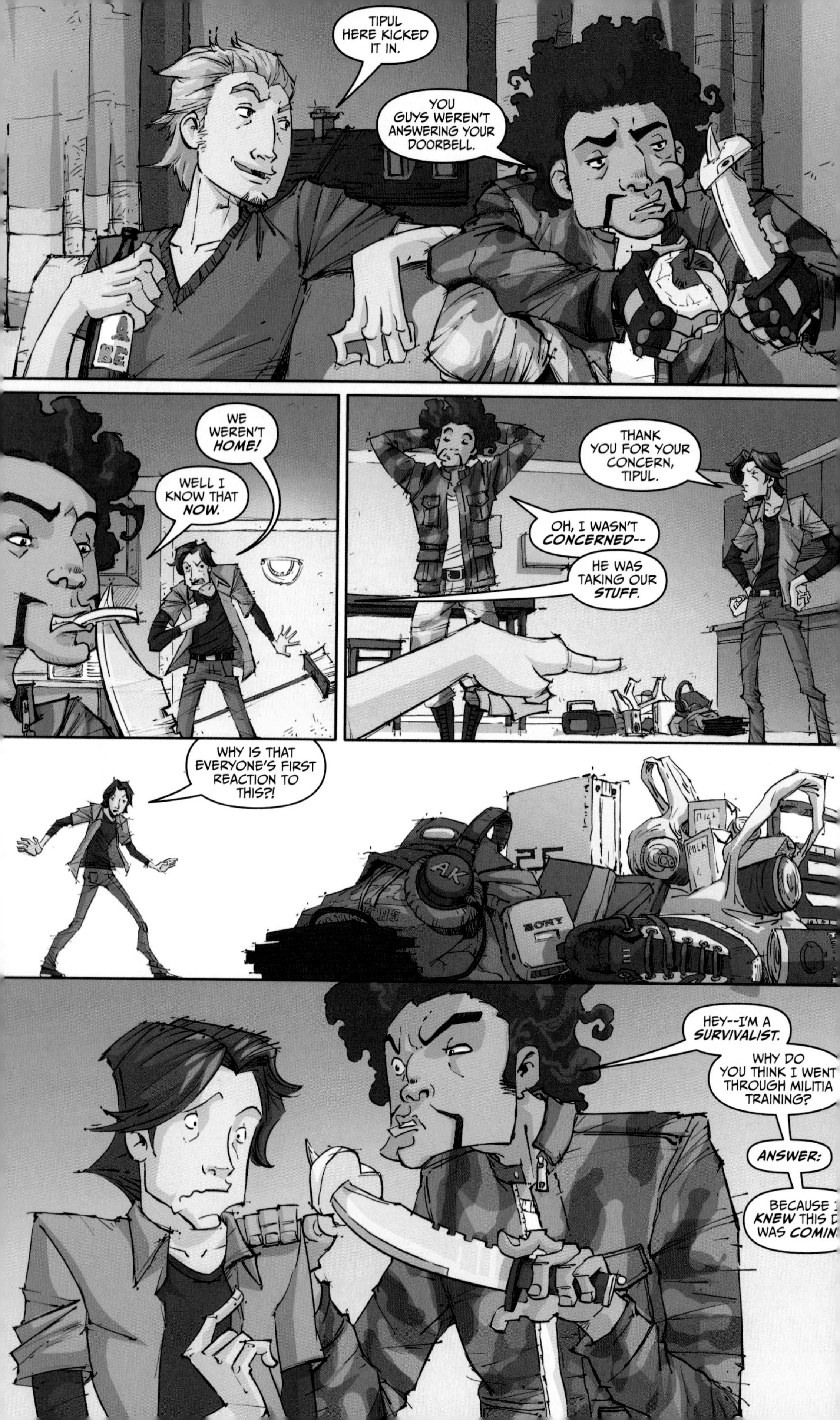
TIPUL HERE KICKED IT IN.
YOU GUYS WEREN'T ANSWERING YOUR DOORBELL.
WE WEREN'T *HOME!*
WELL I KNOW THAT *NOW.*
THANK YOU FOR YOUR CONCERN, TIPUL.
OH, I WASN'T *CONCERNED--*
HE WAS TAKING OUR *STUFF.*
WHY IS THAT EVERYONE'S FIRST REACTION TO THIS?!
AK
SONY
MILK
HEY--I'M A *SURVIVALIST.*
WHY DO YOU THINK I WENT THROUGH MILITIA TRAINING?
*ANSWER:*

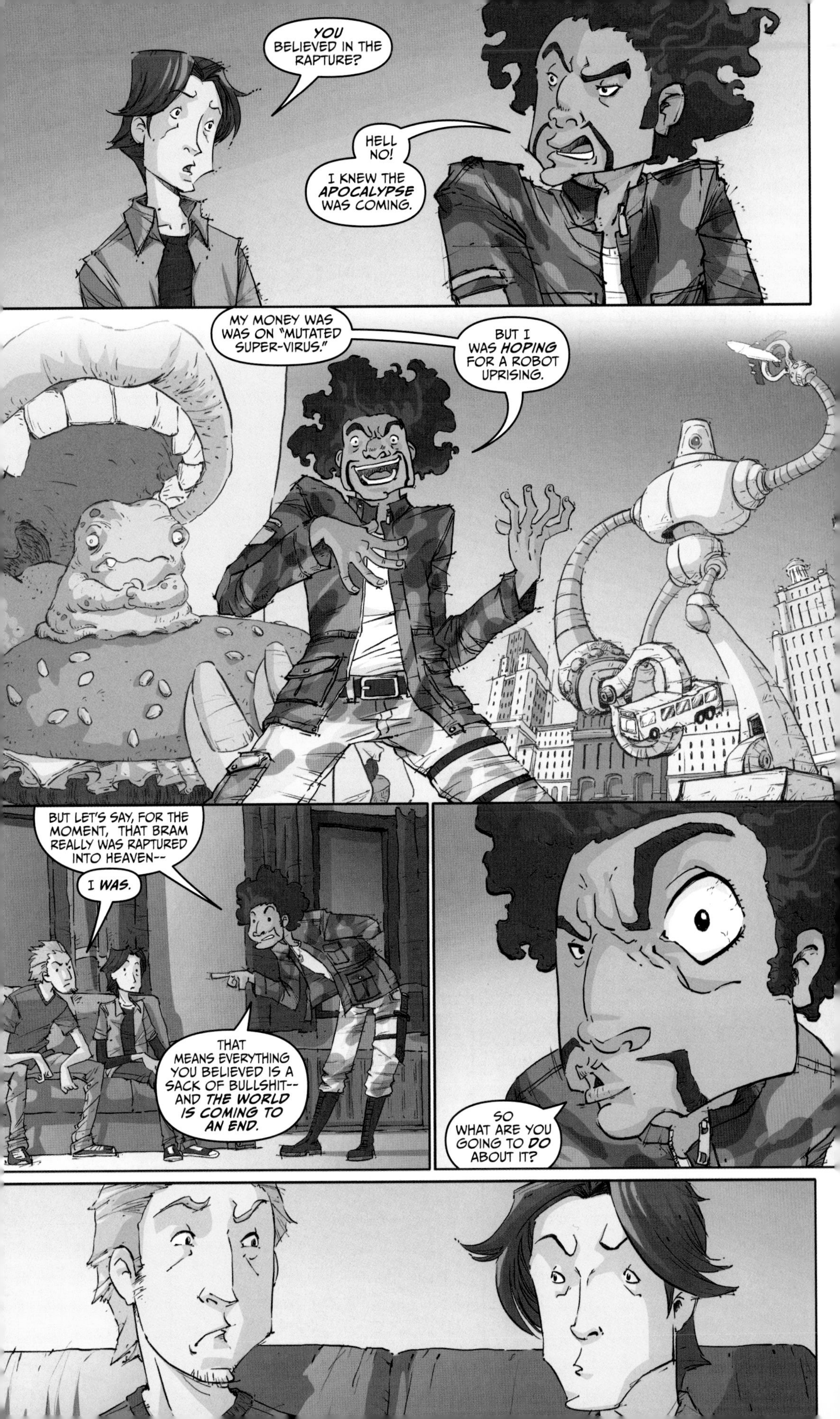
YOU BELIEVED IN THE RAPTURE?
HELL NO!
I KNEW THE APOCALYPSE WAS COMING.
MY MONEY WAS WAS ON "MUTATED SUPER-VIRUS."
BUT I WAS HOPING FOR A ROBOT UPRISING.
BUT LET'S SAY, FOR THE MOMENT, THAT BRAM REALLY WAS RAPTURED INTO HEAVEN--
I WAS.
THAT MEANS EVERYTHING YOU BELIEVED IS A SACK OF BULLSHIT-- AND THE WORLD IS COMING TO AN END.
SO WHAT ARE YOU GOING TO DO ABOUT IT?

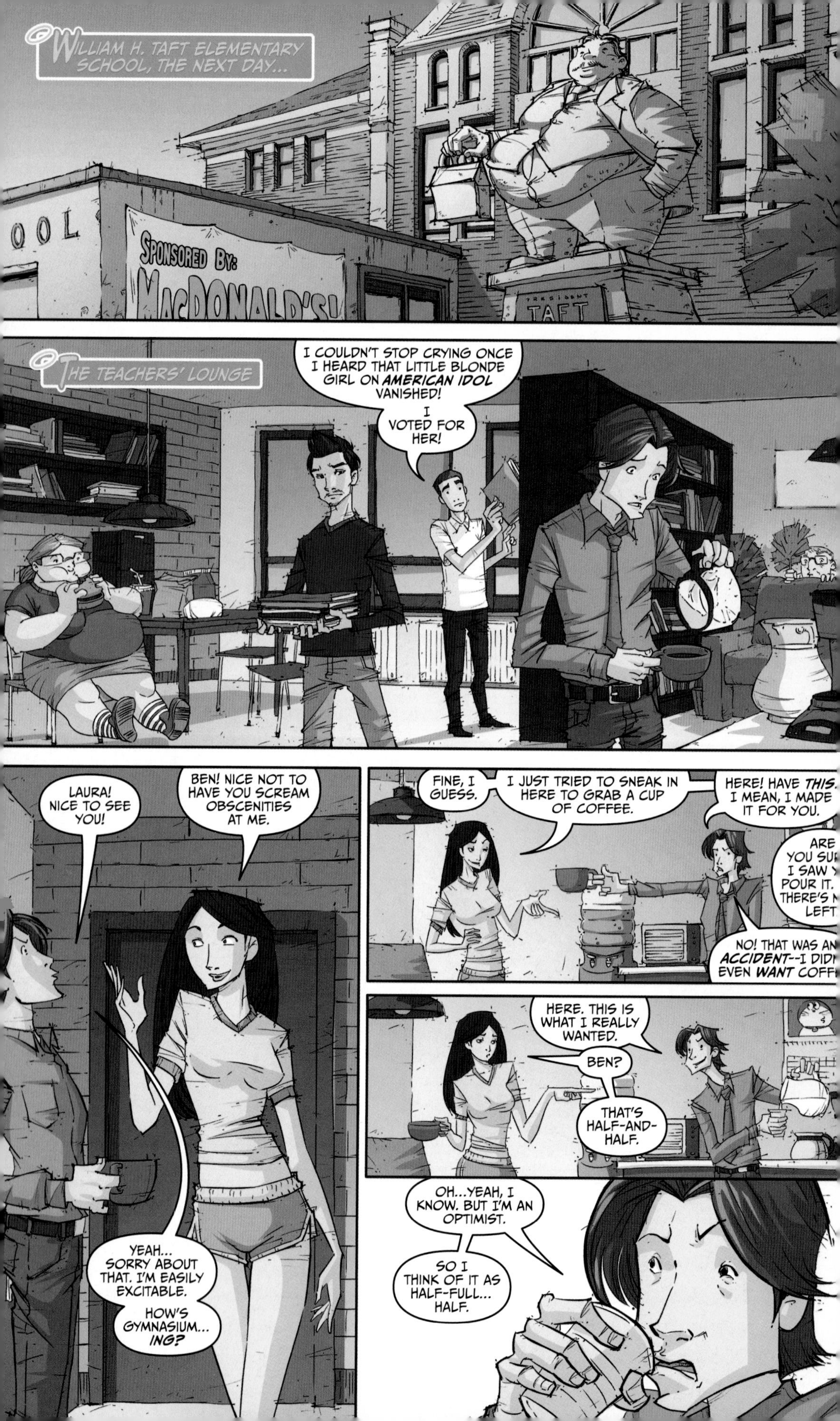
WILLIAM H. TAFT ELEMENTARY SCHOOL, THE NEXT DAY...
OOL
SPONSORED BY: MACDONALD'S!
PRESIDENT TAFT
THE TEACHERS' LOUNGE
I COULDN'T STOP CRYING ONCE I HEARD THAT LITTLE BLONDE GIRL ON AMERICAN IDOL VANISHED!
I VOTED FOR HER!
LAURA! NICE TO SEE YOU!
BEN! NICE NOT TO HAVE YOU SCREAM OBSCENITIES AT ME.
YEAH... SORRY ABOUT THAT. I'M EASILY EXCITABLE.
HOW'S GYMNASIUM... ING?
FINE, I GUESS.
I JUST TRIED TO SNEAK IN HERE TO GRAB A CUP OF COFFEE.
HERE! HAVE THIS. I MEAN, I MADE IT FOR YOU.
ARE YOU SU I SAW POUR IT. THERE'S LEFT
NO! THAT WAS AN ACCIDENT--I DID EVEN WANT COFF
HERE. THIS IS WHAT I REALLY WANTED.
BEN?
THAT'S HALF-AND-HALF.
OH...YEAH, I KNOW. BUT I'M AN OPTIMIST.
SO I THINK OF IT AS HALF-FULL... HALF.

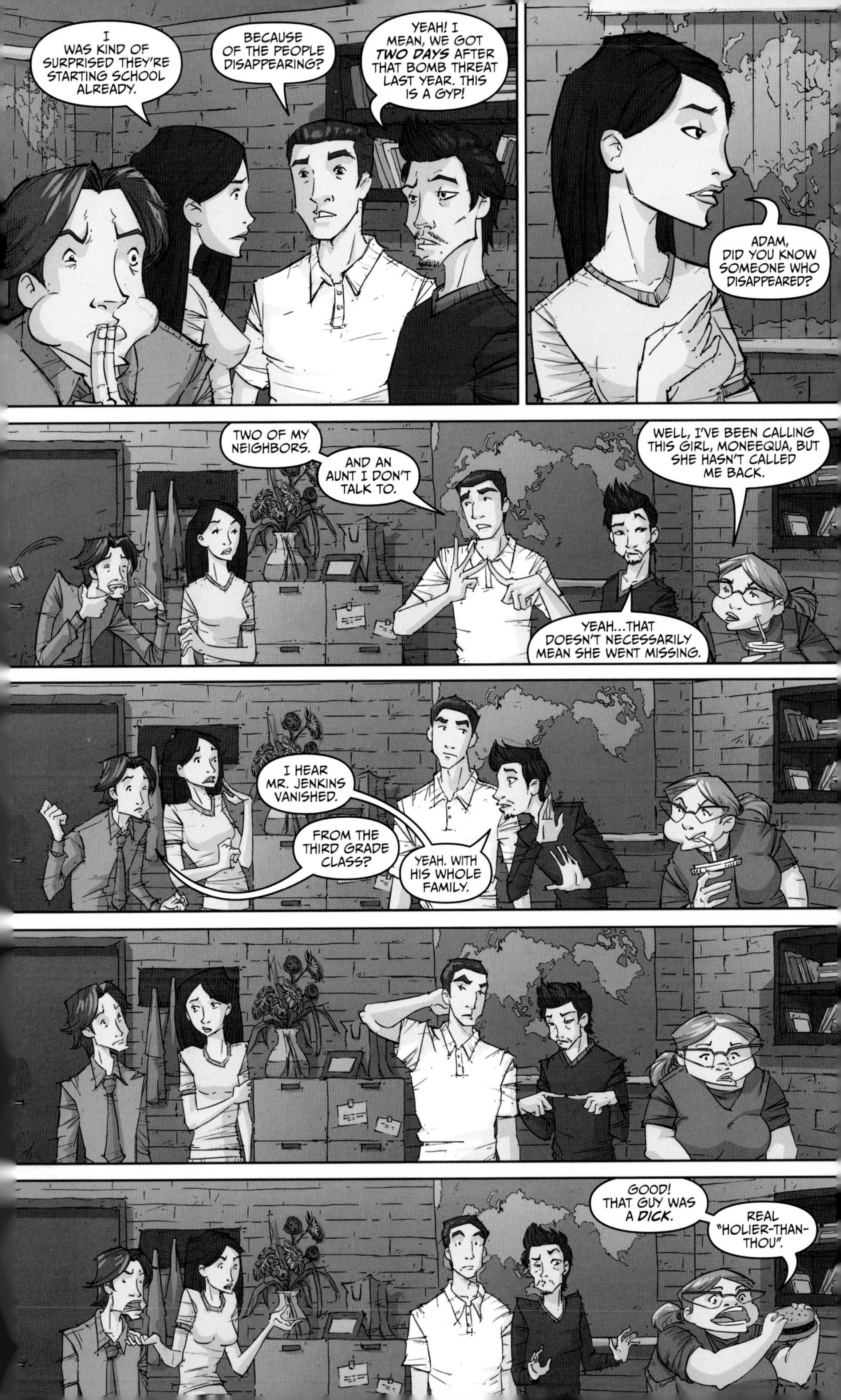
I WAS KIND OF SURPRISED THEY'RE STARTING SCHOOL ALREADY.
BECAUSE OF THE PEOPLE DISAPPEARING?
YEAH! I MEAN, WE GOT *TWO DAYS* AFTER THAT BOMB THREAT LAST YEAR. THIS IS A GYP!
ADAM, DID YOU KNOW SOMEONE WHO DISAPPEARED?
TWO OF MY NEIGHBORS.
AND AN AUNT I DON'T TALK TO.
WELL, I'VE BEEN CALLING THIS GIRL, MONEEQUA, BUT SHE HASN'T CALLED ME BACK.
YEAH...THAT DOESN'T NECESSARILY MEAN SHE WENT MISSING.
I HEAR MR. JENKINS VANISHED.
FROM THE THIRD GRADE CLASS?
YEAH. WITH HIS WHOLE FAMILY.
GOOD! THAT GUY WAS A *DICK*.
REAL "HOLIER-THAN-THOU".

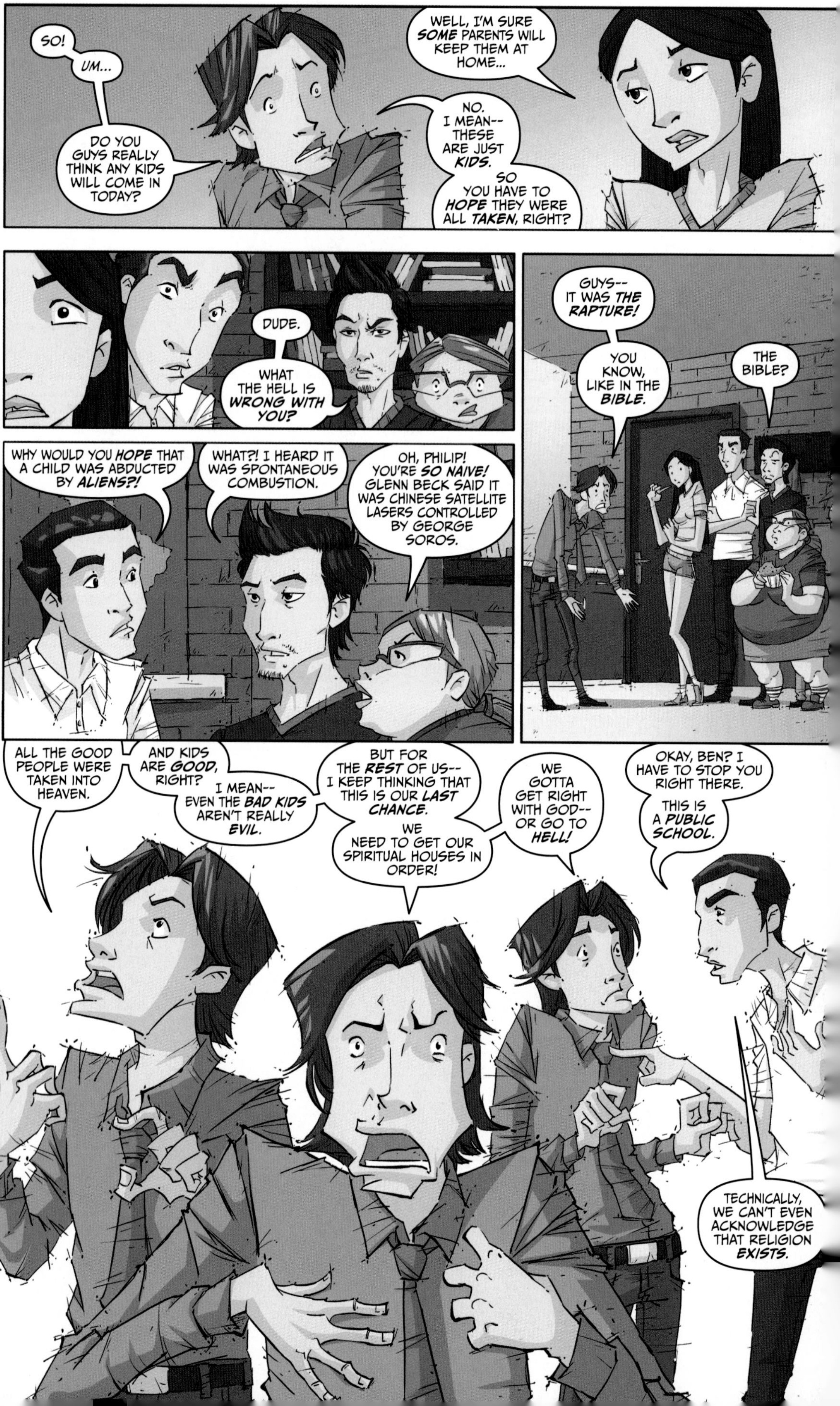
SO!
UM...
DO YOU GUYS REALLY THINK ANY KIDS WILL COME IN TODAY?
WELL, I'M SURE SOME PARENTS WILL KEEP THEM AT HOME...
NO. I MEAN-- THESE ARE JUST KIDS.
SO YOU HAVE TO HOPE THEY WERE ALL TAKEN, RIGHT?
DUDE.
WHAT THE HELL IS WRONG WITH YOU?
WHY WOULD YOU HOPE THAT A CHILD WAS ABDUCTED BY ALIENS?!
WHAT?! I HEARD IT WAS SPONTANEOUS COMBUSTION.
OH, PHILIP! YOU'RE SO NAIVE! GLENN BECK SAID IT WAS CHINESE SATELLITE LASERS CONTROLLED BY GEORGE SOROS.
GUYS-- IT WAS THE RAPTURE!
YOU KNOW, LIKE IN THE BIBLE.
THE BIBLE?
ALL THE GOOD PEOPLE WERE TAKEN INTO HEAVEN.
AND KIDS ARE GOOD, RIGHT?
I MEAN-- EVEN THE BAD KIDS AREN'T REALLY EVIL.
BUT FOR THE REST OF US-- I KEEP THINKING THAT THIS IS OUR LAST CHANCE.
WE NEED TO GET OUR SPIRITUAL HOUSES IN ORDER!
WE GOTTA GET RIGHT WITH GOD-- OR GO TO HELL!
OKAY, BEN? I HAVE TO STOP YOU RIGHT THERE.
THIS IS A PUBLIC SCHOOL.
TECHNICALLY, WE CAN'T EVEN ACKNOWLEDGE THAT RELIGION EXISTS.

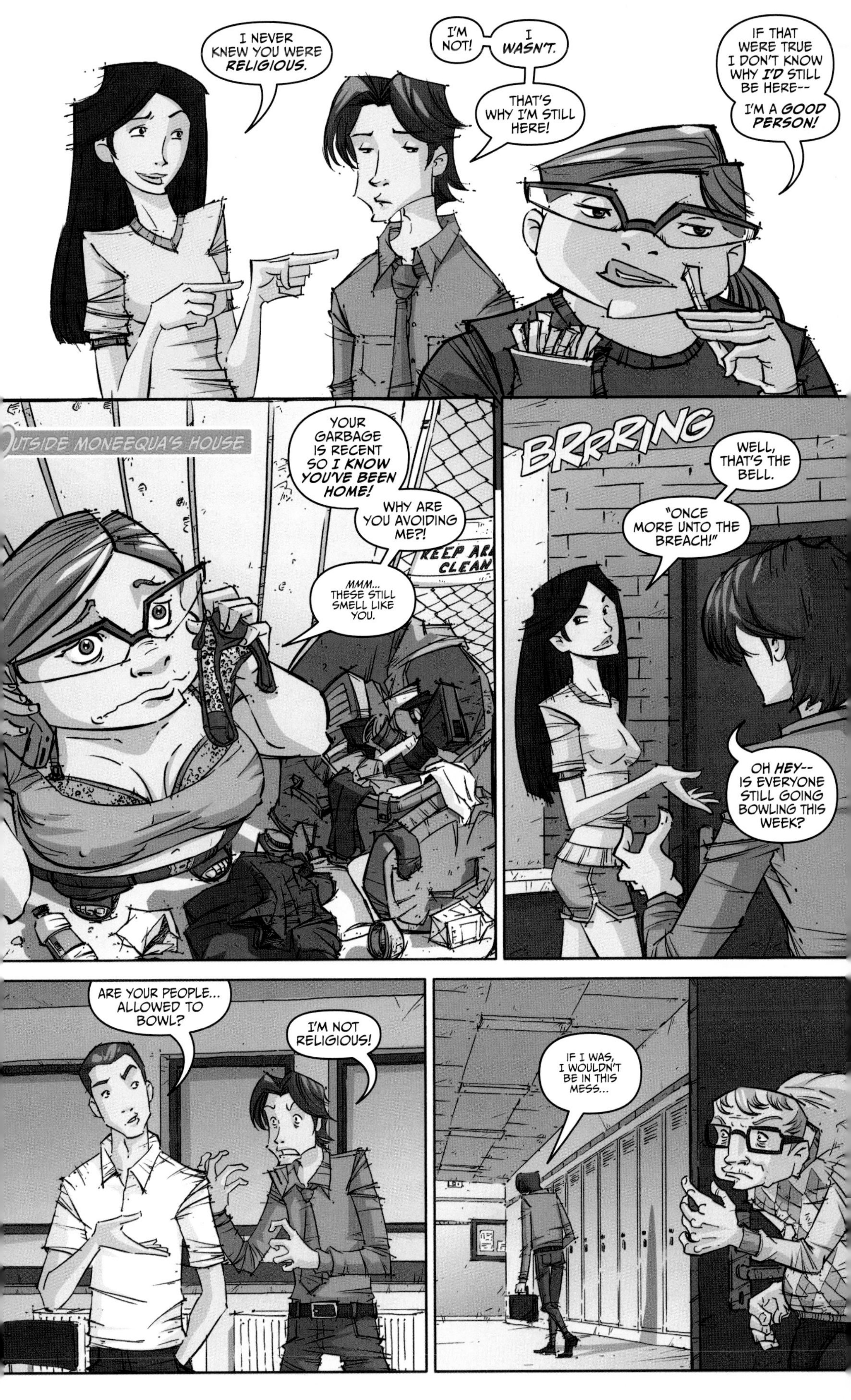

I NEVER KNEW YOU WERE RELIGIOUS.
I'M NOT!
I WASN'T.
THAT'S WHY I'M STILL HERE!
IF THAT WERE TRUE I DON'T KNOW WHY I'D STILL BE HERE--
I'M A GOOD PERSON!
OUTSIDE MONEEQUA'S HOUSE
YOUR GARBAGE IS RECENT SO I KNOW YOU'VE BEEN HOME!
WHY ARE YOU AVOIDING ME?!
KEEP AREA CLEAN
MMM... THESE STILL SMELL LIKE YOU.
BRRRRING
WELL, THAT'S THE BELL.
"ONCE MORE UNTO THE BREACH!"
OH HEY-- IS EVERYONE STILL GOING BOWLING THIS WEEK?
ARE YOUR PEOPLE... ALLOWED TO BOWL?
I'M NOT RELIGIOUS!
IF I WAS, I WOULDN'T BE IN THIS MESS...

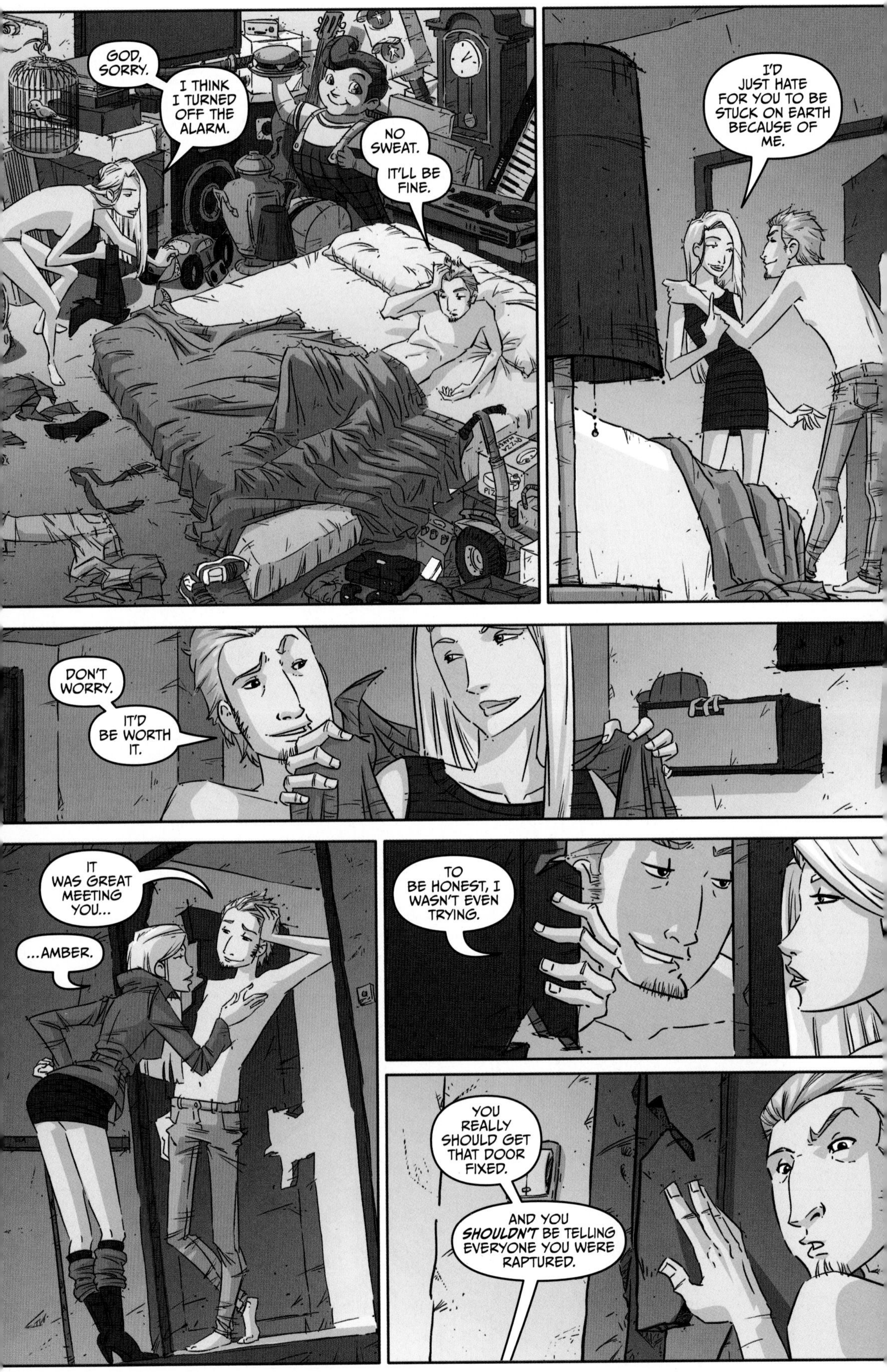
GOD, SORRY.
I THINK I TURNED OFF THE ALARM.
NO SWEAT.
IT'LL BE FINE.
I'D JUST HATE FOR YOU TO BE STUCK ON EARTH BECAUSE OF ME.
DON'T WORRY.
IT'D BE WORTH IT.
IT WAS GREAT MEETING YOU...
...AMBER.
TO BE HONEST, I WASN'T EVEN TRYING.
YOU REALLY SHOULD GET THAT DOOR FIXED.
AND YOU SHOULDN'T BE TELLING EVERYONE YOU WERE RAPTURED.

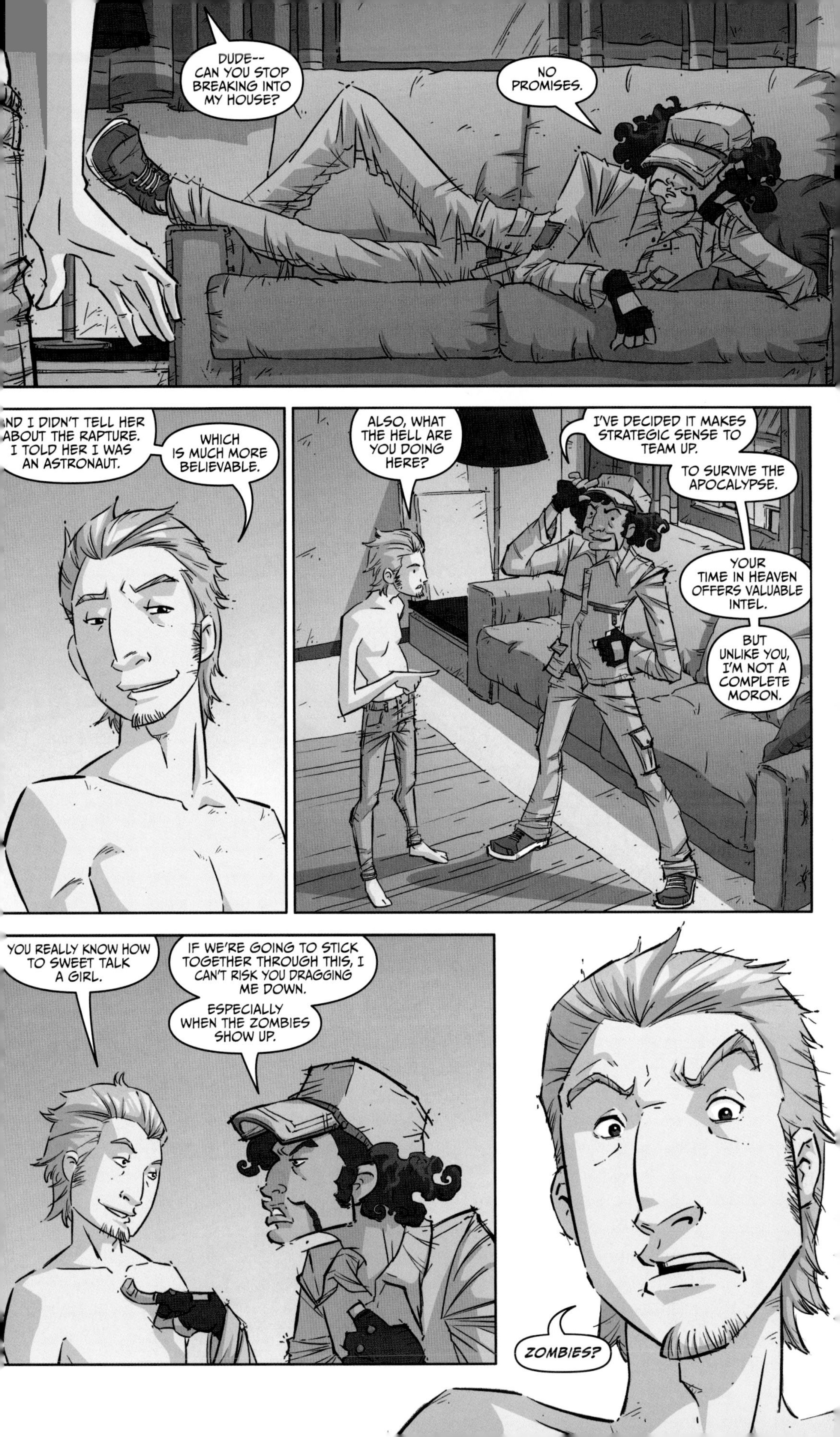
DUDE-- CAN YOU STOP BREAKING INTO MY HOUSE?
NO PROMISES.
ND I DIDN'T TELL HER ABOUT THE RAPTURE. I TOLD HER I WAS AN ASTRONAUT.
WHICH IS MUCH MORE BELIEVABLE.
ALSO, WHAT THE HELL ARE YOU DOING HERE?
I'VE DECIDED IT MAKES STRATEGIC SENSE TO TEAM UP.
TO SURVIVE THE APOCALYPSE.
YOUR TIME IN HEAVEN OFFERS VALUABLE INTEL.
BUT UNLIKE YOU, I'M NOT A COMPLETE MORON.
YOU REALLY KNOW HOW TO SWEET TALK A GIRL.
IF WE'RE GOING TO STICK TOGETHER THROUGH THIS, I CAN'T RISK YOU DRAGGING ME DOWN.
ESPECIALLY WHEN THE ZOMBIES SHOW UP.
ZOMBIES?

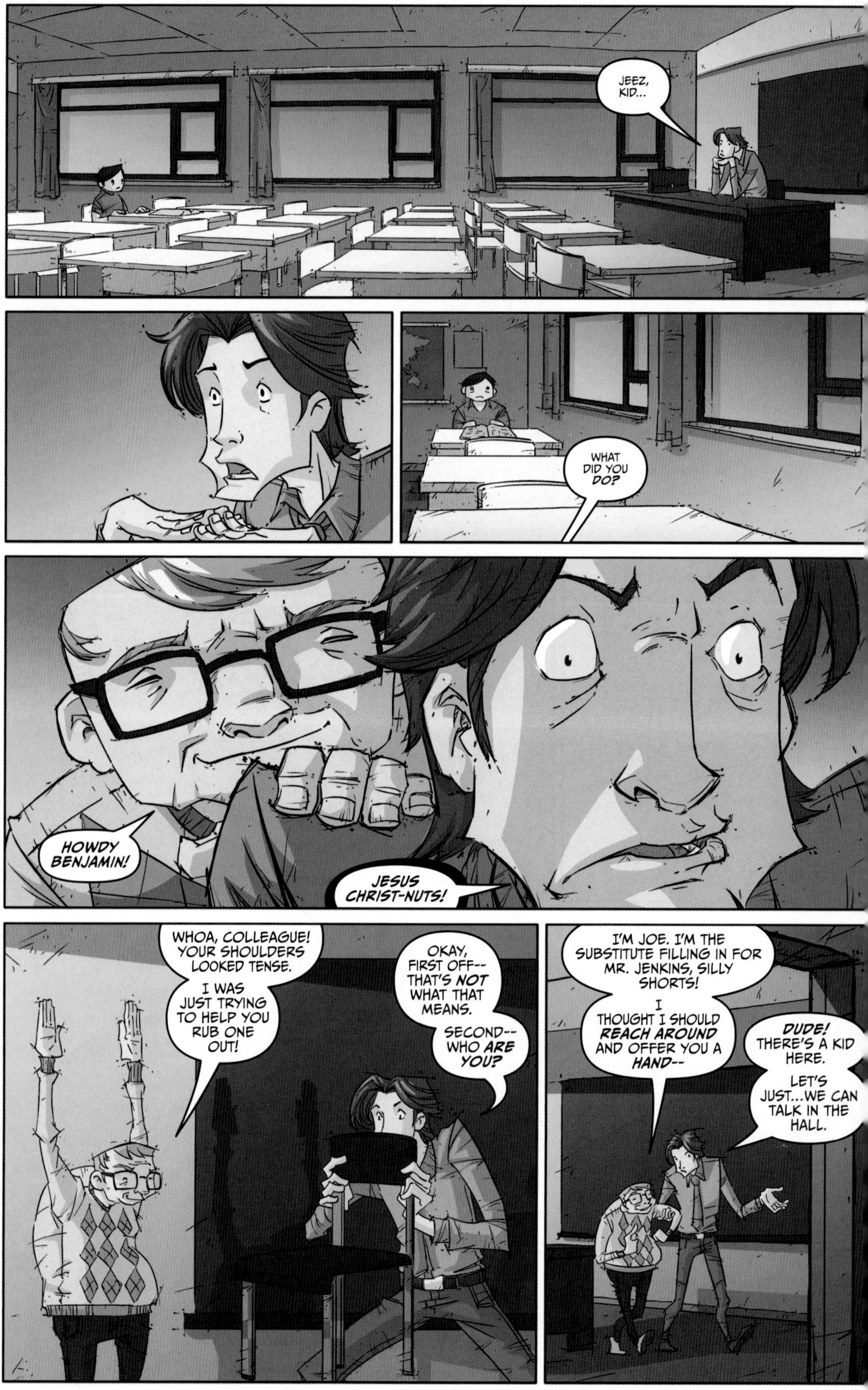
JEEZ, KID...
WHAT DID YOU DO?
HOWDY BENJAMIN!
JESUS CHRIST-NUTS!
WHOA, COLLEAGUE! YOUR SHOULDERS LOOKED TENSE.
I WAS JUST TRYING TO HELP YOU RUB ONE OUT!
OKAY, FIRST OFF-- THAT'S NOT WHAT THAT MEANS.
SECOND-- WHO ARE YOU?
I'M JOE. I'M THE SUBSTITUTE FILLING IN FOR MR. JENKINS, SILLY SHORTS!
I THOUGHT I SHOULD REACH AROUND AND OFFER YOU A HAND--
DUDE! THERE'S A KID HERE.
LET'S JUST...WE CAN TALK IN THE HALL.

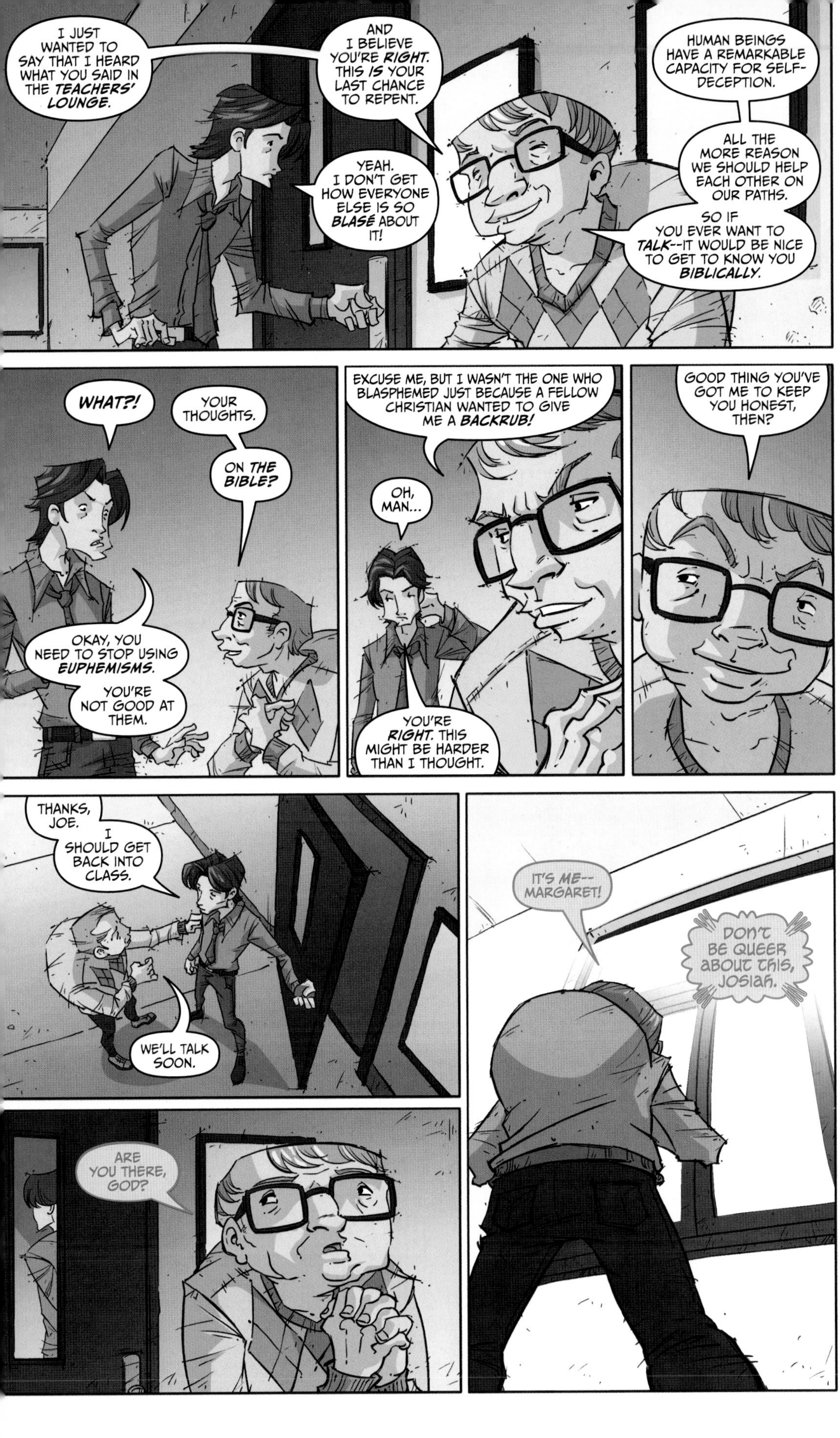
I JUST WANTED TO SAY THAT I HEARD WHAT YOU SAID IN THE TEACHERS' LOUNGE.
AND I BELIEVE YOU'RE RIGHT. THIS IS YOUR LAST CHANCE TO REPENT.
YEAH. I DON'T GET HOW EVERYONE ELSE IS SO BLASÉ ABOUT IT!
HUMAN BEINGS HAVE A REMARKABLE CAPACITY FOR SELF-DECEPTION.
ALL THE MORE REASON WE SHOULD HELP EACH OTHER ON OUR PATHS.
SO IF YOU EVER WANT TO TALK--IT WOULD BE NICE TO GET TO KNOW YOU BIBLICALLY.
WHAT?!
YOUR THOUGHTS.
ON THE BIBLE?
OKAY, YOU NEED TO STOP USING EUPHEMISMS.
YOU'RE NOT GOOD AT THEM.
EXCUSE ME, BUT I WASN'T THE ONE WHO BLASPHEMED JUST BECAUSE A FELLOW CHRISTIAN WANTED TO GIVE ME A BACKRUB!
OH, MAN...
YOU'RE RIGHT. THIS MIGHT BE HARDER THAN I THOUGHT.
GOOD THING YOU'VE GOT ME TO KEEP YOU HONEST, THEN?
THANKS, JOE.
I SHOULD GET BACK INTO CLASS.
WE'LL TALK SOON.
ARE YOU THERE, GOD?
IT'S ME--MARGARET!
DON'T BE QUEER ABOUT THIS, JOSIAH.

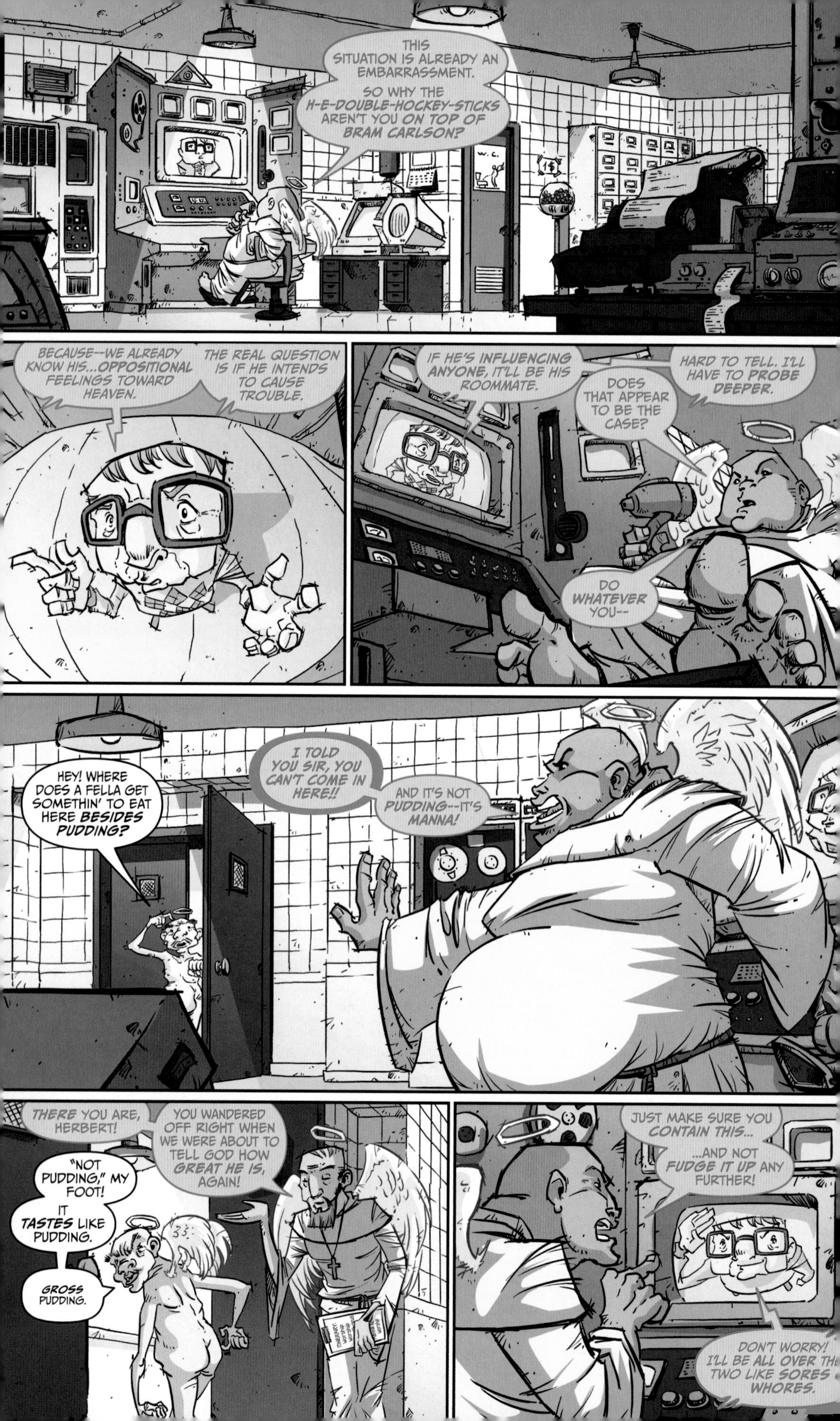
THIS SITUATION IS ALREADY AN EMBARRASSMENT.
SO WHY THE H-E-DOUBLE-HOCKEY-STICKS AREN'T YOU ON TOP OF BRAM CARLSON?
W. C.
BECAUSE--WE ALREADY KNOW HIS...OPPOSITIONAL FEELINGS TOWARD HEAVEN.
THE REAL QUESTION IS IF HE INTENDS TO CAUSE TROUBLE.
IF HE'S INFLUENCING ANYONE, IT'LL BE HIS ROOMMATE.
DOES THAT APPEAR TO BE THE CASE?
HARD TO TELL. I'LL HAVE TO PROBE DEEPER.
DO WHATEVER YOU--
HEY! WHERE DOES A FELLA GET SOMETHIN' TO EAT HERE BESIDES PUDDING?
I TOLD YOU SIR, YOU CAN'T COME IN HERE!!
AND IT'S NOT PUDDING--IT'S MANNA!
THERE YOU ARE, HERBERT!
YOU WANDERED OFF RIGHT WHEN WE WERE ABOUT TO TELL GOD HOW GREAT HE IS, AGAIN!
"NOT PUDDING," MY FOOT!
IT TASTES LIKE PUDDING.
GROSS PUDDING.
JUST MAKE SURE YOU CONTAIN THIS...
...AND NOT FUDGE IT UP ANY FURTHER!
DON'T WORRY! I'LL BE ALL OVER TH TWO LIKE SORES WHORES.

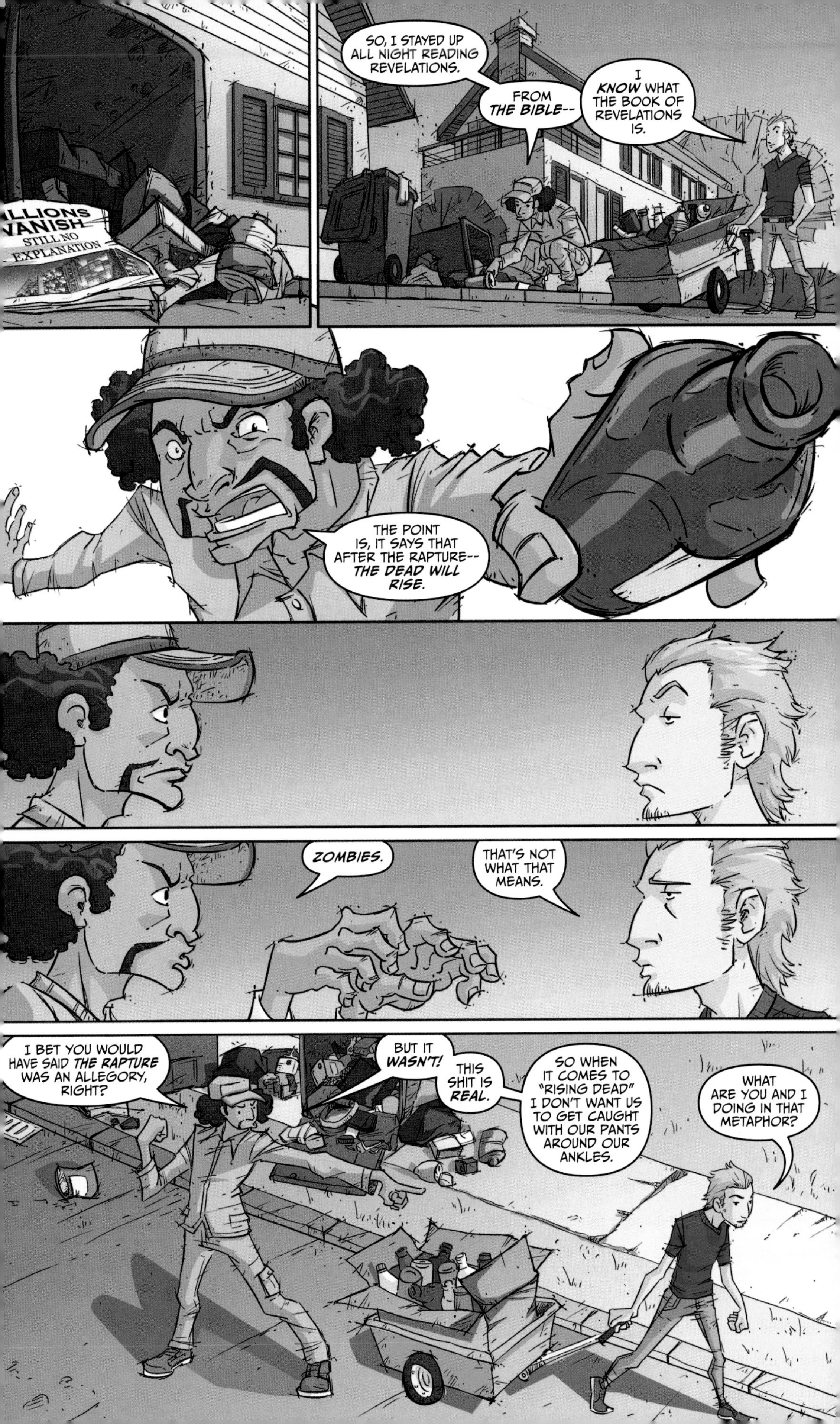
ILLIONS VANISH
STILL NO EXPLANATION
SO, I STAYED UP ALL NIGHT READING REVELATIONS.
FROM *THE BIBLE*--
I *KNOW* WHAT THE BOOK OF REVELATIONS IS.
THE POINT IS, IT SAYS THAT AFTER THE RAPTURE-- *THE DEAD WILL RISE.*
*ZOMBIES.*
THAT'S NOT WHAT THAT MEANS.
I BET YOU WOULD HAVE SAID *THE RAPTURE* WAS AN ALLEGORY, RIGHT?
BUT IT *WASN'T!*
THIS SHIT IS *REAL*.
SO WHEN IT COMES TO "RISING DEAD" I DON'T WANT US TO GET CAUGHT WITH OUR PANTS AROUND OUR ANKLES.
WHAT ARE YOU AND I DOING IN THAT METAPHOR?

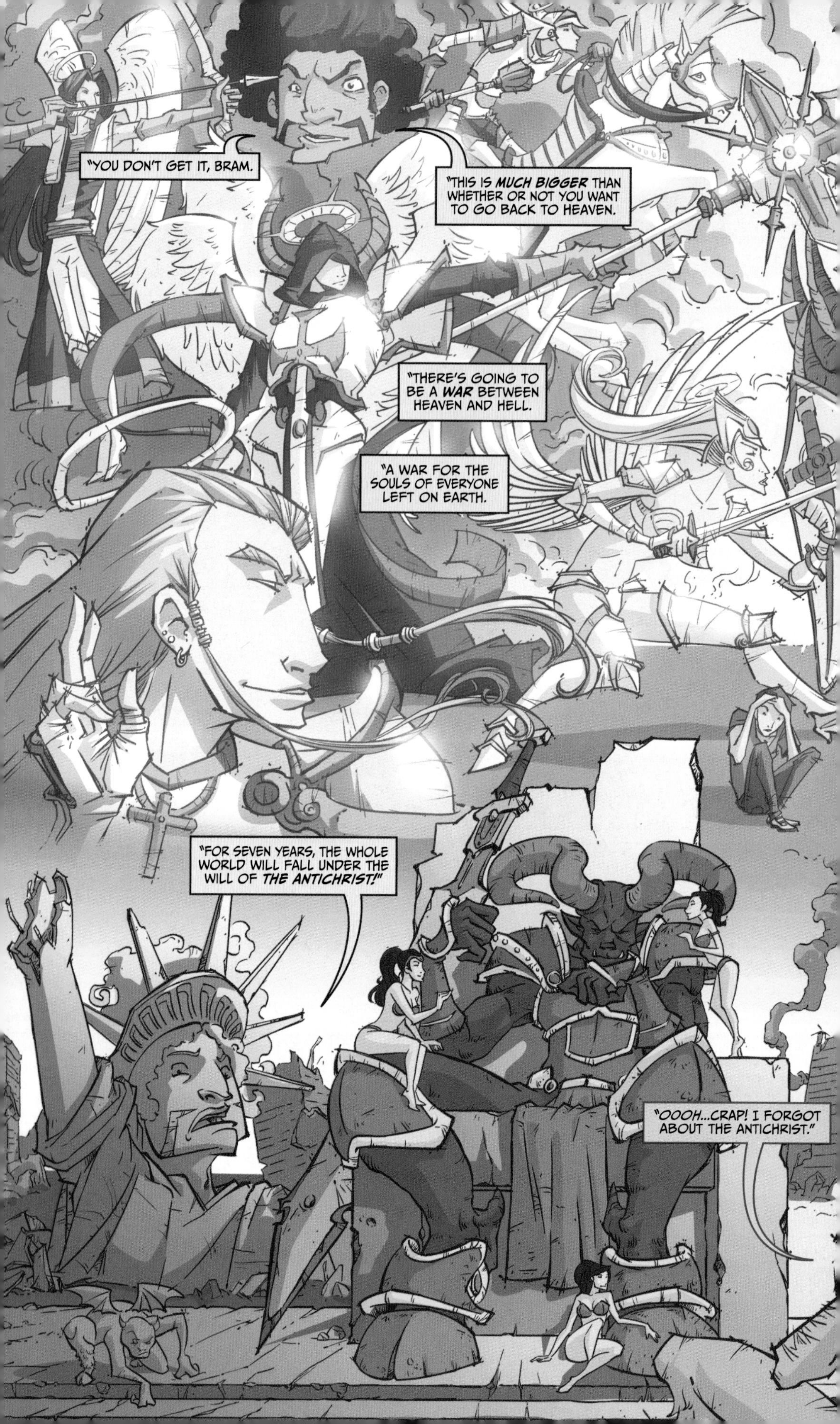
"YOU DON'T GET IT, BRAM.
"THIS IS MUCH BIGGER THAN WHETHER OR NOT YOU WANT TO GO BACK TO HEAVEN.
"THERE'S GOING TO BE A WAR BETWEEN HEAVEN AND HELL.
"A WAR FOR THE SOULS OF EVERYONE LEFT ON EARTH.
"FOR SEVEN YEARS, THE WHOLE WORLD WILL FALL UNDER THE WILL OF THE ANTICHRIST!"
"OOOH...CRAP! I FORGOT ABOUT THE ANTICHRIST."

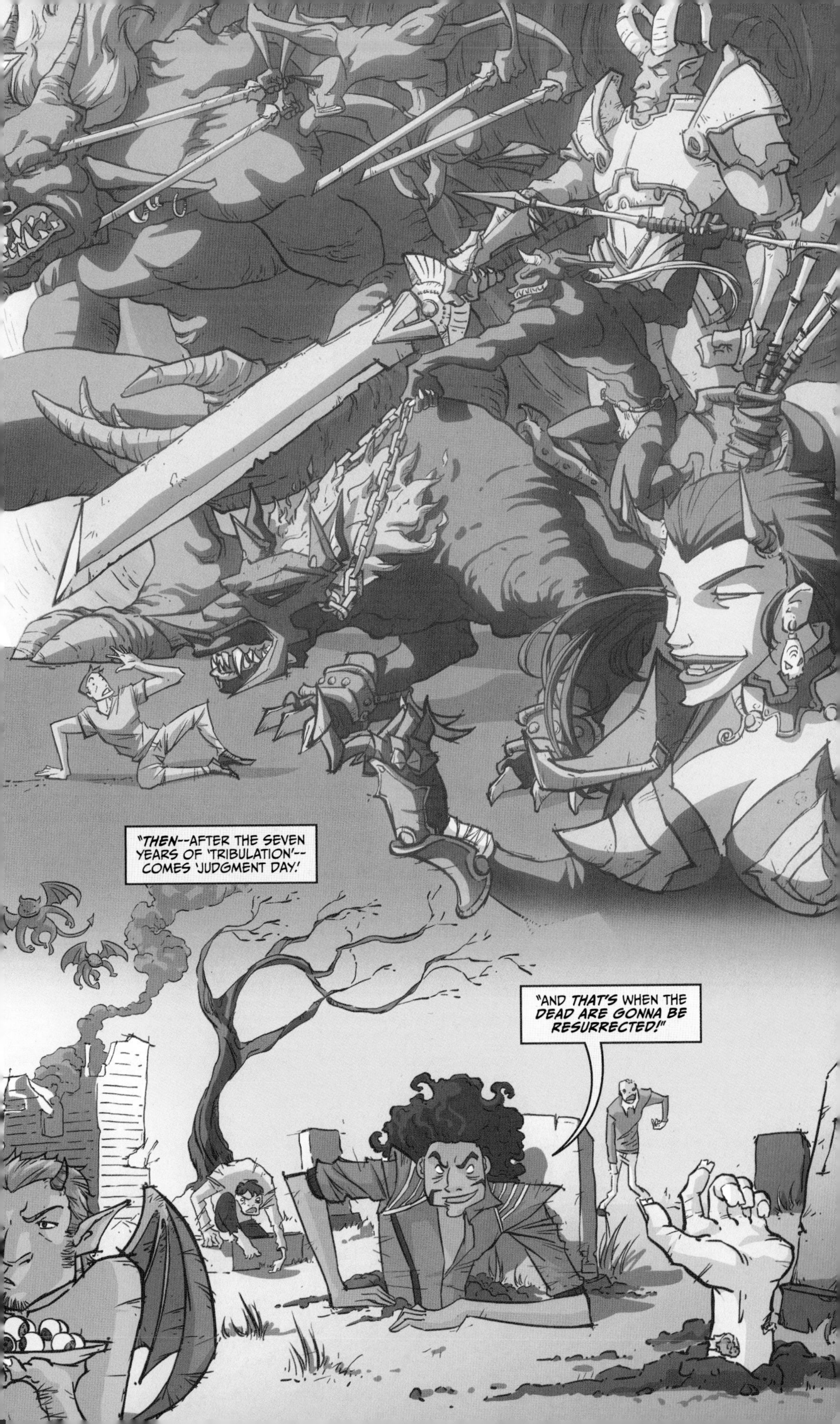
"THEN--AFTER THE SEVEN YEARS OF 'TRIBULATION'--COMES 'JUDGMENT DAY.'
"AND THAT'S WHEN THE DEAD ARE GONNA BE RESURRECTED!"

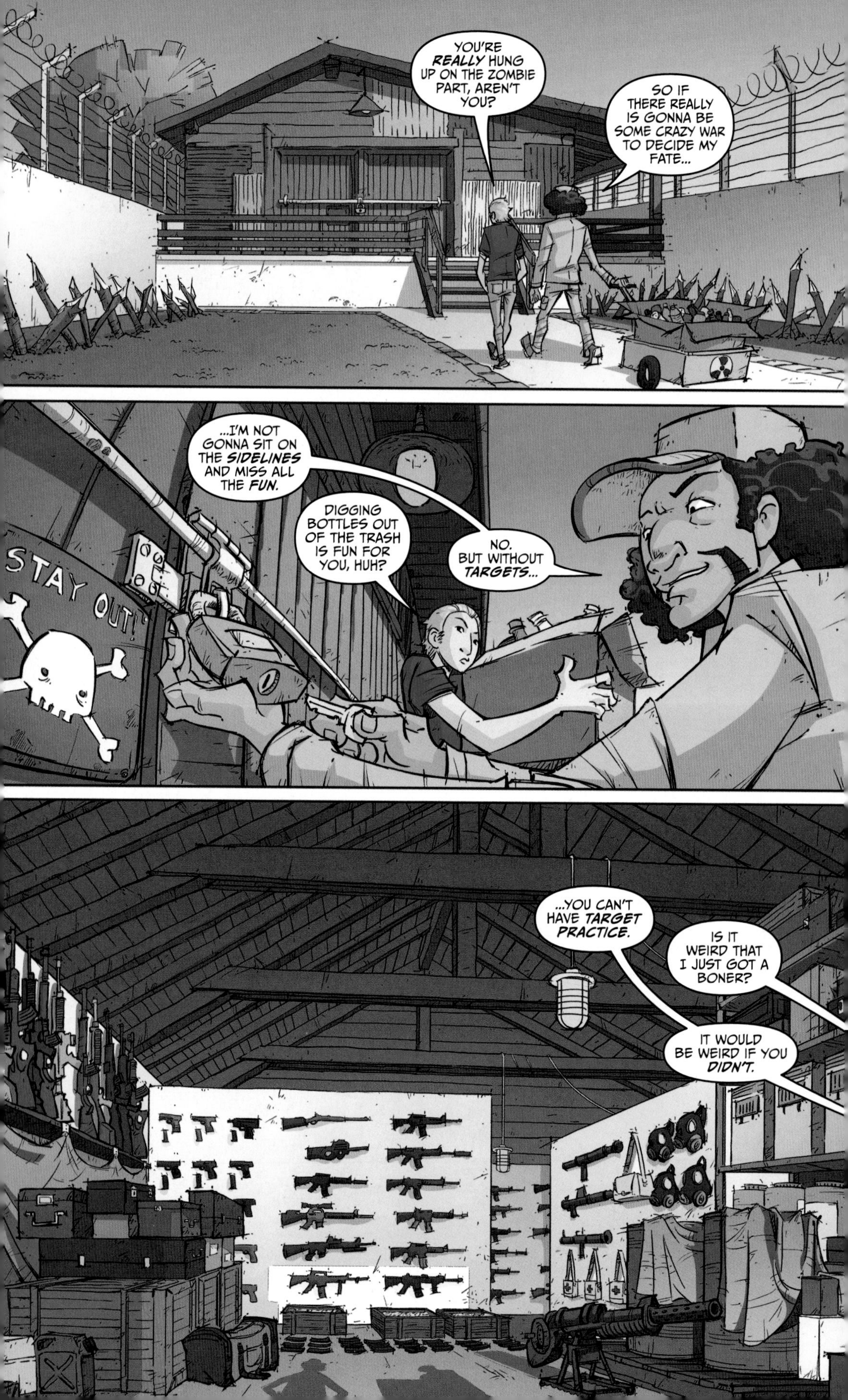
YOU'RE REALLY HUNG UP ON THE ZOMBIE PART, AREN'T YOU?
SO IF THERE REALLY IS GONNA BE SOME CRAZY WAR TO DECIDE MY FATE...
...I'M NOT GONNA SIT ON THE SIDELINES AND MISS ALL THE FUN.
DIGGING BOTTLES OUT OF THE TRASH IS FUN FOR YOU, HUH?
NO. BUT WITHOUT TARGETS...
STAY OUT!
...YOU CAN'T HAVE TARGET PRACTICE.
IS IT WEIRD THAT I JUST GOT A BONER?
IT WOULD BE WEIRD IF YOU DIDN'T.

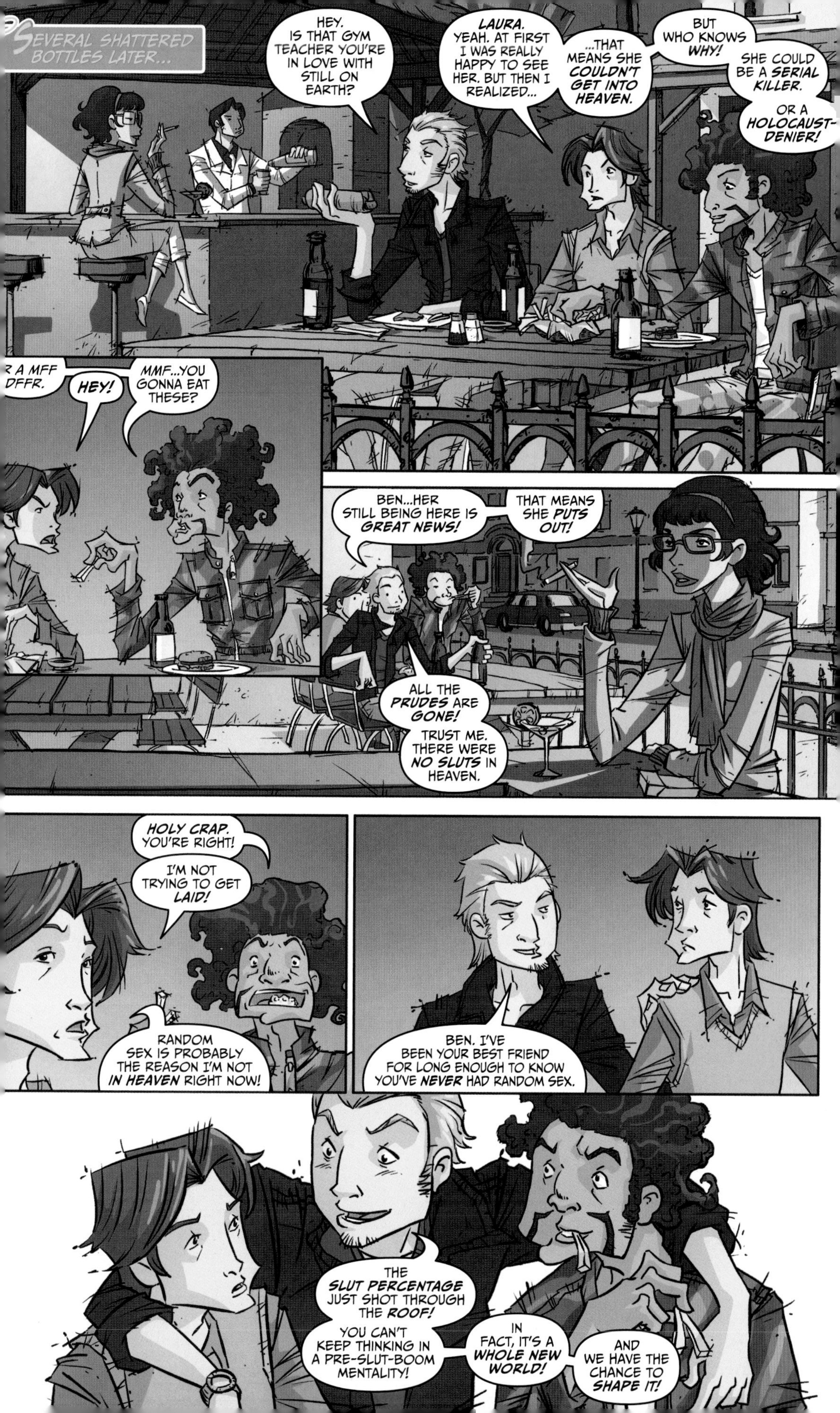
SEVERAL SHATTERED BOTTLES LATER...
HEY. IS THAT GYM TEACHER YOU'RE IN LOVE WITH STILL ON EARTH?
LAURA. YEAH. AT FIRST I WAS REALLY HAPPY TO SEE HER. BUT THEN I REALIZED...
...THAT MEANS SHE COULDN'T GET INTO HEAVEN.
BUT WHO KNOWS WHY!
SHE COULD BE A SERIAL KILLER.
OR A HOLOCAUST-DENIER!
R A MFF DFFR.
HEY!
MMF...YOU GONNA EAT THESE?
BEN...HER STILL BEING HERE IS GREAT NEWS!
THAT MEANS SHE PUTS OUT!
ALL THE PRUDES ARE GONE!
TRUST ME. THERE WERE NO SLUTS IN HEAVEN.
HOLY CRAP. YOU'RE RIGHT!
I'M NOT TRYING TO GET LAID!
RANDOM SEX IS PROBABLY THE REASON I'M NOT IN HEAVEN RIGHT NOW!
BEN. I'VE BEEN YOUR BEST FRIEND FOR LONG ENOUGH TO KNOW YOU'VE NEVER HAD RANDOM SEX.
THE SLUT PERCENTAGE JUST SHOT THROUGH THE ROOF!
YOU CAN'T KEEP THINKING IN A PRE-SLUT-BOOM MENTALITY!
IN FACT, IT'S A WHOLE NEW WORLD!
AND WE HAVE THE CHANCE TO SHAPE IT!

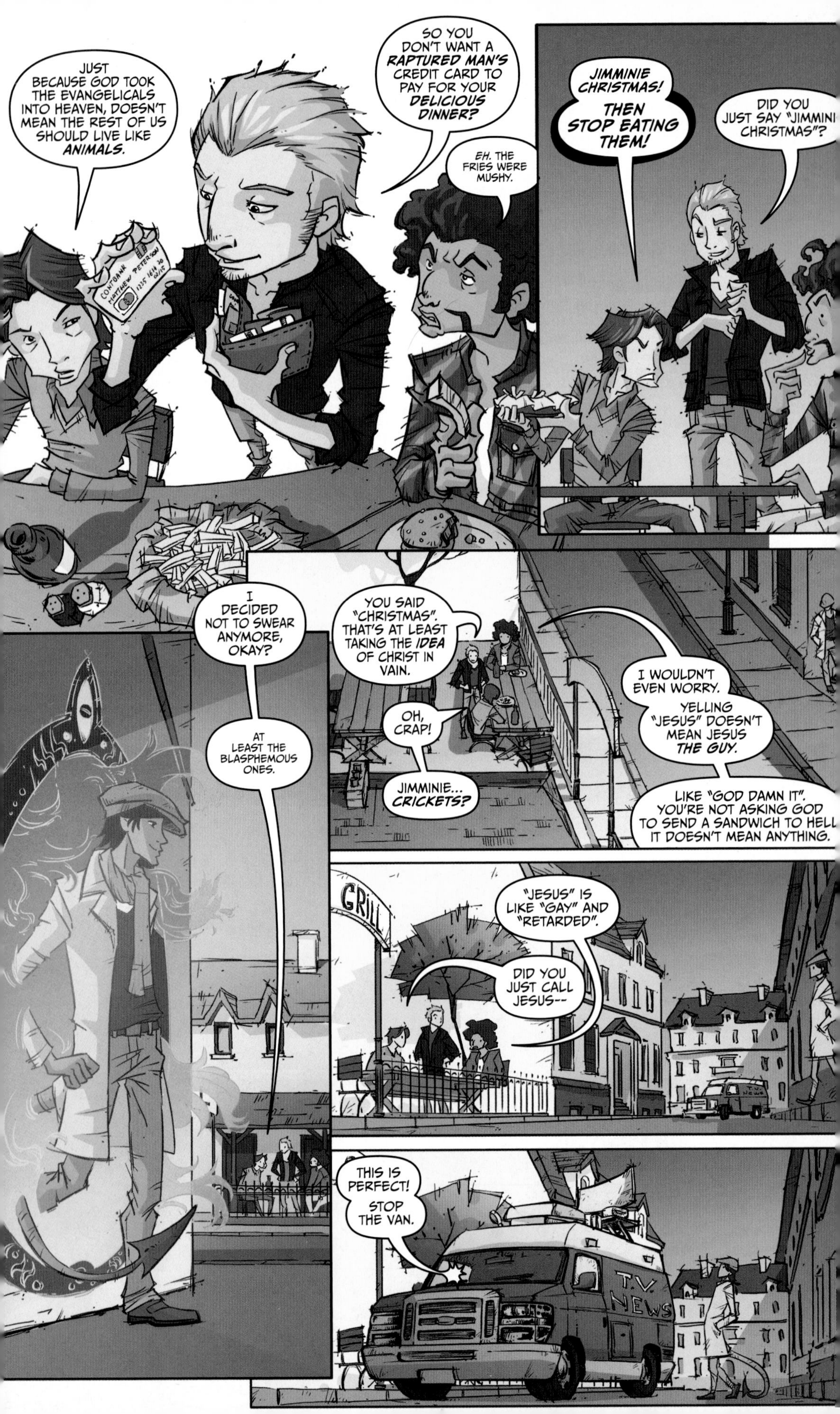
JUST BECAUSE GOD TOOK THE EVANGELICALS INTO HEAVEN, DOESN'T MEAN THE REST OF US SHOULD LIVE LIKE ANIMALS.
SO YOU DON'T WANT A RAPTURED MAN'S CREDIT CARD TO PAY FOR YOUR DELICIOUS DINNER?
EH. THE FRIES WERE MUSHY.
JIMMINIE CHRISTMAS!
THEN STOP EATING THEM!
DID YOU JUST SAY "JIMMINI CHRISTMAS"?
I DECIDED NOT TO SWEAR ANYMORE, OKAY?
AT LEAST THE BLASPHEMOUS ONES.
YOU SAID "CHRISTMAS". THAT'S AT LEAST TAKING THE IDEA OF CHRIST IN VAIN.
OH, CRAP!
JIMMINIE... CRICKETS?
I WOULDN'T EVEN WORRY.
YELLING "JESUS" DOESN'T MEAN JESUS THE GUY.
LIKE "GOD DAMN IT". YOU'RE NOT ASKING GOD TO SEND A SANDWICH TO HELL IT DOESN'T MEAN ANYTHING.
GRILL
"JESUS" IS LIKE "GAY" AND "RETARDED".
DID YOU JUST CALL JESUS--
THIS IS PERFECT!
STOP THE VAN.
T.V. NEWS

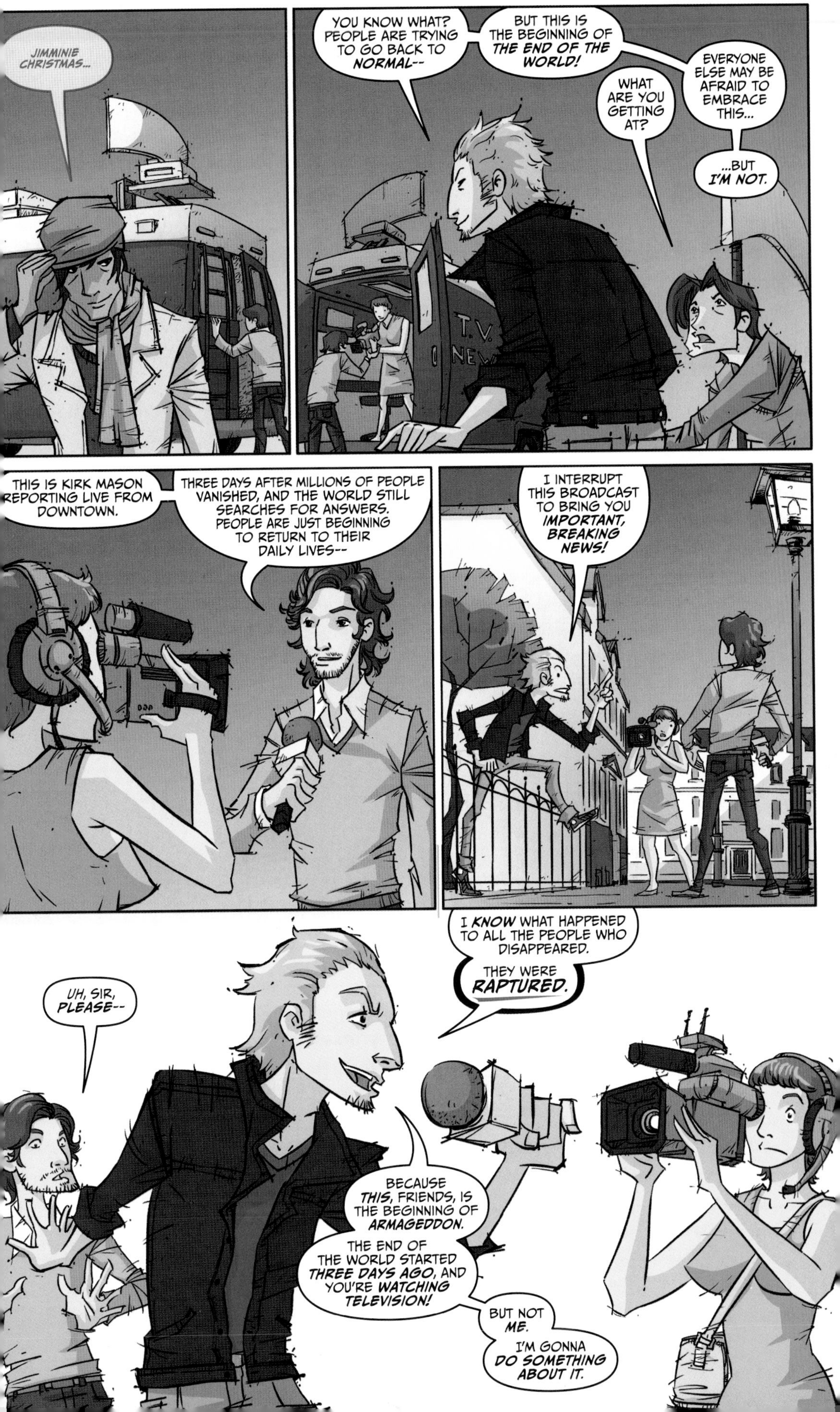
JIMMINIE CHRISTMAS...
YOU KNOW WHAT? PEOPLE ARE TRYING TO GO BACK TO NORMAL--
BUT THIS IS THE BEGINNING OF THE END OF THE WORLD!
WHAT ARE YOU GETTING AT?
EVERYONE ELSE MAY BE AFRAID TO EMBRACE THIS...
...BUT I'M NOT.
T.V. NEWS
THIS IS KIRK MASON REPORTING LIVE FROM DOWNTOWN.
THREE DAYS AFTER MILLIONS OF PEOPLE VANISHED, AND THE WORLD STILL SEARCHES FOR ANSWERS. PEOPLE ARE JUST BEGINNING TO RETURN TO THEIR DAILY LIVES--
I INTERRUPT THIS BROADCAST TO BRING YOU IMPORTANT, BREAKING NEWS!
I KNOW WHAT HAPPENED TO ALL THE PEOPLE WHO DISAPPEARED.
THEY WERE RAPTURED.
UH, SIR, PLEASE--
BECAUSE THIS, FRIENDS, IS THE BEGINNING OF ARMAGEDDON.
THE END OF THE WORLD STARTED THREE DAYS AGO, AND YOU'RE WATCHING TELEVISION!
BUT NOT ME.
I'M GONNA DO SOMETHING ABOUT IT.

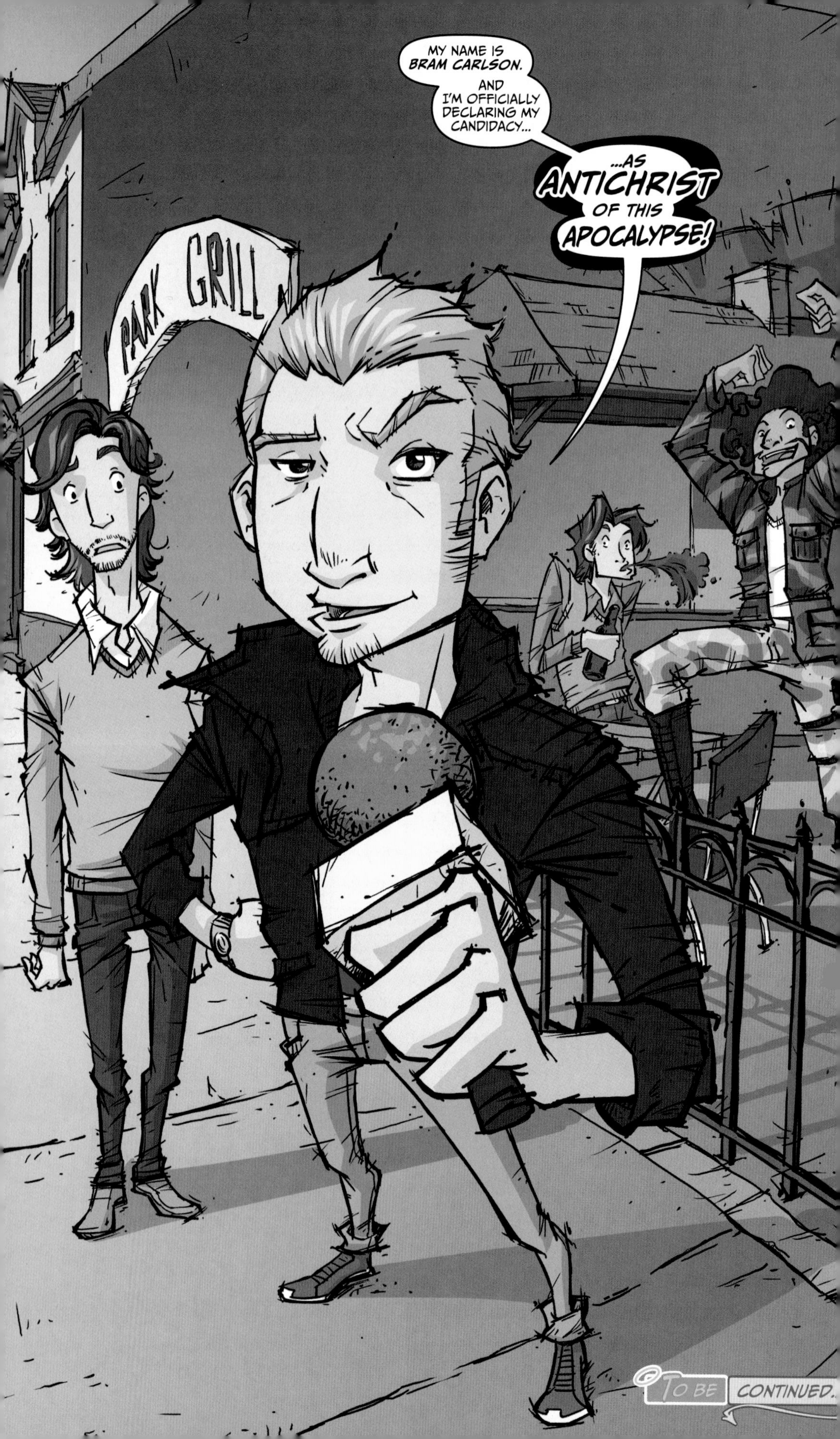
MY NAME IS BRAM CARLSON.
AND I'M OFFICIALLY DECLARING MY CANDIDACY...
...AS ANTICHRIST OF THIS APOCALYPSE!
PARK GRILL
TO BE CONTINUED.

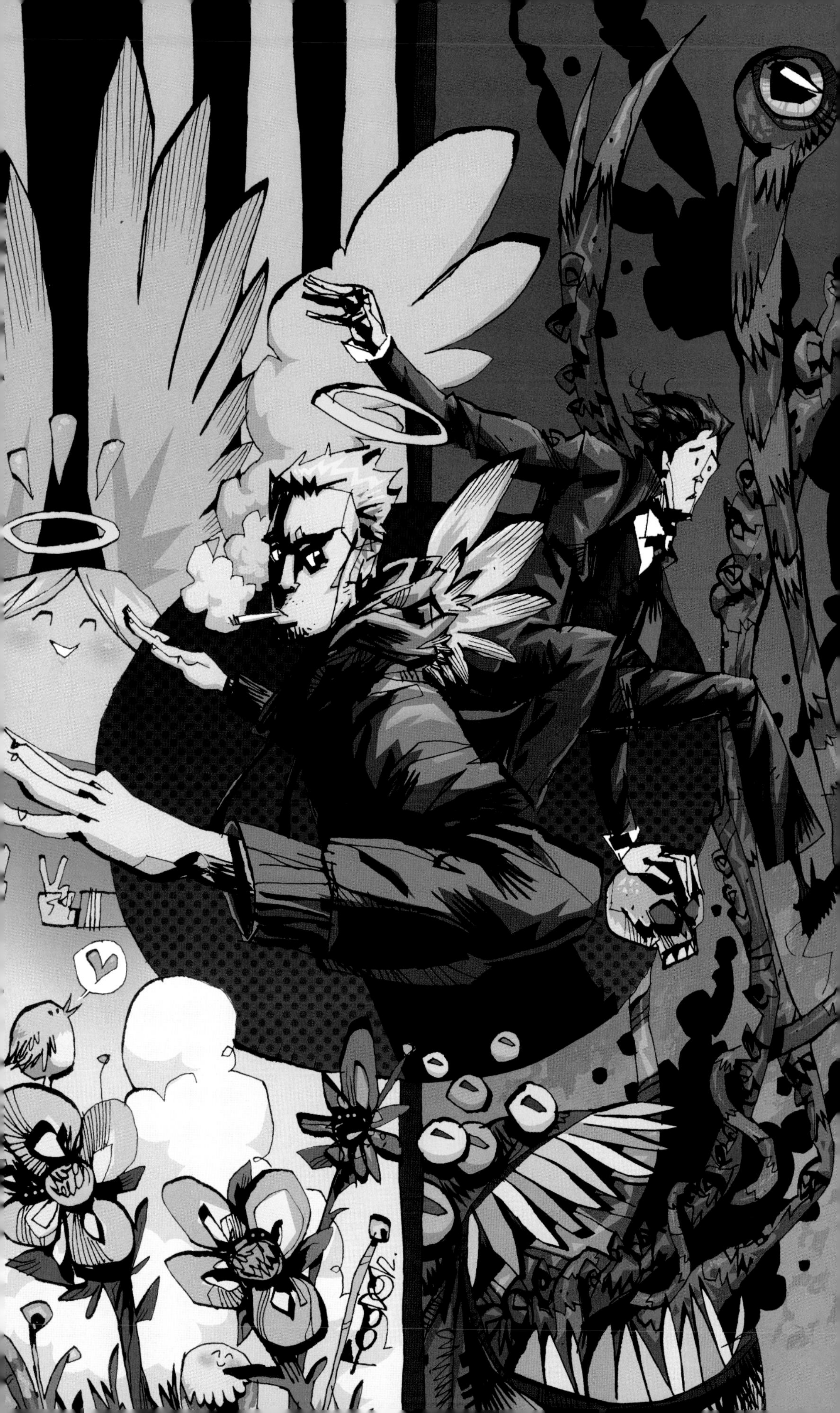

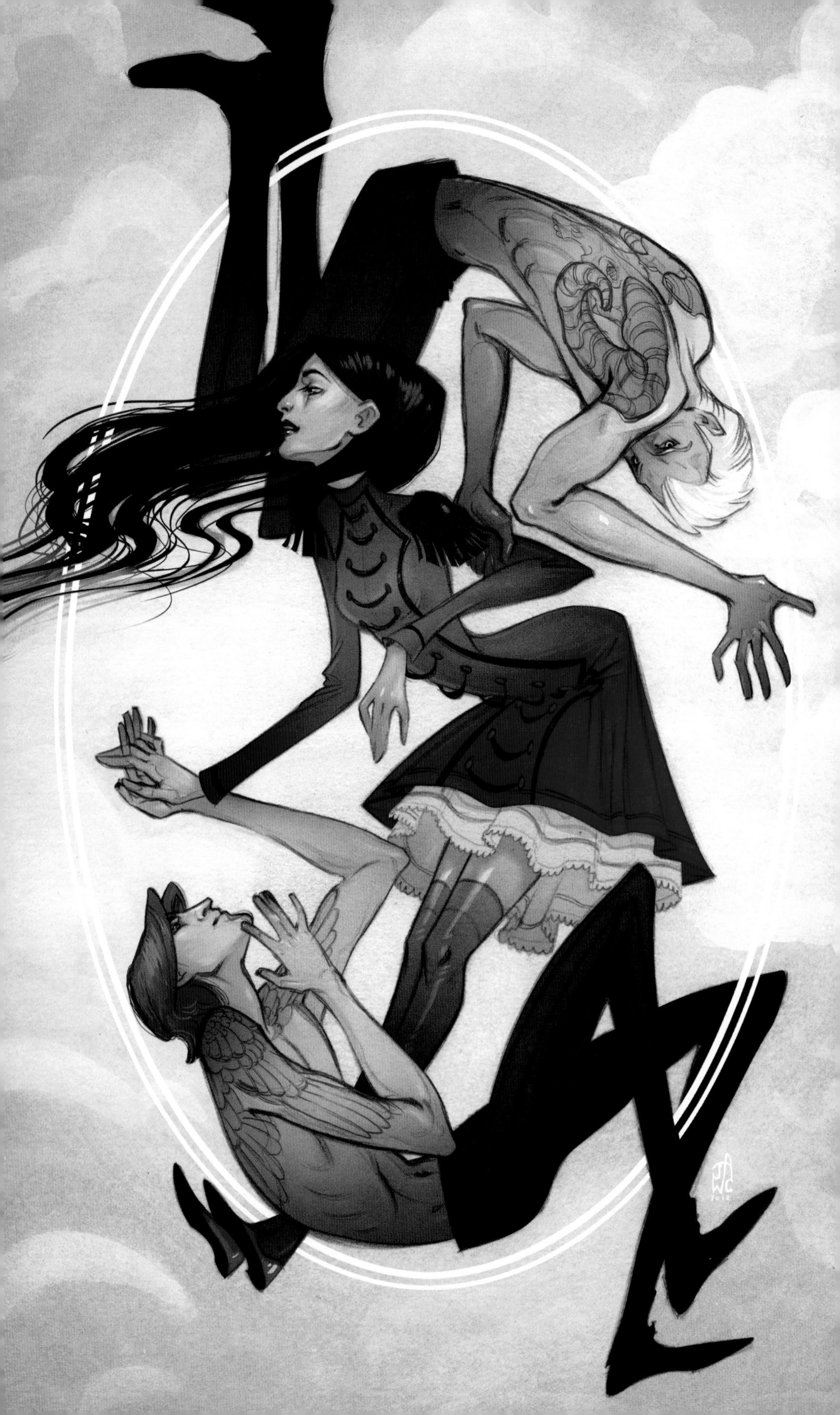

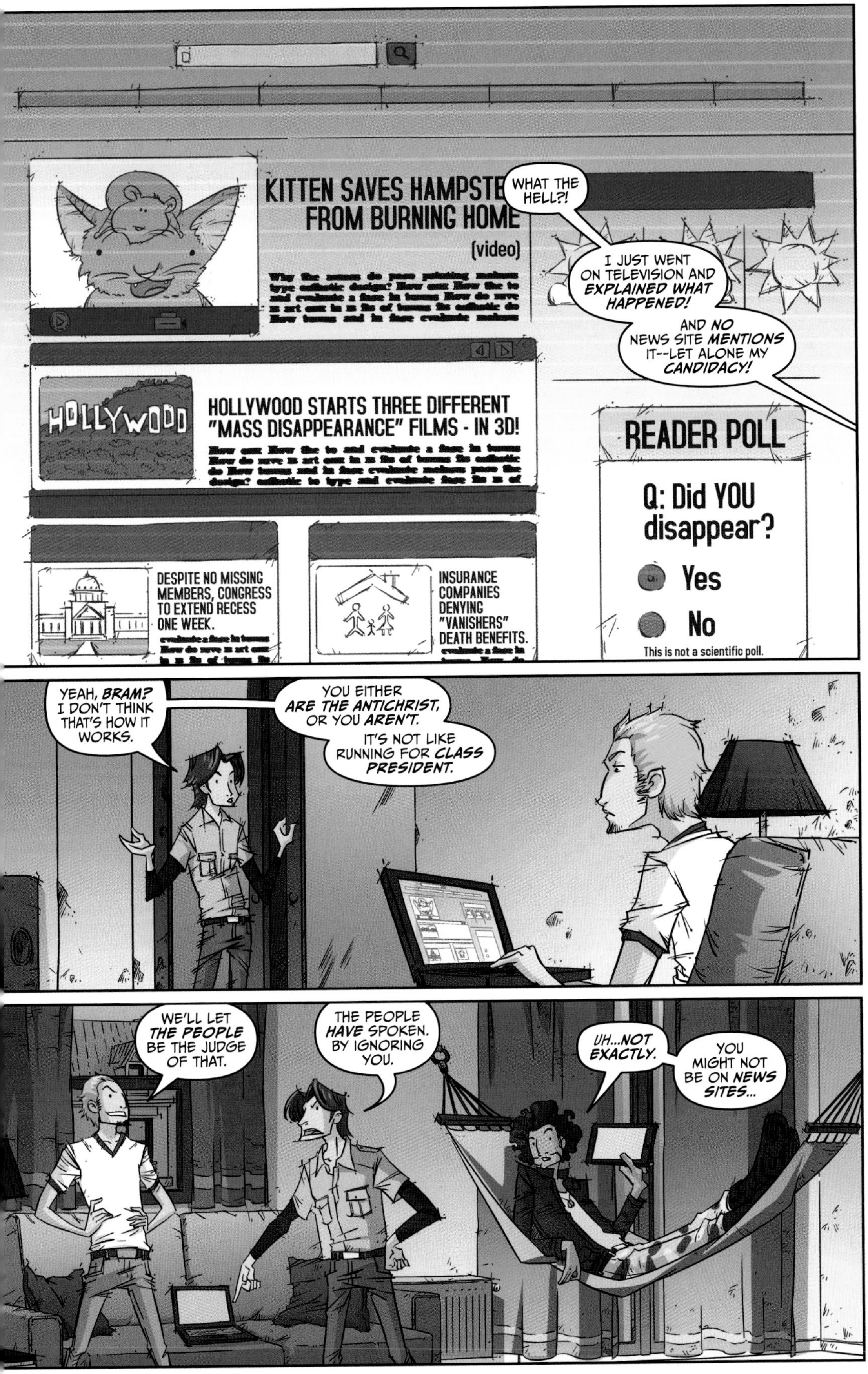
KITTEN SAVES HAMPSTE
FROM BURNING HOME
(video)
WHAT THE HELL?!
I JUST WENT ON TELEVISION AND EXPLAINED WHAT HAPPENED!
AND NO NEWS SITE MENTIONS IT--LET ALONE MY CANDIDACY!
HOLLYWOOD
HOLLYWOOD STARTS THREE DIFFERENT "MASS DISAPPEARANCE" FILMS - IN 3D!
READER POLL
Q: Did YOU disappear?
Yes
No
This is not a scientific poll.
DESPITE NO MISSING MEMBERS, CONGRESS TO EXTEND RECESS ONE WEEK.
INSURANCE COMPANIES DENYING "VANISHERS" DEATH BENEFITS.
YEAH, BRAM? I DON'T THINK THAT'S HOW IT WORKS.
YOU EITHER ARE THE ANTICHRIST, OR YOU AREN'T.
IT'S NOT LIKE RUNNING FOR CLASS PRESIDENT.
WE'LL LET THE PEOPLE BE THE JUDGE OF THAT.
THE PEOPLE HAVE SPOKEN. BY IGNORING YOU.
UH...NOT EXACTLY.
YOU MIGHT NOT BE ON NEWS SITES...

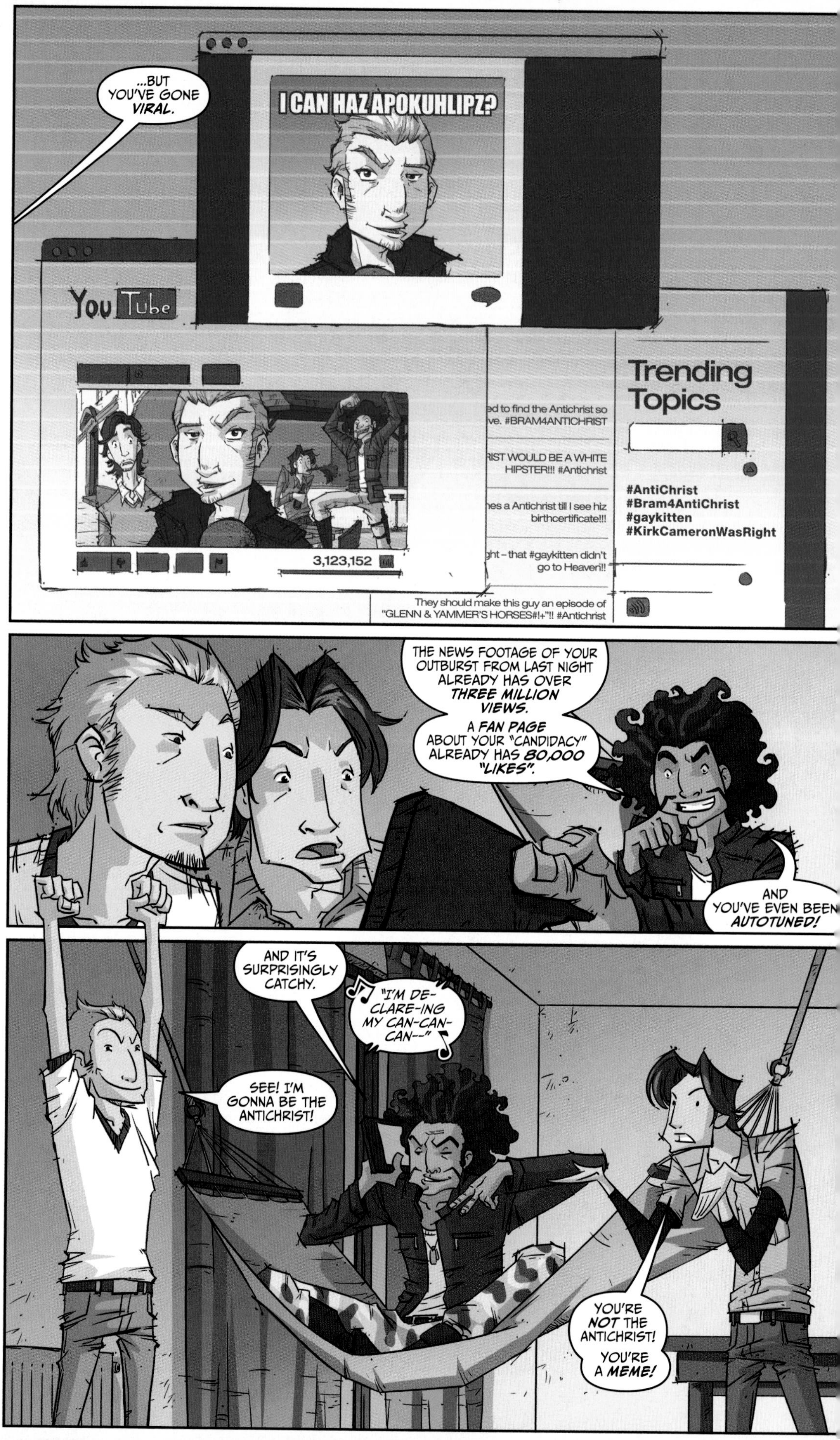
...BUT YOU'VE GONE *VIRAL*.
I CAN HAZ APOKUHLIPZ?
YouTube
3,123,152
ed to find the Antichrist so
ve. #BRAM4ANTICHRIST
RIST WOULD BE A WHITE HIPSTER!!! #Antichrist
nes a Antichrist till I see hiz birthcertificate!!!
ght – that #gaykitten didn't go to Heaven!!
They should make this guy an episode of "GLENN & YAMMER'S HORSES#!+"!! #Antichrist
Trending Topics
#AntiChrist
#Bram4AntiChrist
#gaykitten
#KirkCameronWasRight
THE NEWS FOOTAGE OF YOUR OUTBURST FROM LAST NIGHT ALREADY HAS OVER *THREE MILLION VIEWS*.
A *FAN PAGE* ABOUT YOUR "CANDIDACY" ALREADY HAS *80,000 "LIKES"*.
AND YOU'VE EVEN BEEN *AUTOTUNED!*
AND IT'S SURPRISINGLY CATCHY.
"I'M DE-CLARE-ING MY CAN-CAN-CAN--"
SEE! I'M GONNA BE THE ANTICHRIST!
YOU'RE *NOT* THE ANTICHRIST!
YOU'RE A *MEME!*

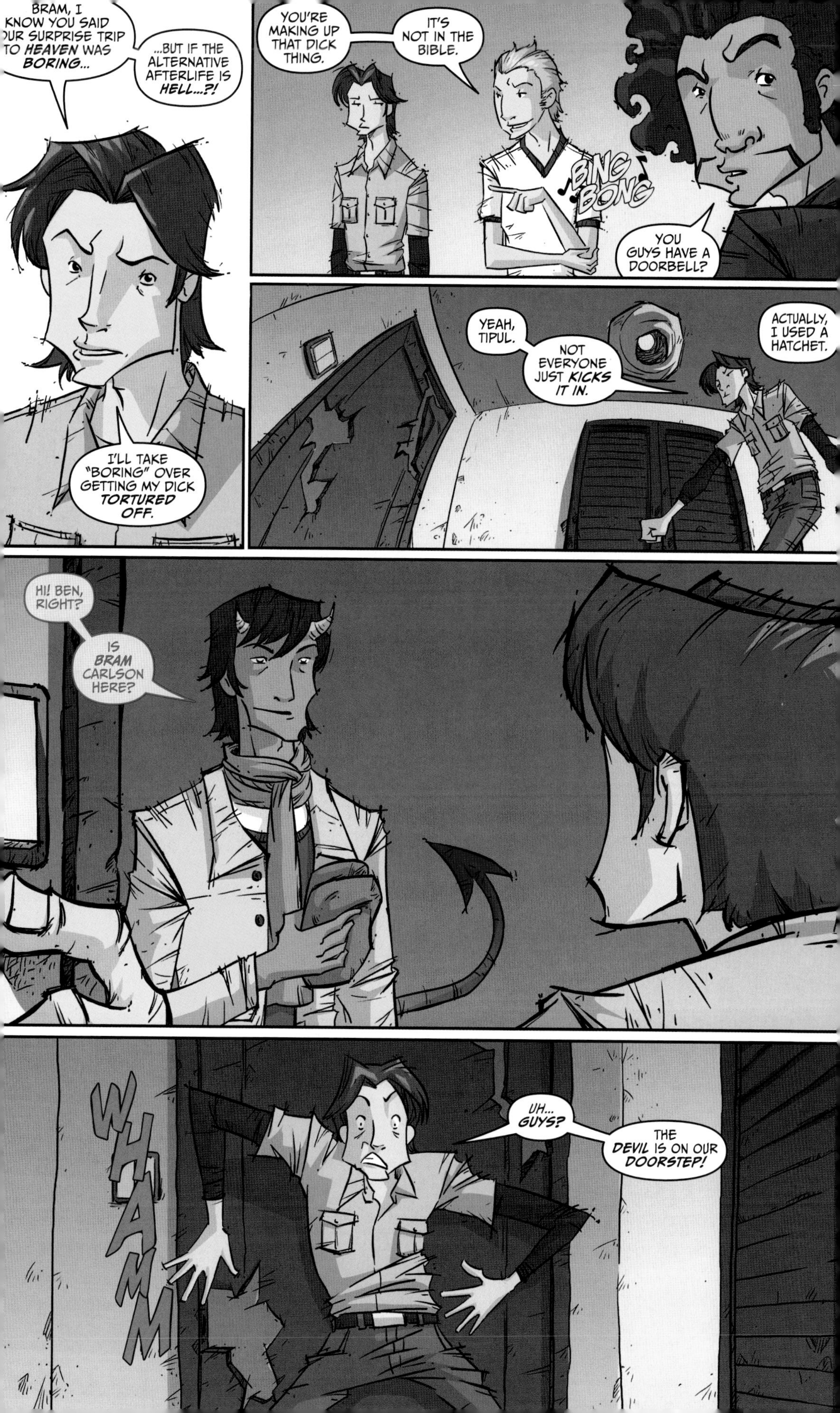
BRAM, I KNOW YOU SAID OUR SURPRISE TRIP TO HEAVEN WAS BORING...
...BUT IF THE ALTERNATIVE AFTERLIFE IS HELL...?!
I'LL TAKE "BORING" OVER GETTING MY DICK TORTURED OFF.
YOU'RE MAKING UP THAT DICK THING.
IT'S NOT IN THE BIBLE.
BING BONG
YOU GUYS HAVE A DOORBELL?
YEAH, TIPUL.
NOT EVERYONE JUST KICKS IT IN.
ACTUALLY, I USED A HATCHET.
HI! BEN, RIGHT?
IS BRAM CARLSON HERE?
WHAMM
UH... GUYS?
THE DEVIL IS ON OUR DOORSTEP!

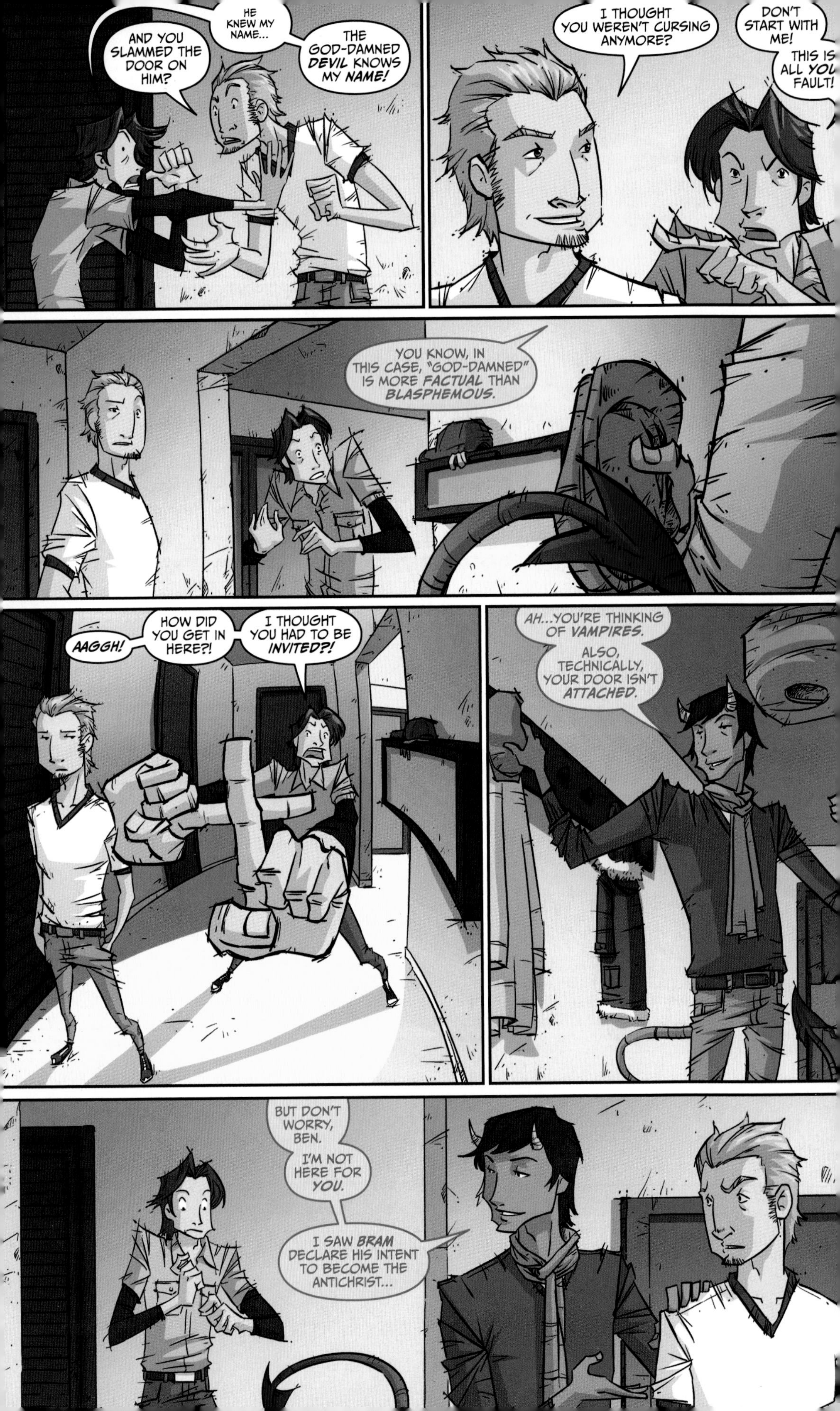
AND YOU SLAMMED THE DOOR ON HIM?
HE KNEW MY NAME...
THE GOD-DAMNED DEVIL KNOWS MY NAME!
I THOUGHT YOU WEREN'T CURSING ANYMORE?
DON'T START WITH ME!
THIS IS ALL YOU FAULT!
YOU KNOW, IN THIS CASE, "GOD-DAMNED" IS MORE FACTUAL THAN BLASPHEMOUS.
AAGGH!
HOW DID YOU GET IN HERE?!
I THOUGHT YOU HAD TO BE INVITED?!
AH...YOU'RE THINKING OF VAMPIRES.
ALSO, TECHNICALLY, YOUR DOOR ISN'T ATTACHED.
BUT DON'T WORRY, BEN.
I'M NOT HERE FOR YOU.
I SAW BRAM DECLARE HIS INTENT TO BECOME THE ANTICHRIST...

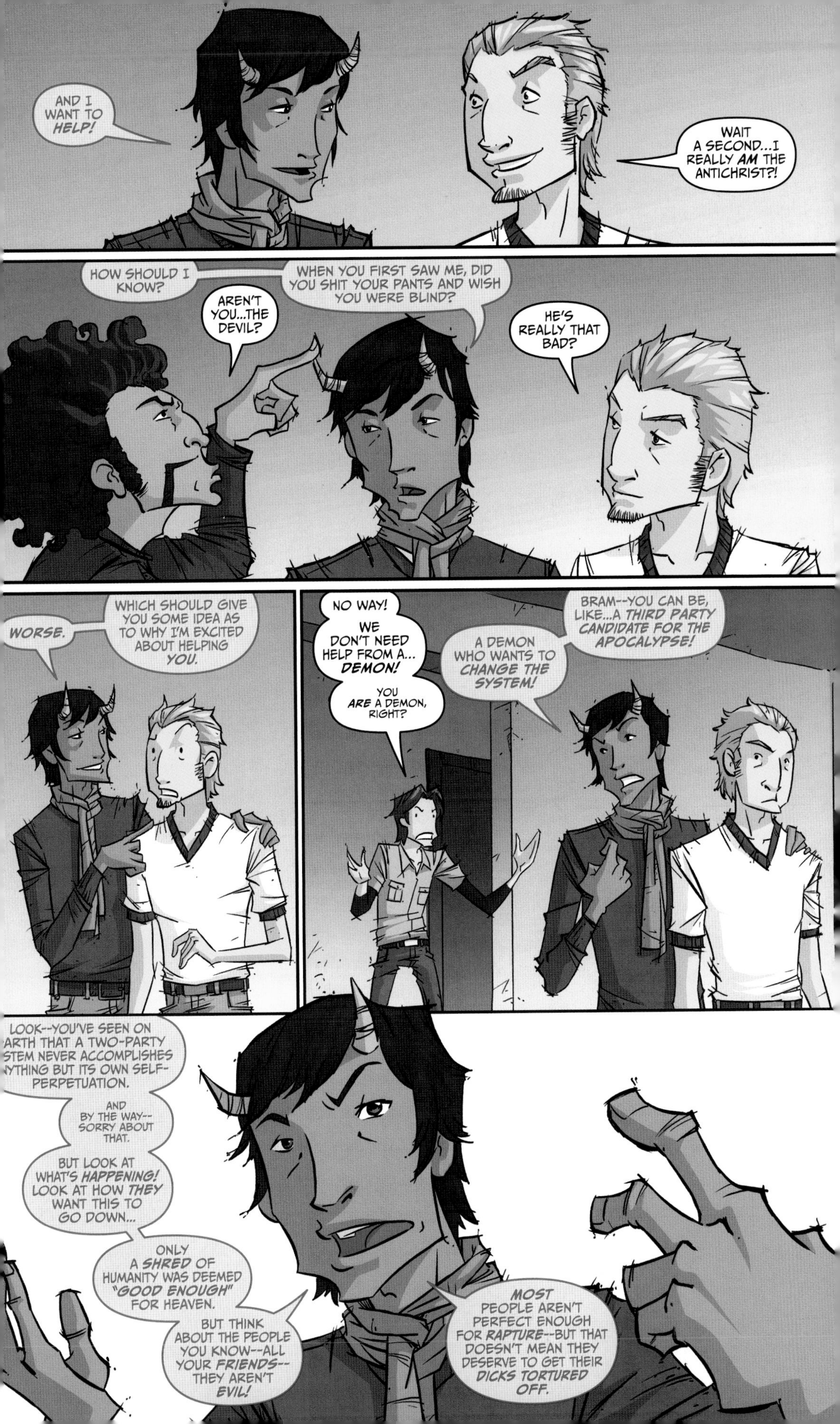
AND I WANT TO HELP!
WAIT A SECOND...I REALLY AM THE ANTICHRIST?!
HOW SHOULD I KNOW?
WHEN YOU FIRST SAW ME, DID YOU SHIT YOUR PANTS AND WISH YOU WERE BLIND?
AREN'T YOU...THE DEVIL?
HE'S REALLY THAT BAD?
WORSE.
WHICH SHOULD GIVE YOU SOME IDEA AS TO WHY I'M EXCITED ABOUT HELPING YOU.
NO WAY!
WE DON'T NEED HELP FROM A... DEMON!
YOU ARE A DEMON, RIGHT?
A DEMON WHO WANTS TO CHANGE THE SYSTEM!
BRAM--YOU CAN BE, LIKE...A THIRD PARTY CANDIDATE FOR THE APOCALYPSE!
LOOK--YOU'VE SEEN ON ARTH THAT A TWO-PARTY STEM NEVER ACCOMPLISHES YTHING BUT ITS OWN SELF-PERPETUATION.
AND BY THE WAY--SORRY ABOUT THAT.
BUT LOOK AT WHAT'S HAPPENING! LOOK AT HOW THEY WANT THIS TO GO DOWN...
ONLY A SHRED OF HUMANITY WAS DEEMED "GOOD ENOUGH" FOR HEAVEN.
BUT THINK ABOUT THE PEOPLE YOU KNOW--ALL YOUR FRIENDS--THEY AREN'T EVIL!
MOST PEOPLE AREN'T PERFECT ENOUGH FOR RAPTURE--BUT THAT DOESN'T MEAN THEY DESERVE TO GET THEIR DICKS TORTURED OFF.

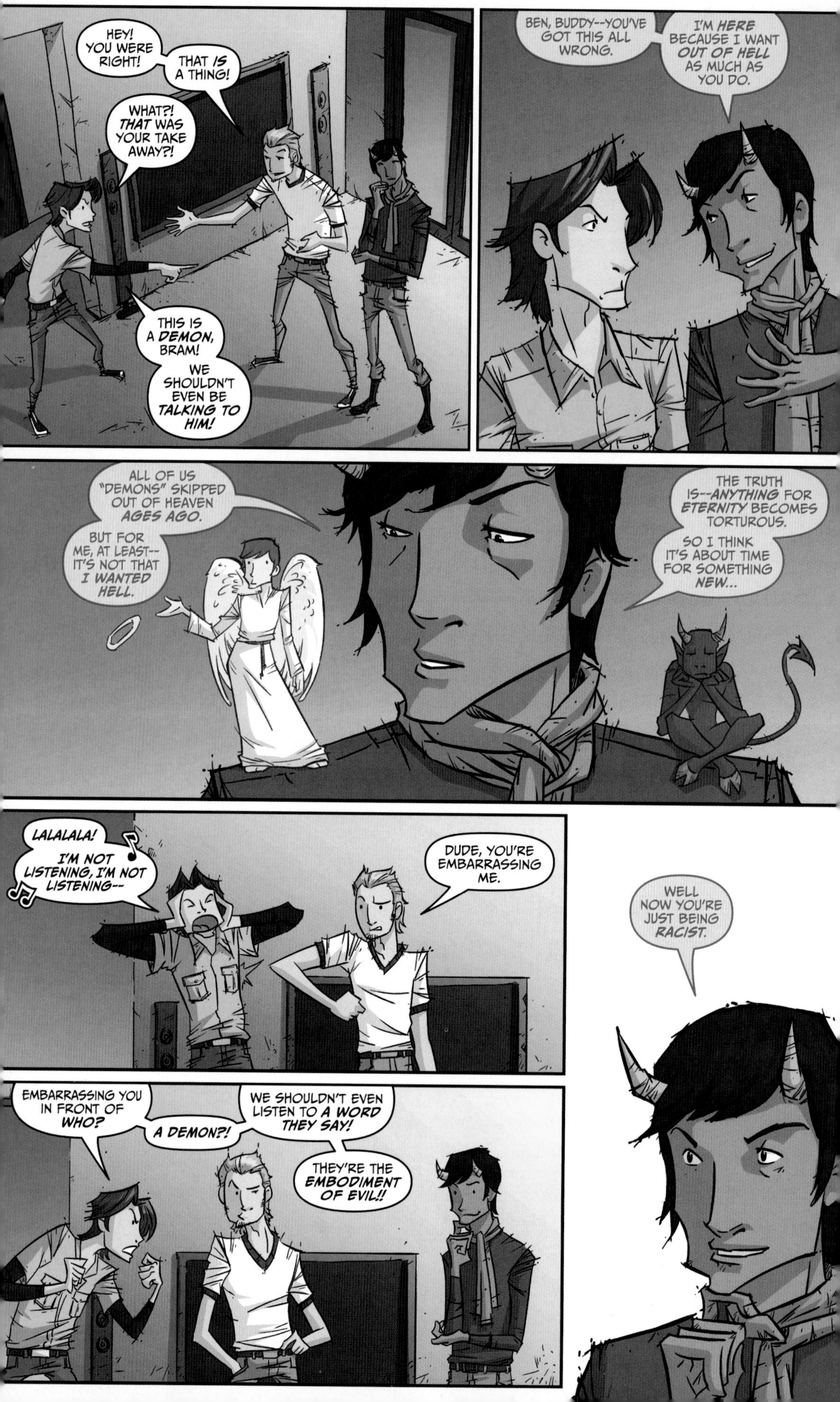

HEY! YOU WERE RIGHT!
THAT IS A THING!
WHAT?! THAT WAS YOUR TAKE AWAY?!
THIS IS A DEMON, BRAM!
WE SHOULDN'T EVEN BE TALKING TO HIM!
BEN, BUDDY--YOU'VE GOT THIS ALL WRONG.
I'M HERE BECAUSE I WANT OUT OF HELL AS MUCH AS YOU DO.
ALL OF US "DEMONS" SKIPPED OUT OF HEAVEN AGES AGO.
BUT FOR ME, AT LEAST--IT'S NOT THAT I WANTED HELL.
THE TRUTH IS--ANYTHING FOR ETERNITY BECOMES TORTUROUS.
SO I THINK IT'S ABOUT TIME FOR SOMETHING NEW...
LALALALA!
I'M NOT LISTENING, I'M NOT LISTENING--
DUDE, YOU'RE EMBARRASSING ME.
EMBARRASSING YOU IN FRONT OF WHO?
A DEMON?!
WE SHOULDN'T EVEN LISTEN TO A WORD THEY SAY!
THEY'RE THE EMBODIMENT OF EVIL!!
WELL NOW YOU'RE JUST BEING RACIST.

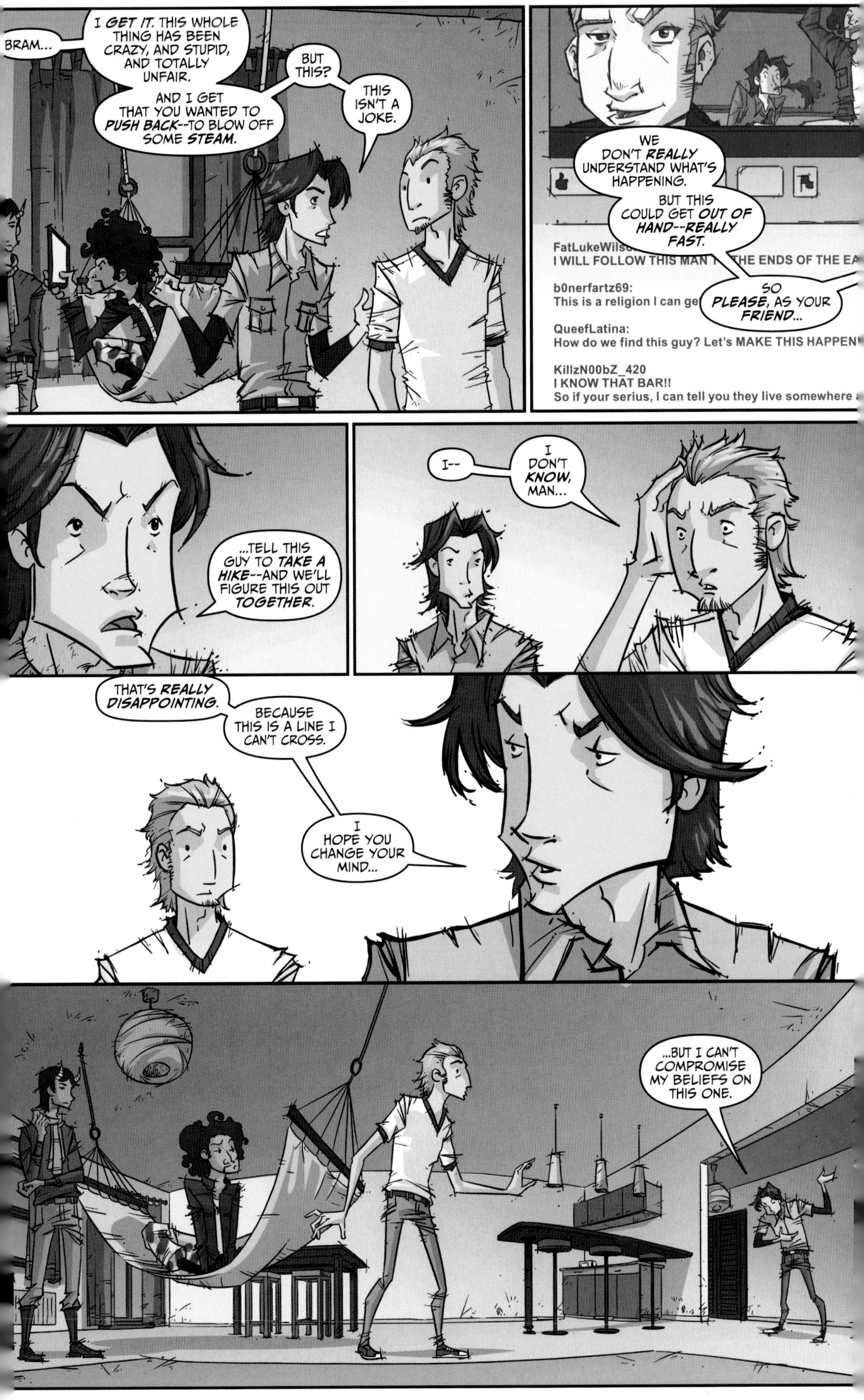
BRAM...
I GET IT. THIS WHOLE THING HAS BEEN CRAZY, AND STUPID, AND TOTALLY UNFAIR.
AND I GET THAT YOU WANTED TO PUSH BACK--TO BLOW OFF SOME STEAM.
BUT THIS?
THIS ISN'T A JOKE.
WE DON'T REALLY UNDERSTAND WHAT'S HAPPENING.
BUT THIS COULD GET OUT OF HAND--REALLY FAST.
FatLukeWils
I WILL FOLLOW THIS MAN T THE ENDS OF THE EA
b0nerfartz69:
This is a religion I can ge
SO PLEASE, AS YOUR FRIEND...
QueefLatina:
How do we find this guy? Let's MAKE THIS HAPPEN
KillzN00bZ_420
I KNOW THAT BAR!!
So if your serius, I can tell you they live somewhere
...TELL THIS GUY TO TAKE A HIKE--AND WE'LL FIGURE THIS OUT TOGETHER.
I--
I DON'T KNOW, MAN...
THAT'S REALLY DISAPPOINTING.
BECAUSE THIS IS A LINE I CAN'T CROSS.
I HOPE YOU CHANGE YOUR MIND...
...BUT I CAN'T COMPROMISE MY BELIEFS ON THIS ONE.

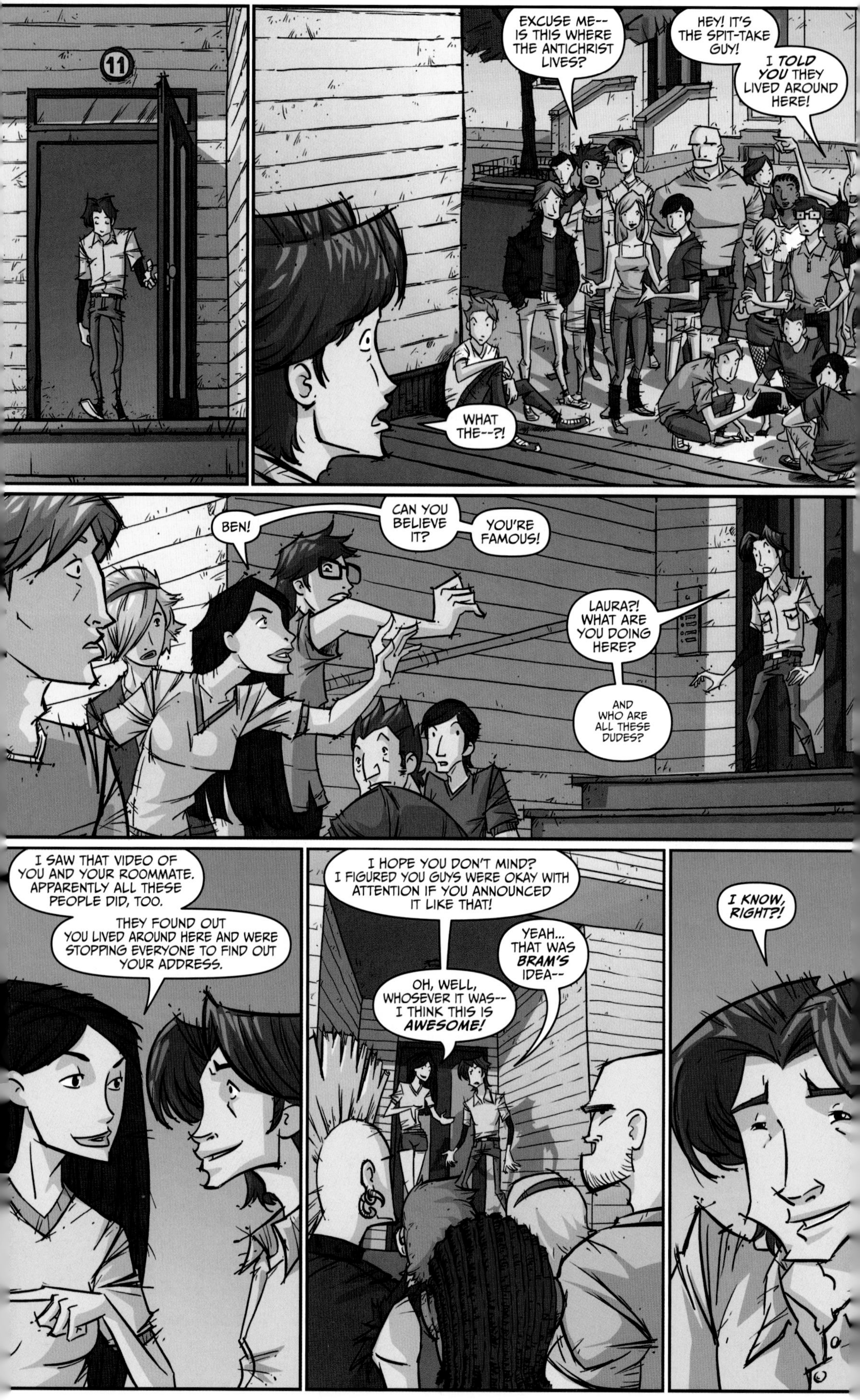
EXCUSE ME-- IS THIS WHERE THE ANTICHRIST LIVES?
HEY! IT'S THE SPIT-TAKE GUY!
I TOLD YOU THEY LIVED AROUND HERE!
WHAT THE--?!
BEN!
CAN YOU BELIEVE IT?
YOU'RE FAMOUS!
LAURA?! WHAT ARE YOU DOING HERE?
AND WHO ARE ALL THESE DUDES?
I SAW THAT VIDEO OF YOU AND YOUR ROOMMATE. APPARENTLY ALL THESE PEOPLE DID, TOO.
THEY FOUND OUT YOU LIVED AROUND HERE AND WERE STOPPING EVERYONE TO FIND OUT YOUR ADDRESS.
I HOPE YOU DON'T MIND? I FIGURED YOU GUYS WERE OKAY WITH ATTENTION IF YOU ANNOUNCED IT LIKE THAT!
YEAH... THAT WAS BRAM'S IDEA--
OH, WELL, WHOSEVER IT WAS-- I THINK THIS IS AWESOME!
I KNOW, RIGHT?!

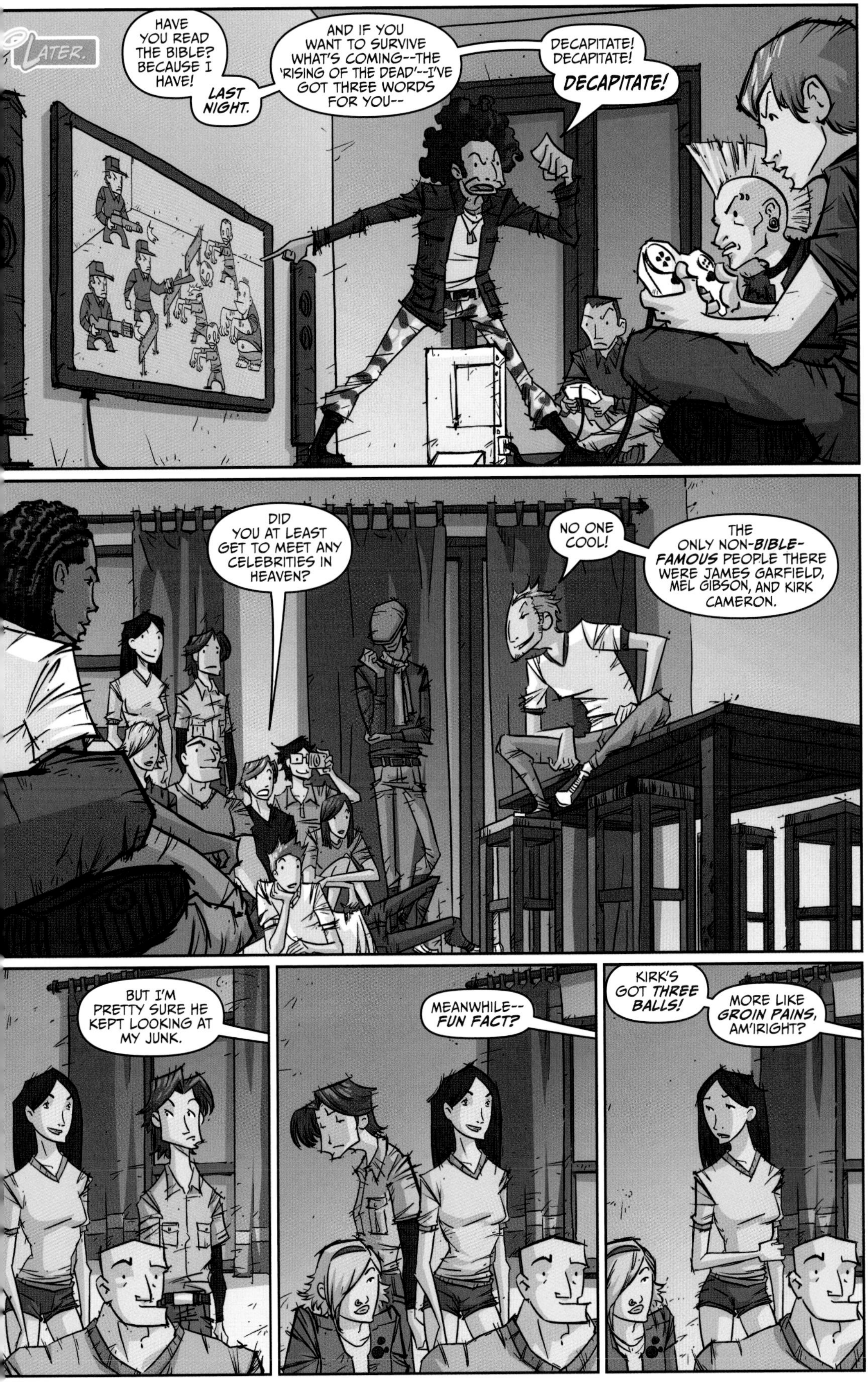
LATER.
HAVE YOU READ THE BIBLE? BECAUSE I HAVE!
LAST NIGHT.
AND IF YOU WANT TO SURVIVE WHAT'S COMING--THE 'RISING OF THE DEAD'--I'VE GOT THREE WORDS FOR YOU--
DECAPITATE! DECAPITATE! DECAPITATE!
DID YOU AT LEAST GET TO MEET ANY CELEBRITIES IN HEAVEN?
NO ONE COOL!
THE ONLY NON-BIBLE-FAMOUS PEOPLE THERE WERE JAMES GARFIELD, MEL GIBSON, AND KIRK CAMERON.
BUT I'M PRETTY SURE HE KEPT LOOKING AT MY JUNK.
MEANWHILE-- FUN FACT?
KIRK'S GOT THREE BALLS!
MORE LIKE GROIN PAINS, AM'IRIGHT?

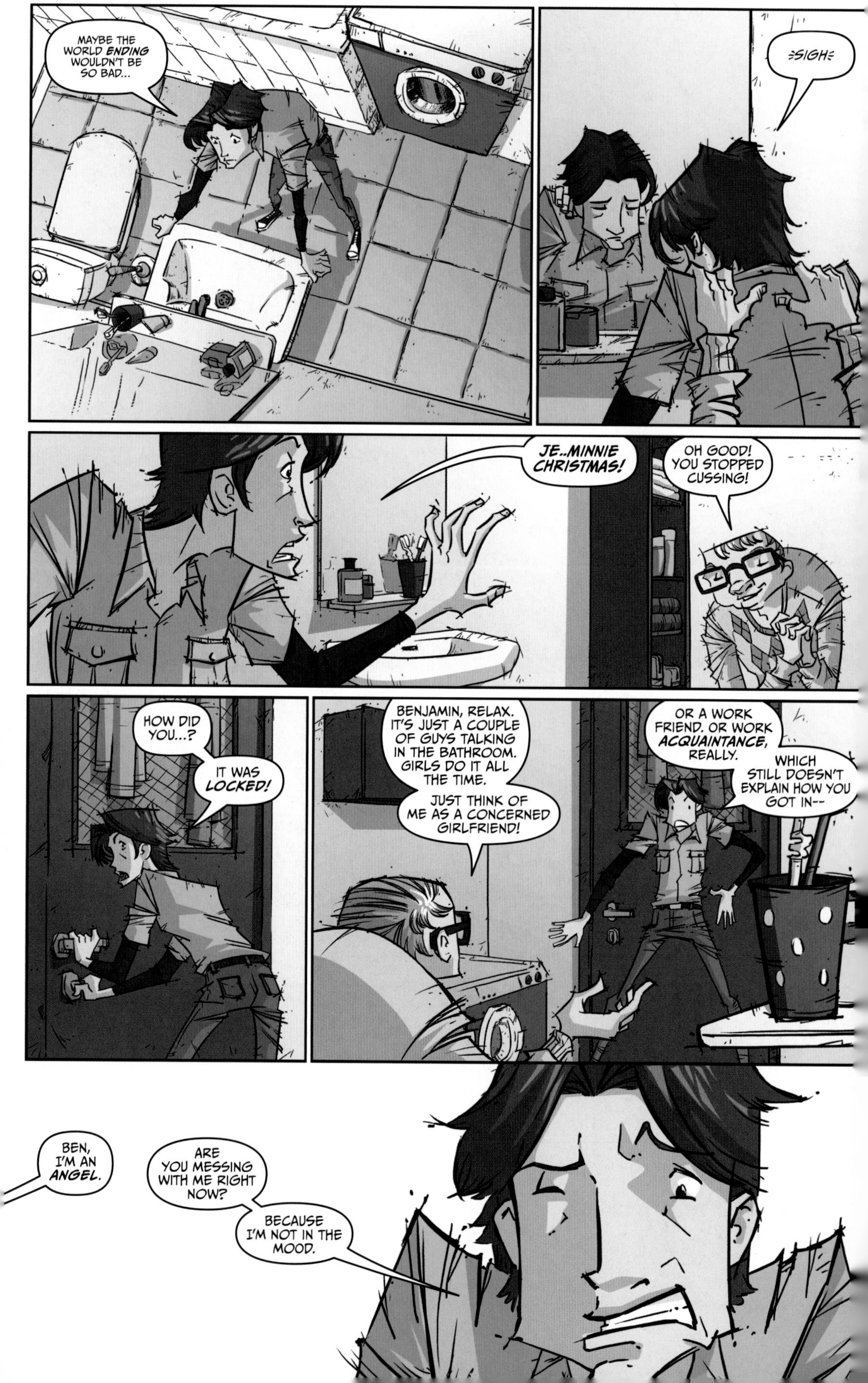
MAYBE THE WORLD ENDING WOULDN'T BE SO BAD...
SIGH
JE..MINNIE CHRISTMAS!
OH GOOD! YOU STOPPED CUSSING!
HOW DID YOU...?
IT WAS LOCKED!
BENJAMIN, RELAX. IT'S JUST A COUPLE OF GUYS TALKING IN THE BATHROOM. GIRLS DO IT ALL THE TIME.
JUST THINK OF ME AS A CONCERNED GIRLFRIEND!
OR A WORK FRIEND. OR WORK ACQUAINTANCE, REALLY.
WHICH STILL DOESN'T EXPLAIN HOW YOU GOT IN--
BEN, I'M AN ANGEL.
ARE YOU MESSING WITH ME RIGHT NOW?
BECAUSE I'M NOT IN THE MOOD.

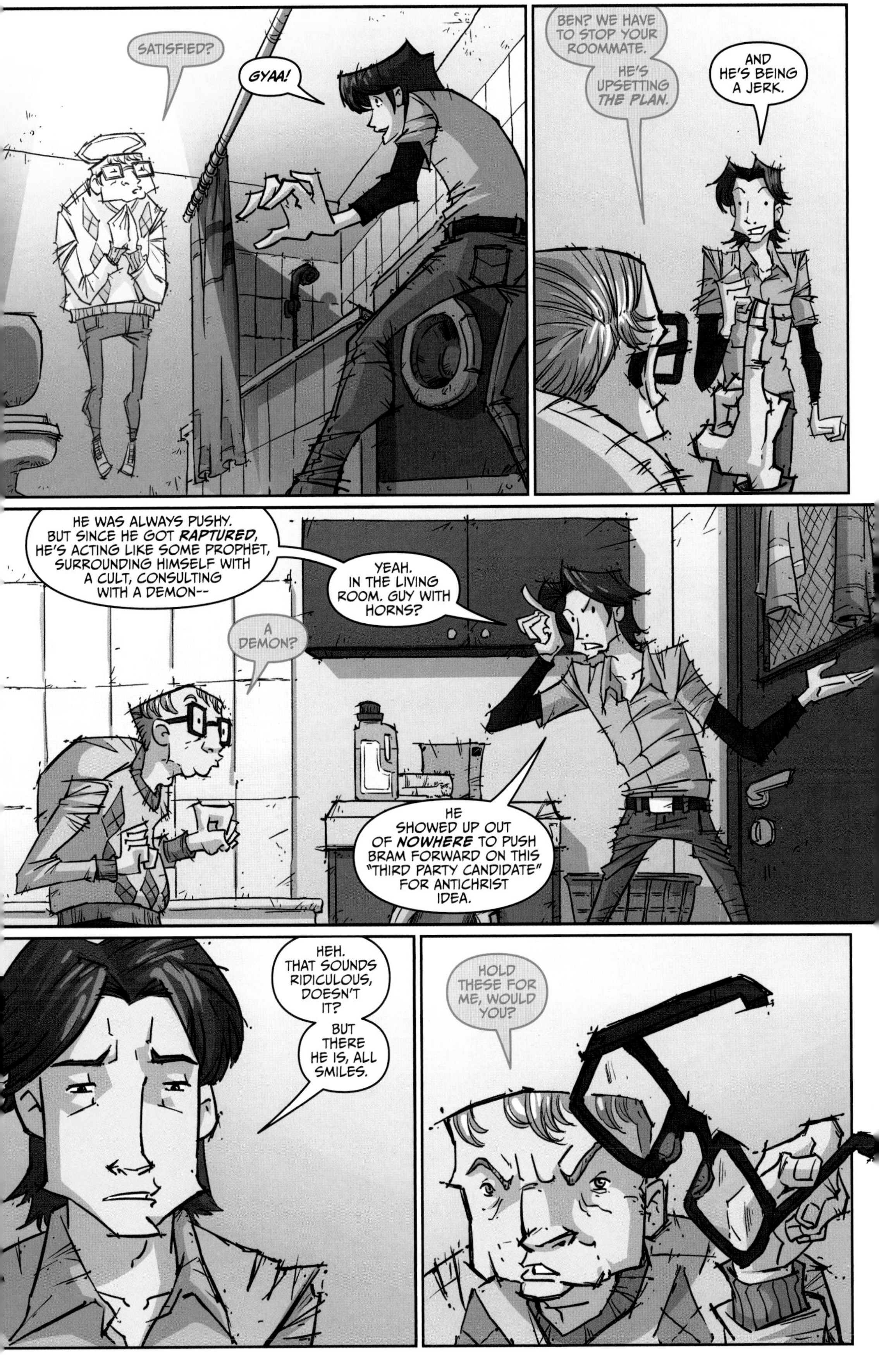
SATISFIED?
GYAA!
BEN? WE HAVE TO STOP YOUR ROOMMATE.
HE'S UPSETTING THE PLAN.
AND HE'S BEING A JERK.
HE WAS ALWAYS PUSHY. BUT SINCE HE GOT RAPTURED, HE'S ACTING LIKE SOME PROPHET, SURROUNDING HIMSELF WITH A CULT, CONSULTING WITH A DEMON--
YEAH. IN THE LIVING ROOM. GUY WITH HORNS?
A DEMON?
HE SHOWED UP OUT OF NOWHERE TO PUSH BRAM FORWARD ON THIS "THIRD PARTY CANDIDATE" FOR ANTICHRIST IDEA.
HEH. THAT SOUNDS RIDICULOUS, DOESN'T IT?
BUT THERE HE IS, ALL SMILES.
HOLD THESE FOR ME, WOULD YOU?

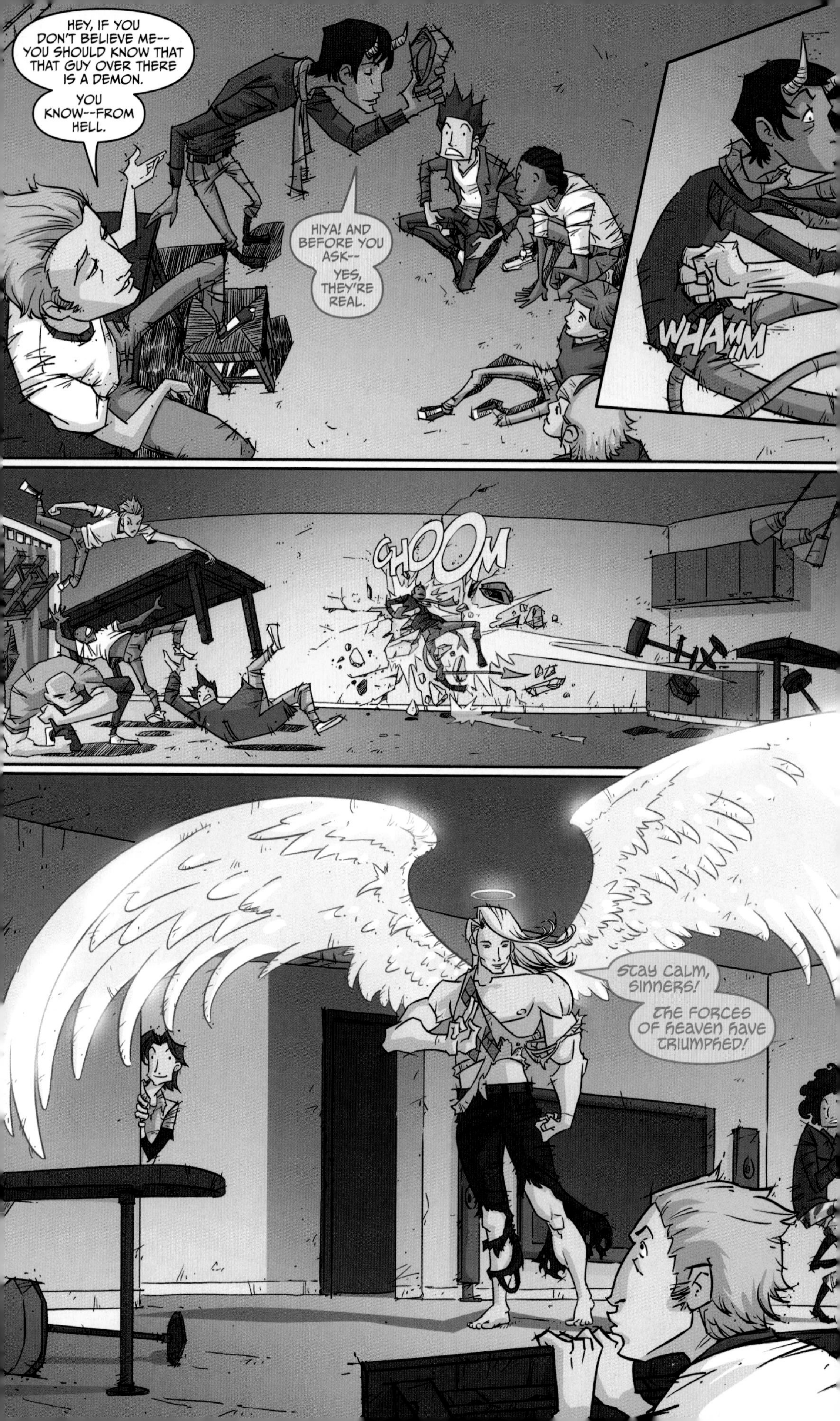
HEY, IF YOU DON'T BELIEVE ME-- YOU SHOULD KNOW THAT THAT GUY OVER THERE IS A DEMON.
YOU KNOW--FROM HELL.
HIYA! AND BEFORE YOU ASK--
YES, THEY'RE REAL.
WHAMM
CHOOM
STAY CALM, SINNERS!
THE FORCES OF HEAVEN HAVE TRIUMPHED!

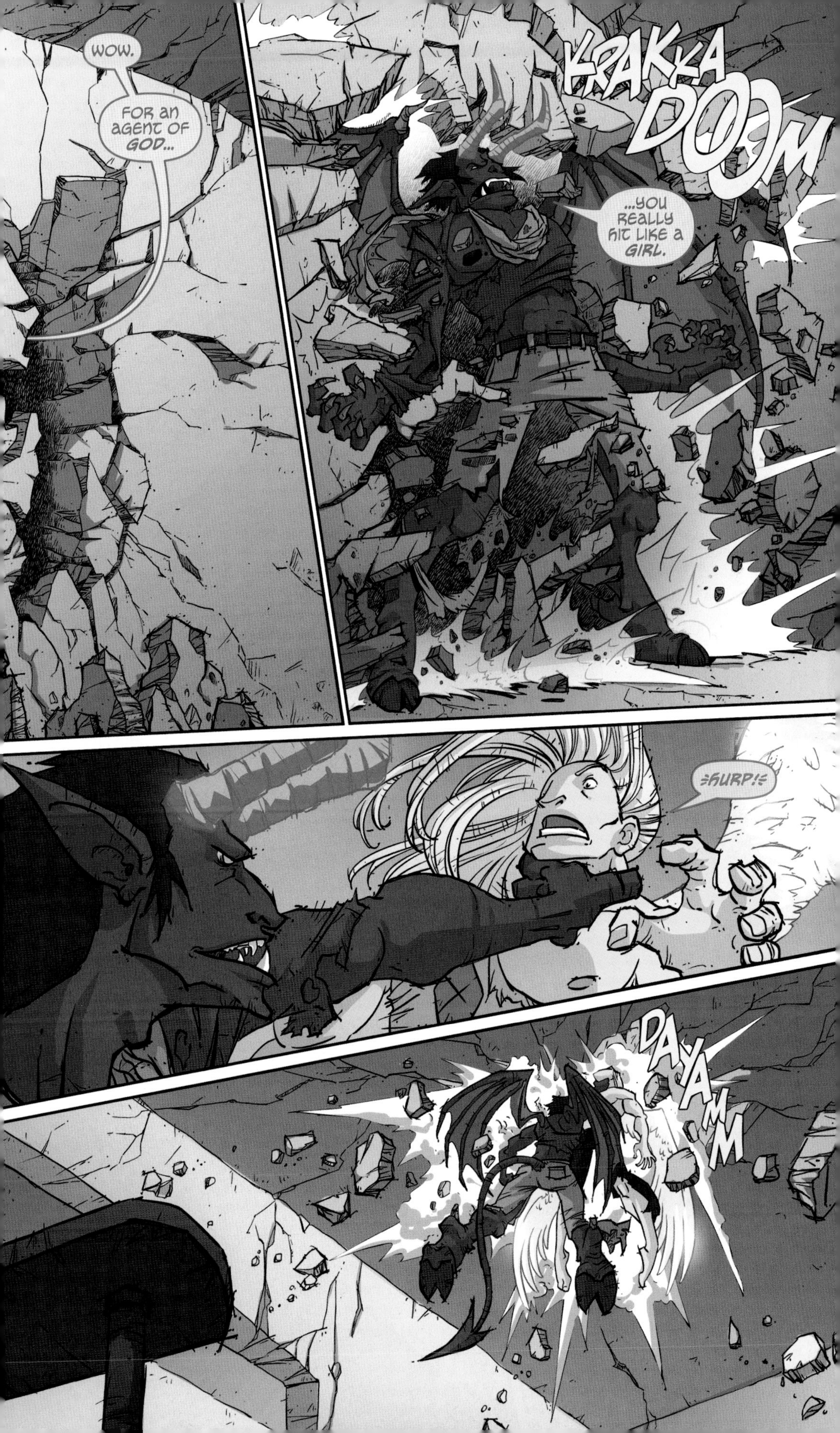
WOW.
FOR an agent OF GOD...
KRAKKA DOOOM
...YOU REALLY HIT LIKE A GIRL.
HURP!
DAYAMM

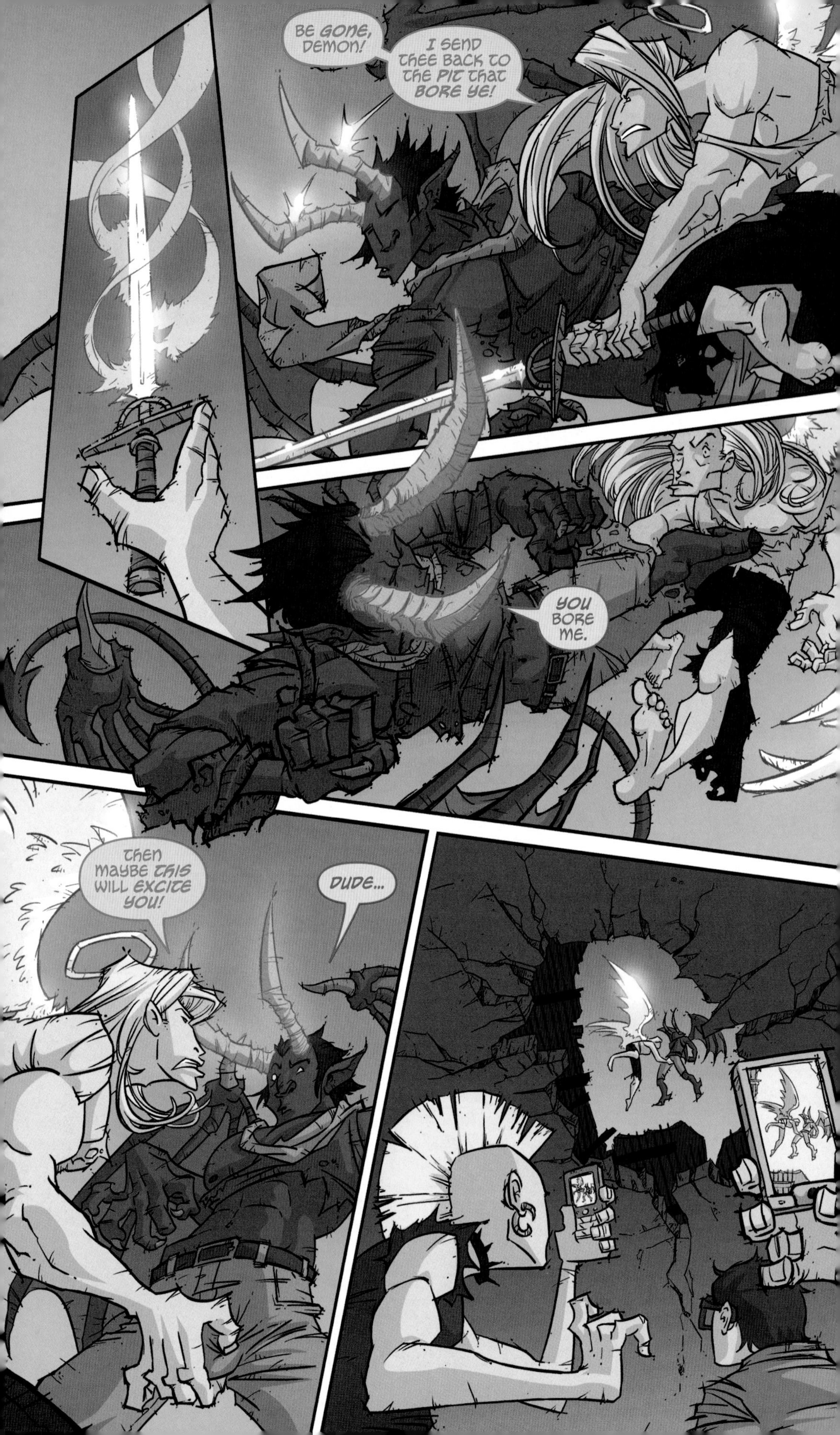
BE GONE, DEMON!
I SEND THEE BACK TO THE PIT THAT BORE YE!
YOU BORE ME.
THEN MAYBE THIS WILL EXCITE YOU!
DUDE...

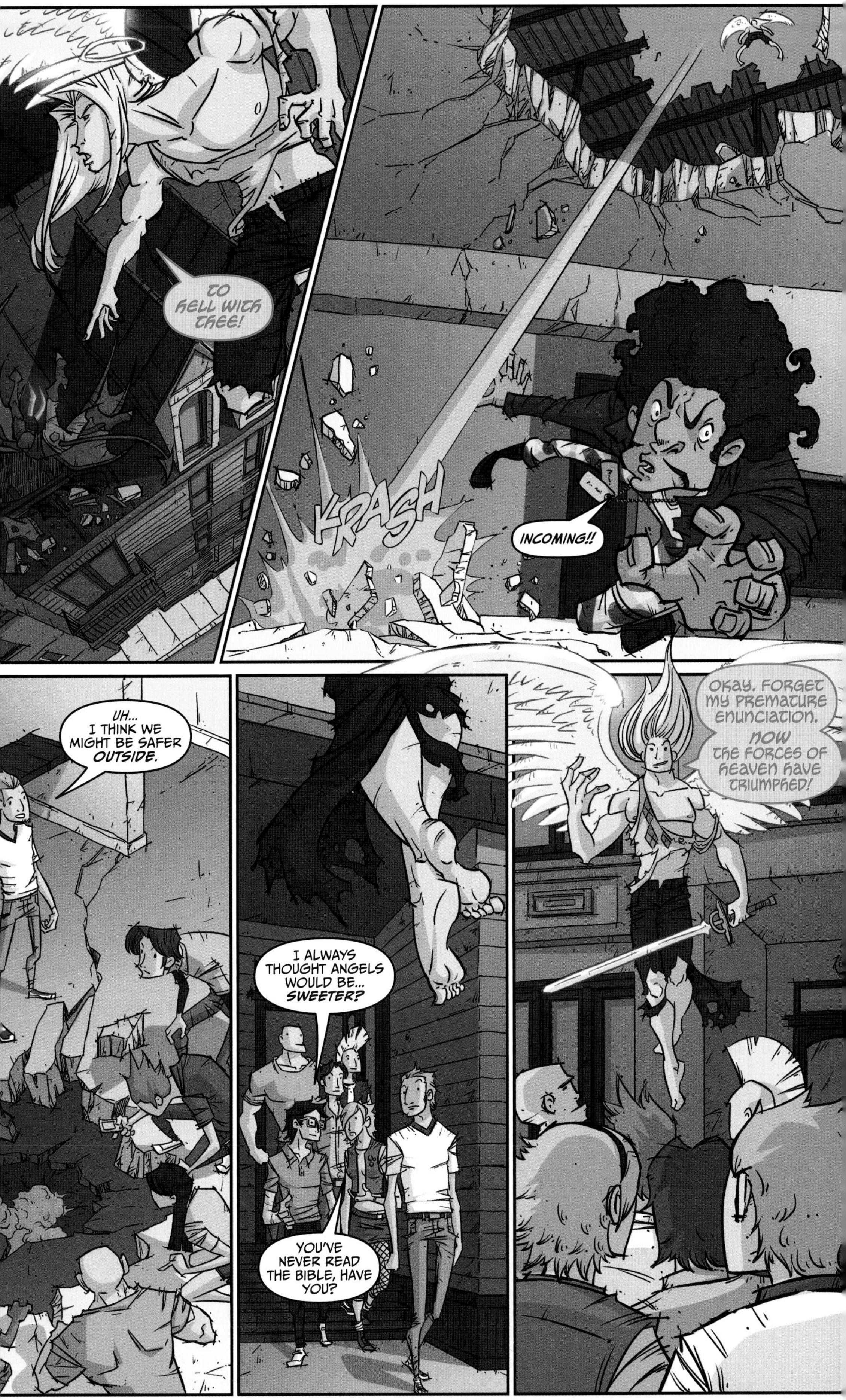
TO HELL WITH THEE!
KRASH
INCOMING!!
UH... I THINK WE MIGHT BE SAFER OUTSIDE.
I ALWAYS THOUGHT ANGELS WOULD BE... SWEETER?
YOU'VE NEVER READ THE BIBLE, HAVE YOU?
OKAY. FORGET MY PREMATURE ENUNCIATION. NOW THE FORCES OF HEAVEN HAVE TRIUMPHED!

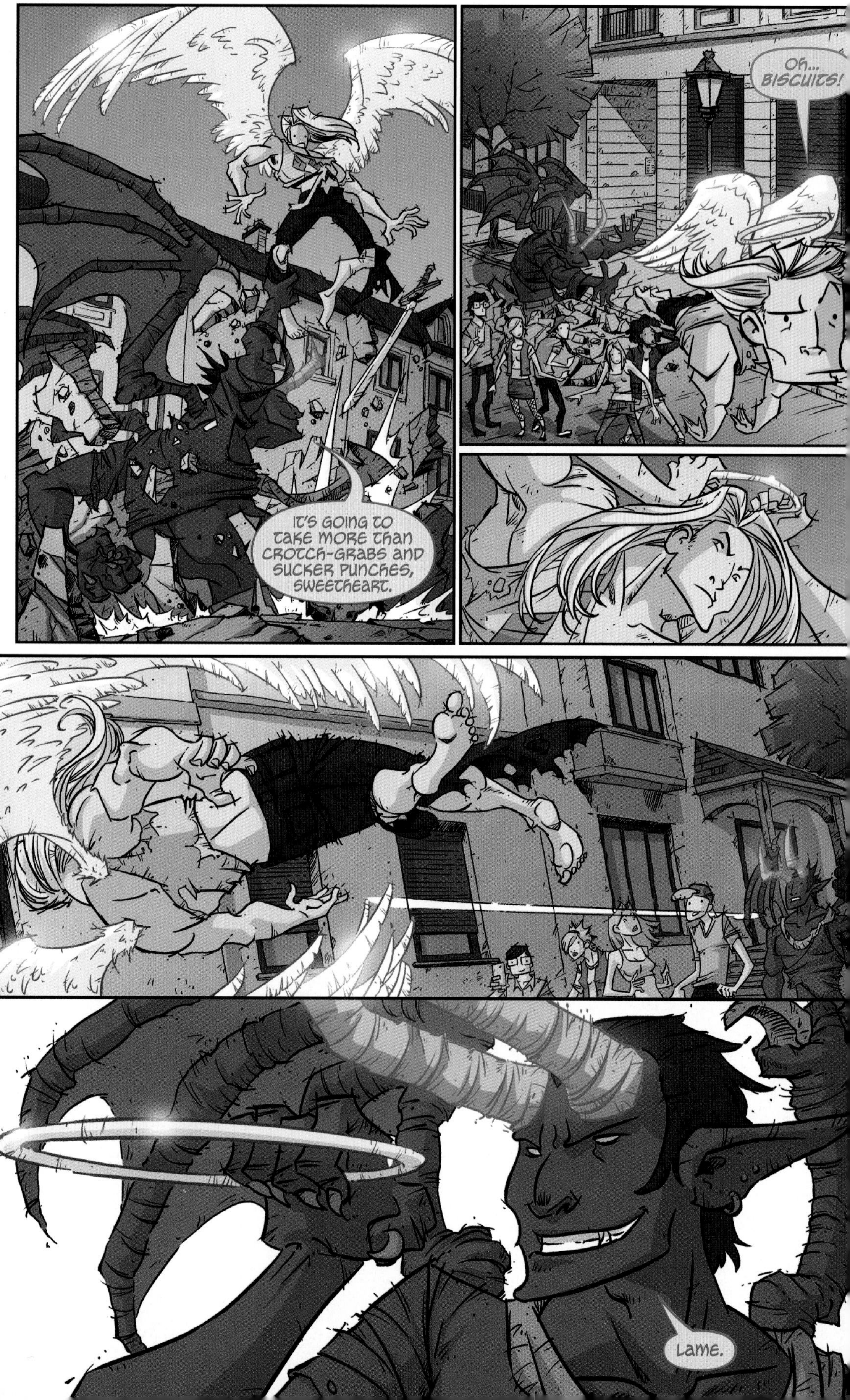
IT'S GOING TO TAKE MORE THAN CROTCH-GRABS AND SUCKER PUNCHES, SWEETHEART.
Oh... BISCUITS!
Lame.

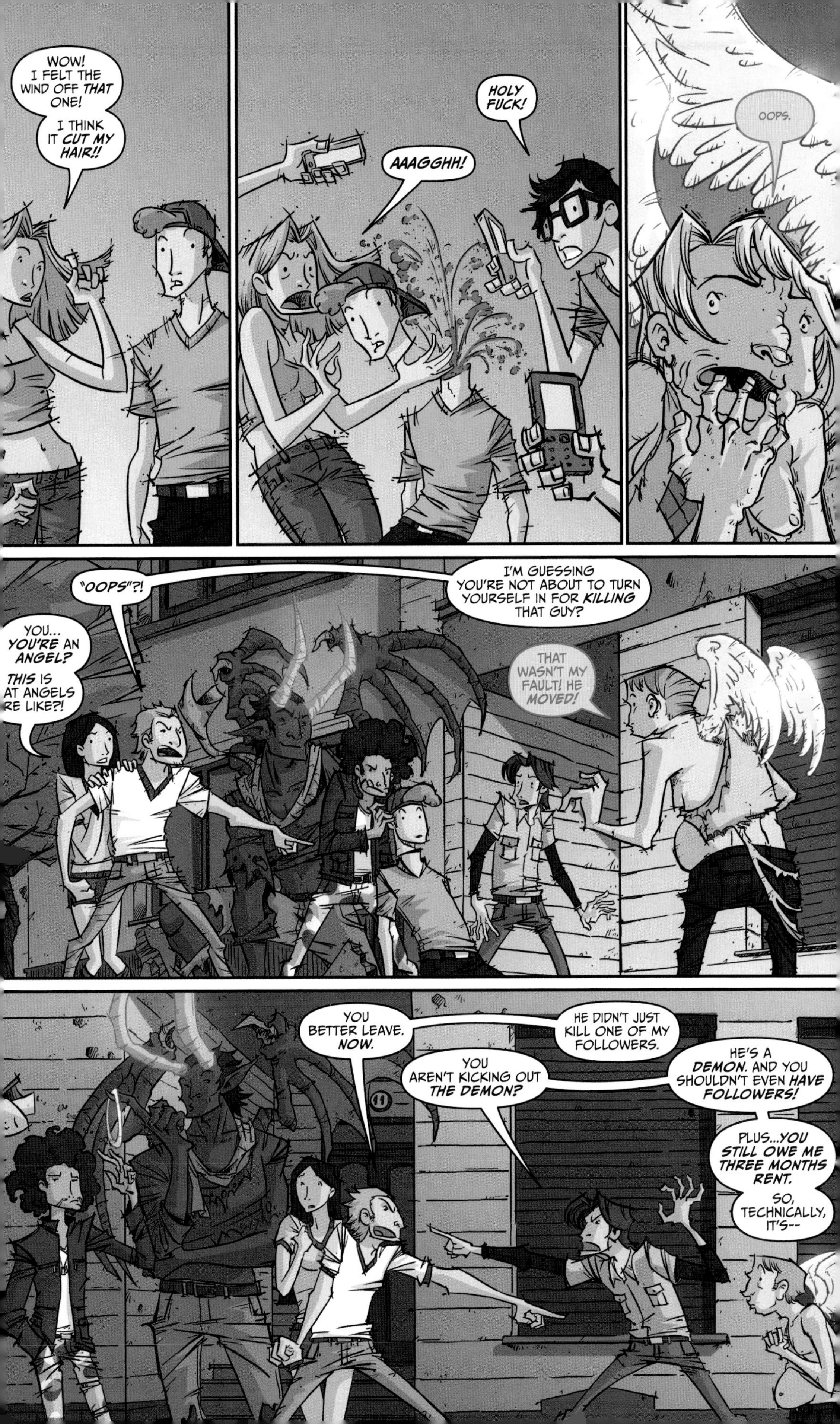
WOW! I FELT THE WIND OFF THAT ONE!
I THINK IT CUT MY HAIR!!
HOLY FUCK!
AAAGGHH!
OOPS.
"OOPS"?!
I'M GUESSING YOU'RE NOT ABOUT TO TURN YOURSELF IN FOR KILLING THAT GUY?
YOU... YOU'RE AN ANGEL?
THIS IS AT ANGELS RE LIKE?!
THAT WASN'T MY FAULT! HE MOVED!
YOU BETTER LEAVE. NOW.
HE DIDN'T JUST KILL ONE OF MY FOLLOWERS.
YOU AREN'T KICKING OUT THE DEMON?
HE'S A DEMON. AND YOU SHOULDN'T EVEN HAVE FOLLOWERS!
PLUS...YOU STILL OWE ME THREE MONTHS RENT.
SO, TECHNICALLY, IT'S--

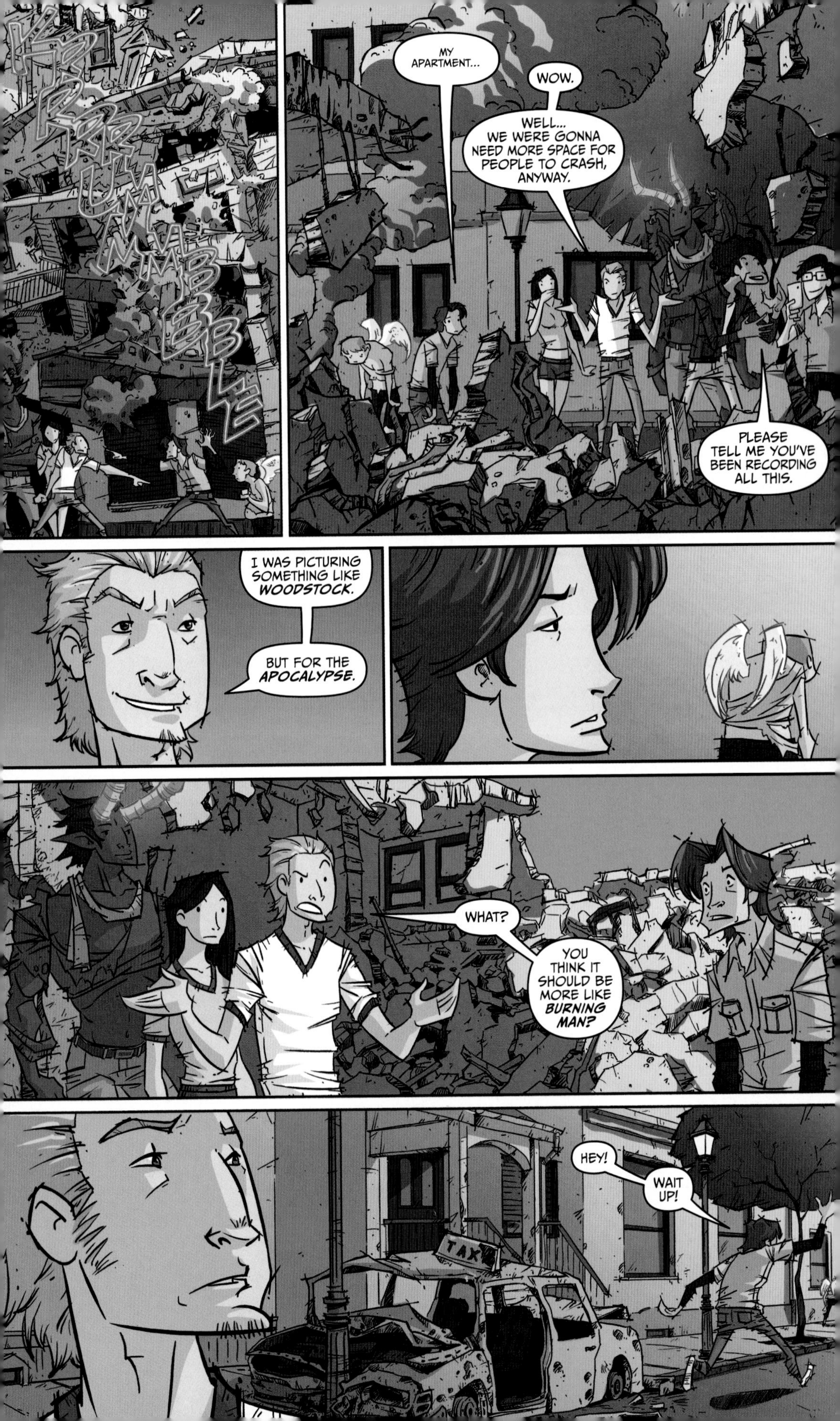
KRRRUMMBBLE
MY APARTMENT...
WOW.
WELL... WE WERE GONNA NEED MORE SPACE FOR PEOPLE TO CRASH, ANYWAY.
PLEASE TELL ME YOU'VE BEEN RECORDING ALL THIS.
I WAS PICTURING SOMETHING LIKE *WOODSTOCK*.
BUT FOR THE *APOCALYPSE*.
WHAT?
YOU THINK IT SHOULD BE MORE LIKE *BURNING MAN?*
TAXI
HEY!
WAIT UP!

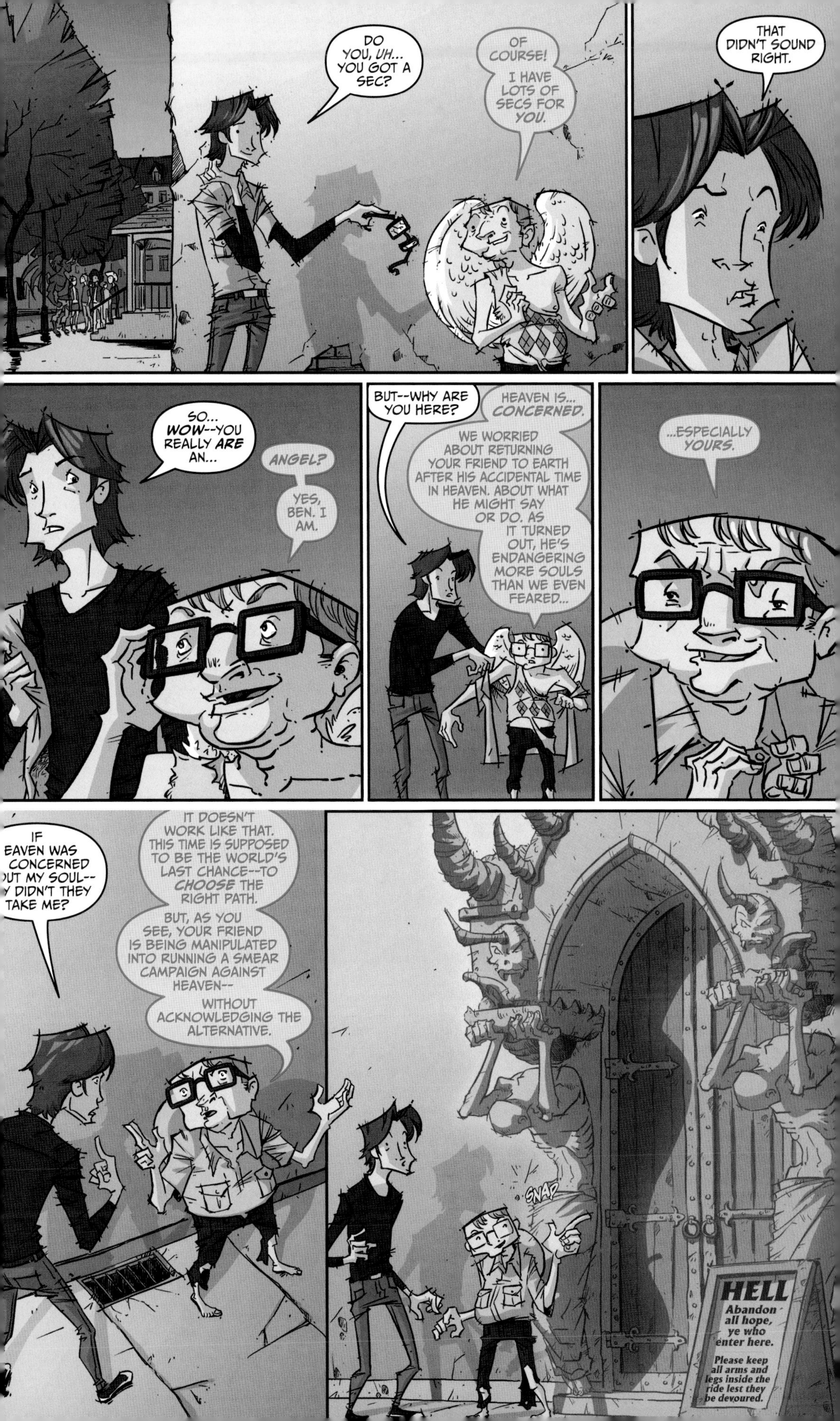
DO YOU, UH... YOU GOT A SEC?
OF COURSE!
I HAVE LOTS OF SECS FOR YOU.
THAT DIDN'T SOUND RIGHT.
SO... WOW--YOU REALLY ARE AN...
ANGEL?
YES, BEN. I AM.
BUT--WHY ARE YOU HERE?
HEAVEN IS... CONCERNED.
WE WORRIED ABOUT RETURNING YOUR FRIEND TO EARTH AFTER HIS ACCIDENTAL TIME IN HEAVEN. ABOUT WHAT HE MIGHT SAY OR DO. AS IT TURNED OUT, HE'S ENDANGERING MORE SOULS THAN WE EVEN FEARED...
...ESPECIALLY YOURS.
IF EAVEN WAS CONCERNED UT MY SOUL-- Y DIDN'T THEY TAKE ME?
IT DOESN'T WORK LIKE THAT. THIS TIME IS SUPPOSED TO BE THE WORLD'S LAST CHANCE--TO CHOOSE THE RIGHT PATH.
BUT, AS YOU SEE, YOUR FRIEND IS BEING MANIPULATED INTO RUNNING A SMEAR CAMPAIGN AGAINST HEAVEN--
WITHOUT ACKNOWLEDGING THE ALTERNATIVE.
SNAP
HELL
Abandon all hope, ye who enter here.
Please keep all arms and legs inside the ride lest they be devoured.

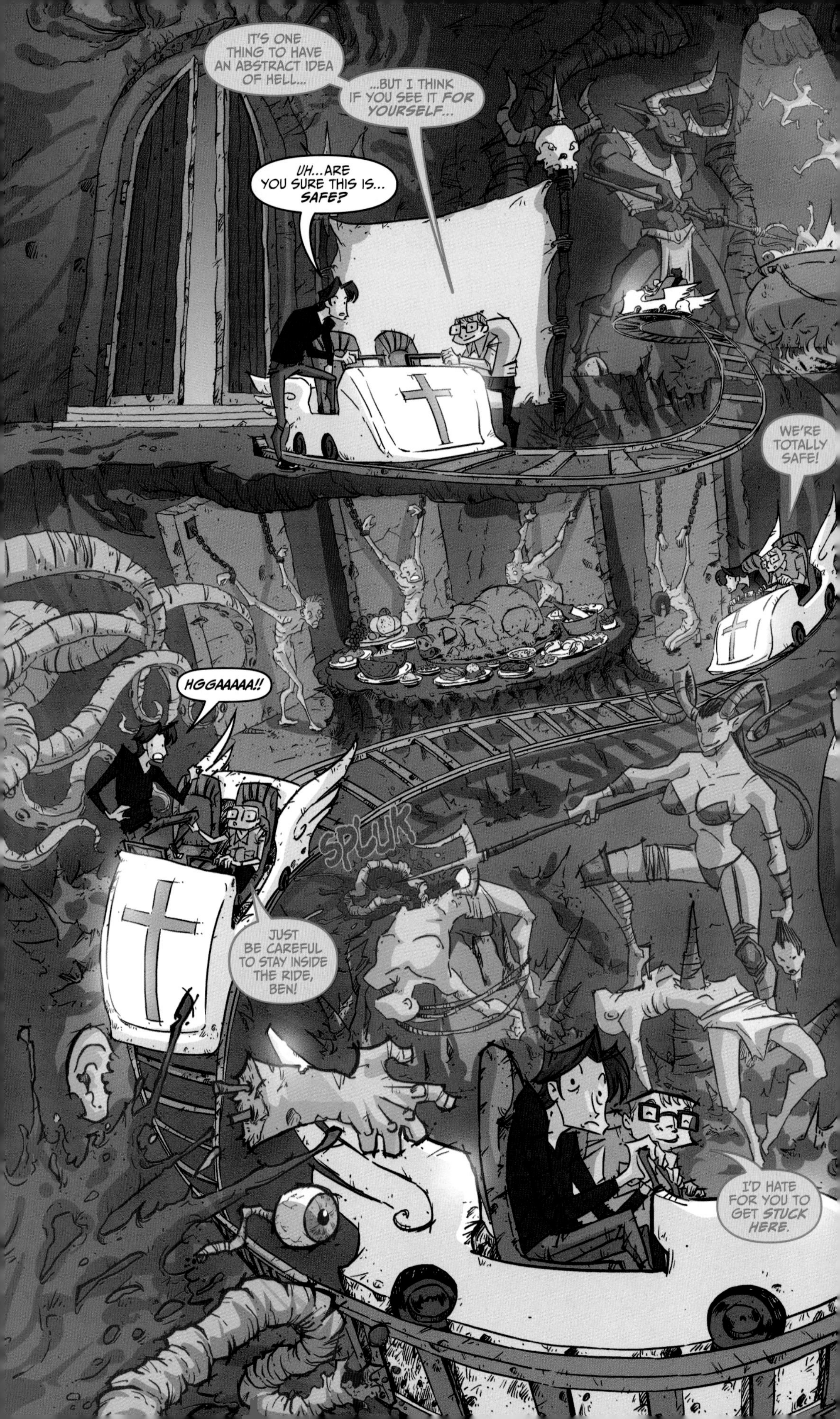

IT'S ONE THING TO HAVE AN ABSTRACT IDEA OF HELL...
...BUT I THINK IF YOU SEE IT FOR YOURSELF...
UH...ARE YOU SURE THIS IS... SAFE?
WE'RE TOTALLY SAFE!
HGGAAAAA!!
SPLUK
JUST BE CAREFUL TO STAY INSIDE THE RIDE, BEN!
I'D HATE FOR YOU TO GET STUCK HERE.

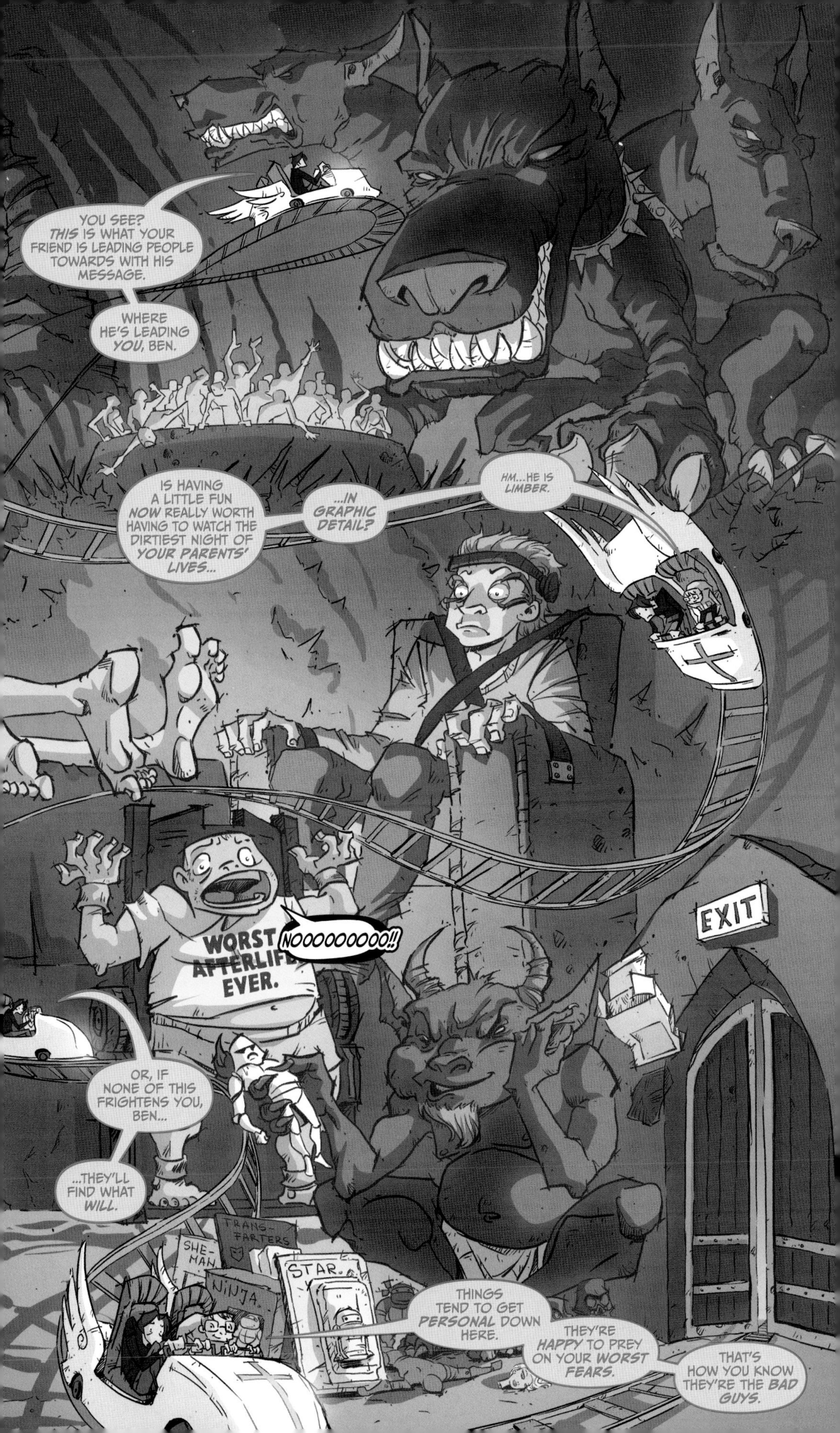

YOU SEE? THIS IS WHAT YOUR FRIEND IS LEADING PEOPLE TOWARDS WITH HIS MESSAGE.
WHERE HE'S LEADING YOU, BEN.
IS HAVING A LITTLE FUN NOW REALLY WORTH HAVING TO WATCH THE DIRTIEST NIGHT OF YOUR PARENTS' LIVES...
...IN GRAPHIC DETAIL?
HM...HE IS LIMBER.
WORST AFTERLIFE EVER.
NOOOOOOOOO!!
EXIT
OR, IF NONE OF THIS FRIGHTENS YOU, BEN...
...THEY'LL FIND WHAT WILL.
TRANS-FARTERS
SHE-MAN
NINJA
STAR
THINGS TEND TO GET PERSONAL DOWN HERE.
THEY'RE HAPPY TO PREY ON YOUR WORST FEARS.
THAT'S HOW YOU KNOW THEY'RE THE BAD GUYS.

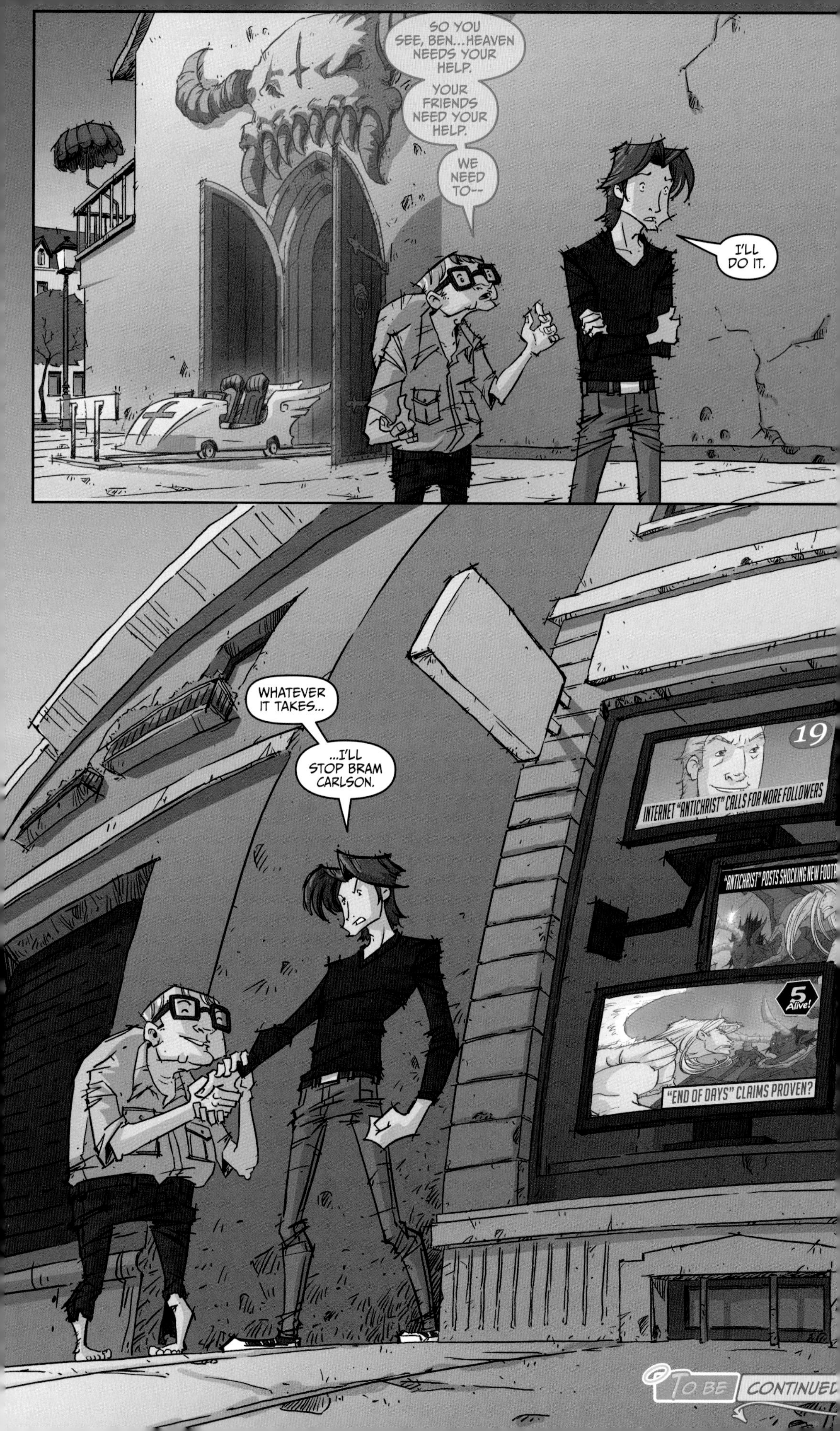
SO YOU SEE, BEN...HEAVEN NEEDS YOUR HELP.
YOUR FRIENDS NEED YOUR HELP.
WE NEED TO--
I'LL DO IT.
WHATEVER IT TAKES...
...I'LL STOP BRAM CARLSON.
19
INTERNET "ANTICHRIST" CALLS FOR MORE FOLLOWERS
"ANTICHRIST" POSTS SHOCKING NEW
5 Alive!
"END OF DAYS" CLAIMS PROVEN?
TO BE CONTINUED

# I WANT YOU*

## FOR THE RAPTURE AT THE END OF DAYS!

*UNLESS YOU ARE: an idol worshipper; a blasphemer; a bad son/daughter; a murderer; an adulterer; a thief; a liar; a hoarder; a sorceress and/or sorceress protector; an interest-charger; a lamb, ox, goat, rabbit, bacon, and/or shellfish eater; a menstruating woman and/or someone who's touched one; a wearer of mixed fiber clothing; someone who shaves; someone with tattoos; an illegal alien-surpressor; married to a widow (and are not said widow's brother-in-law). For further details, exclusions, and punishments - see *The Bible*. **Meanwhile, enjoy the apocalyptic misadventures of those left behind at:** LIFEandENDTIMES.com

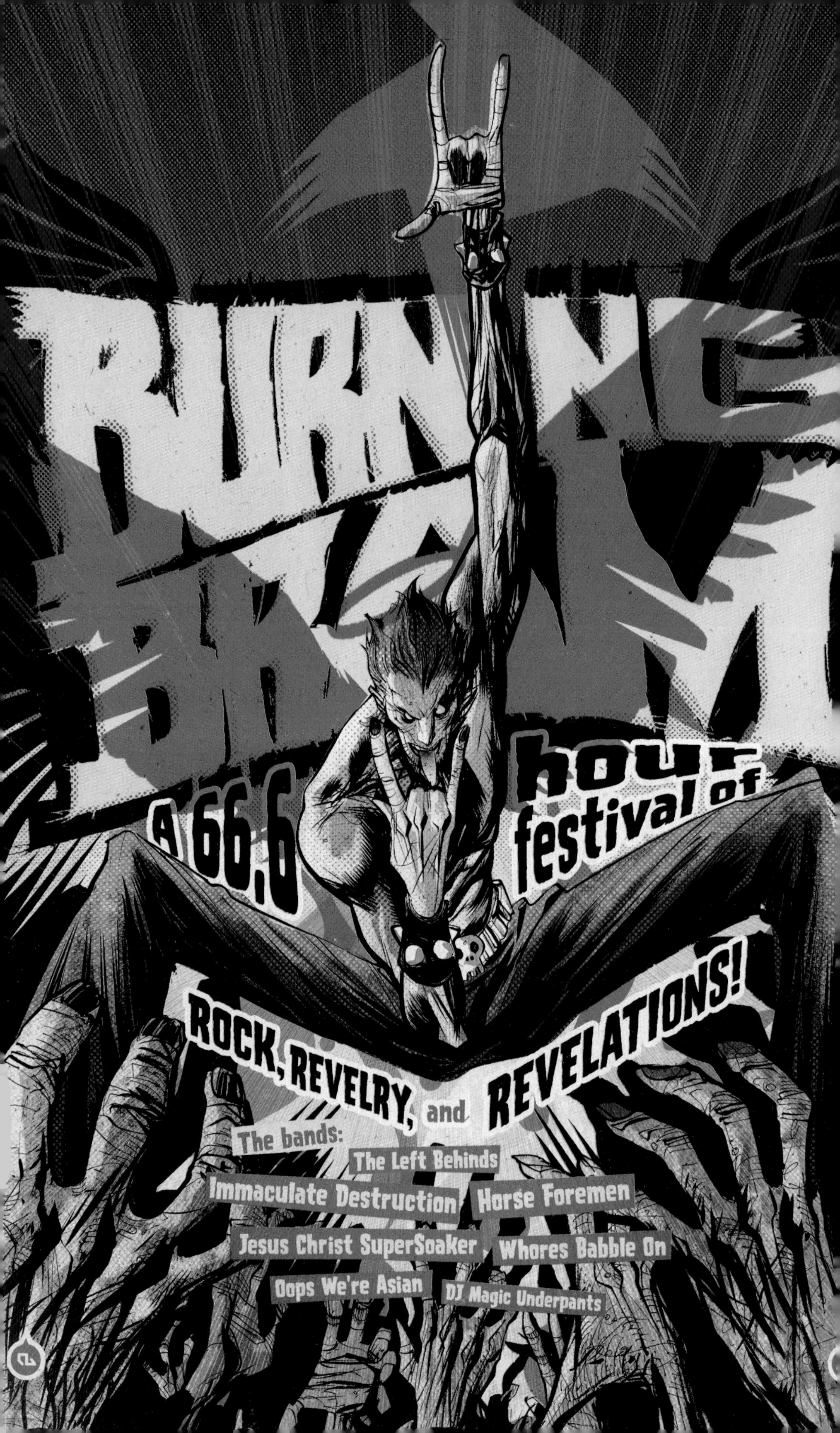
A 66.6 hour festival of
ROCK, REVELRY, and REVELATIONS!
The bands:
The Left Behinds
Immaculate Destruction
Horse Foremen
Jesus Christ SuperSoaker
Whores Babble On
Oops We're Asian
DJ Magic Underpants

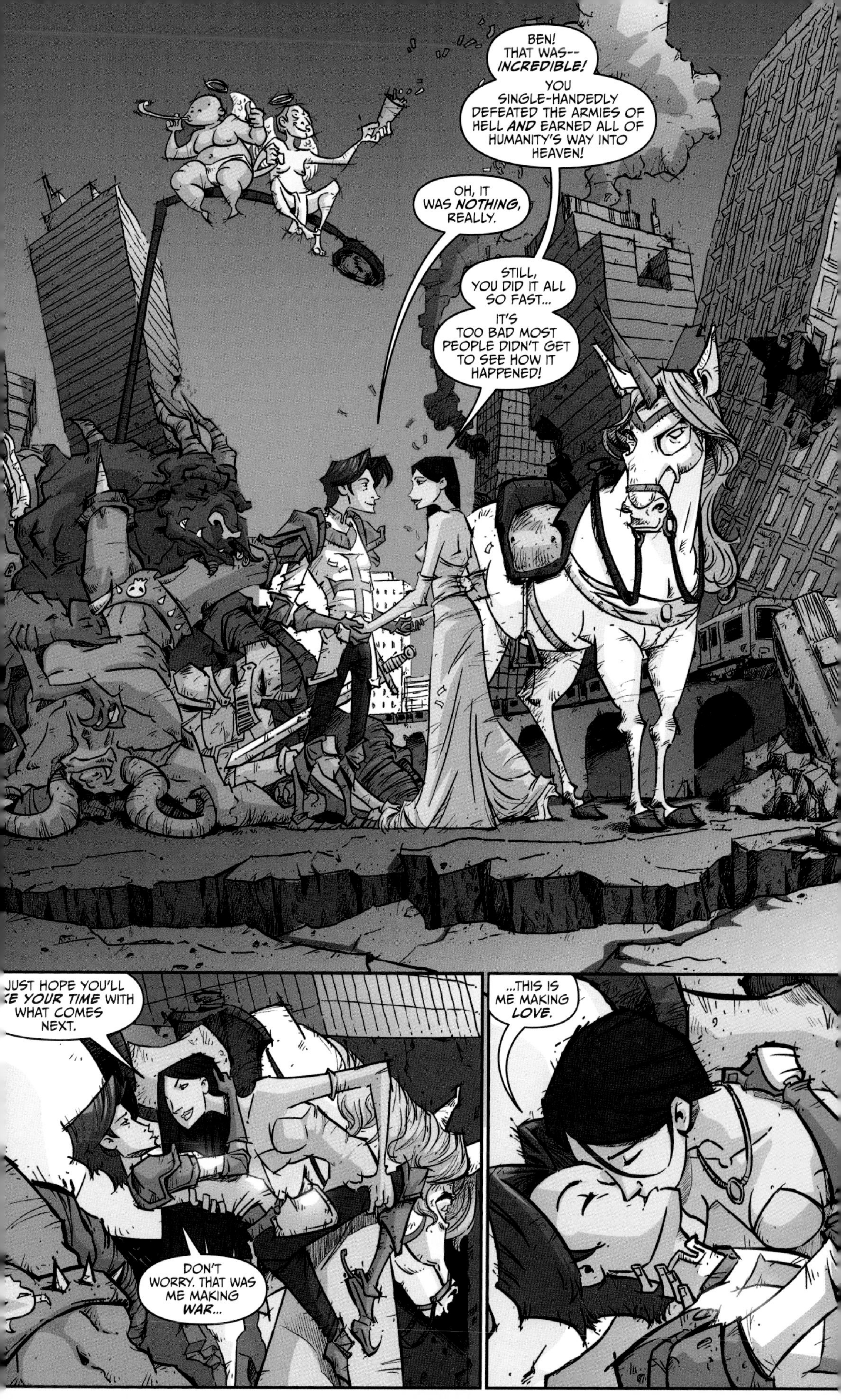
BEN! THAT WAS-- INCREDIBLE!
YOU SINGLE-HANDEDLY DEFEATED THE ARMIES OF HELL AND EARNED ALL OF HUMANITY'S WAY INTO HEAVEN!
OH, IT WAS NOTHING, REALLY.
STILL, YOU DID IT ALL SO FAST...
IT'S TOO BAD MOST PEOPLE DIDN'T GET TO SEE HOW IT HAPPENED!
JUST HOPE YOU'LL E YOUR TIME WITH WHAT COMES NEXT.
DON'T WORRY. THAT WAS ME MAKING WAR...
...THIS IS ME MAKING LOVE.

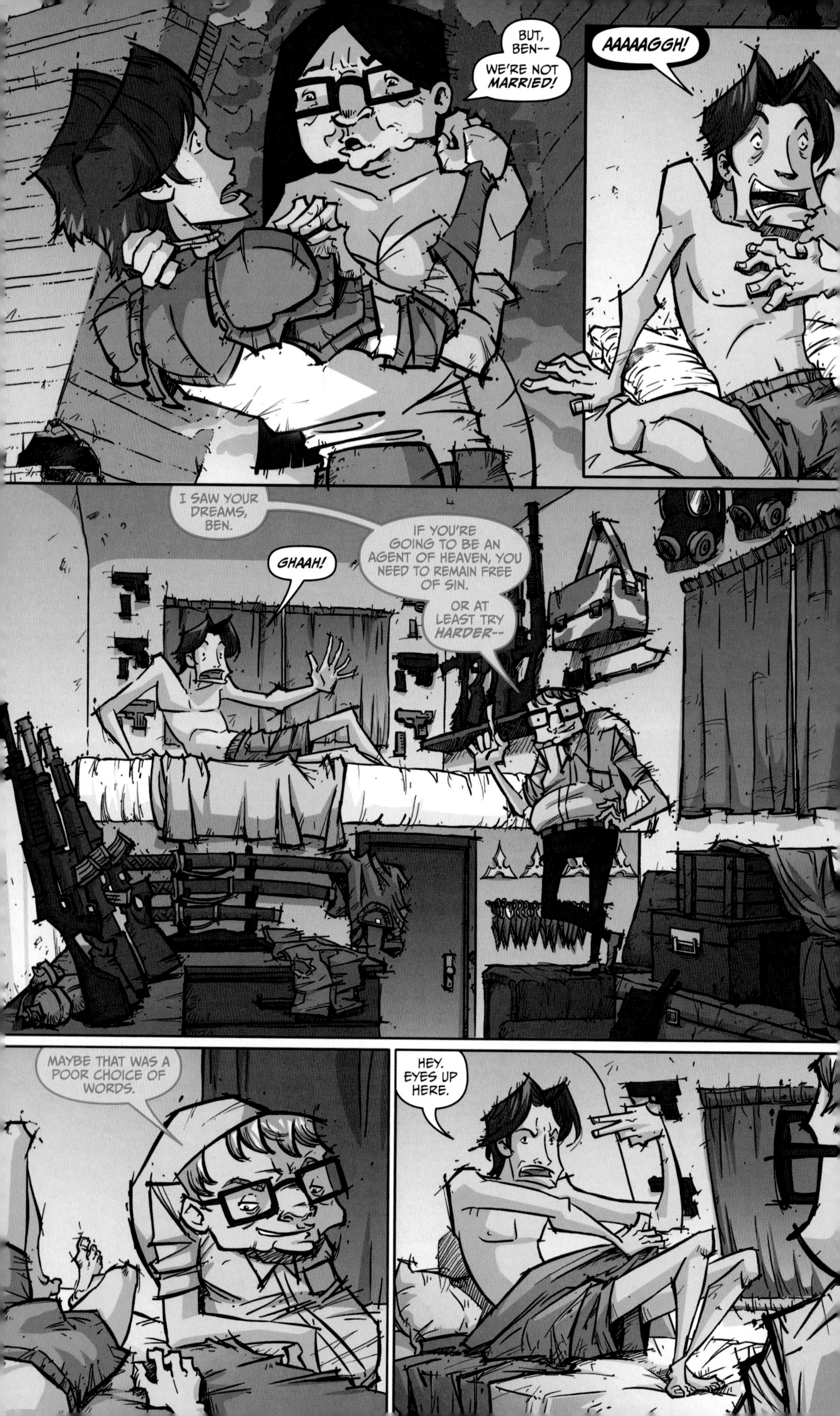
BUT, BEN--
WE'RE NOT MARRIED!
AAAAAGGH!
I SAW YOUR DREAMS, BEN.
GHAAH!
IF YOU'RE GOING TO BE AN AGENT OF HEAVEN, YOU NEED TO REMAIN FREE OF SIN.
OR AT LEAST TRY HARDER--
MAYBE THAT WAS A POOR CHOICE OF WORDS.
HEY. EYES UP HERE.

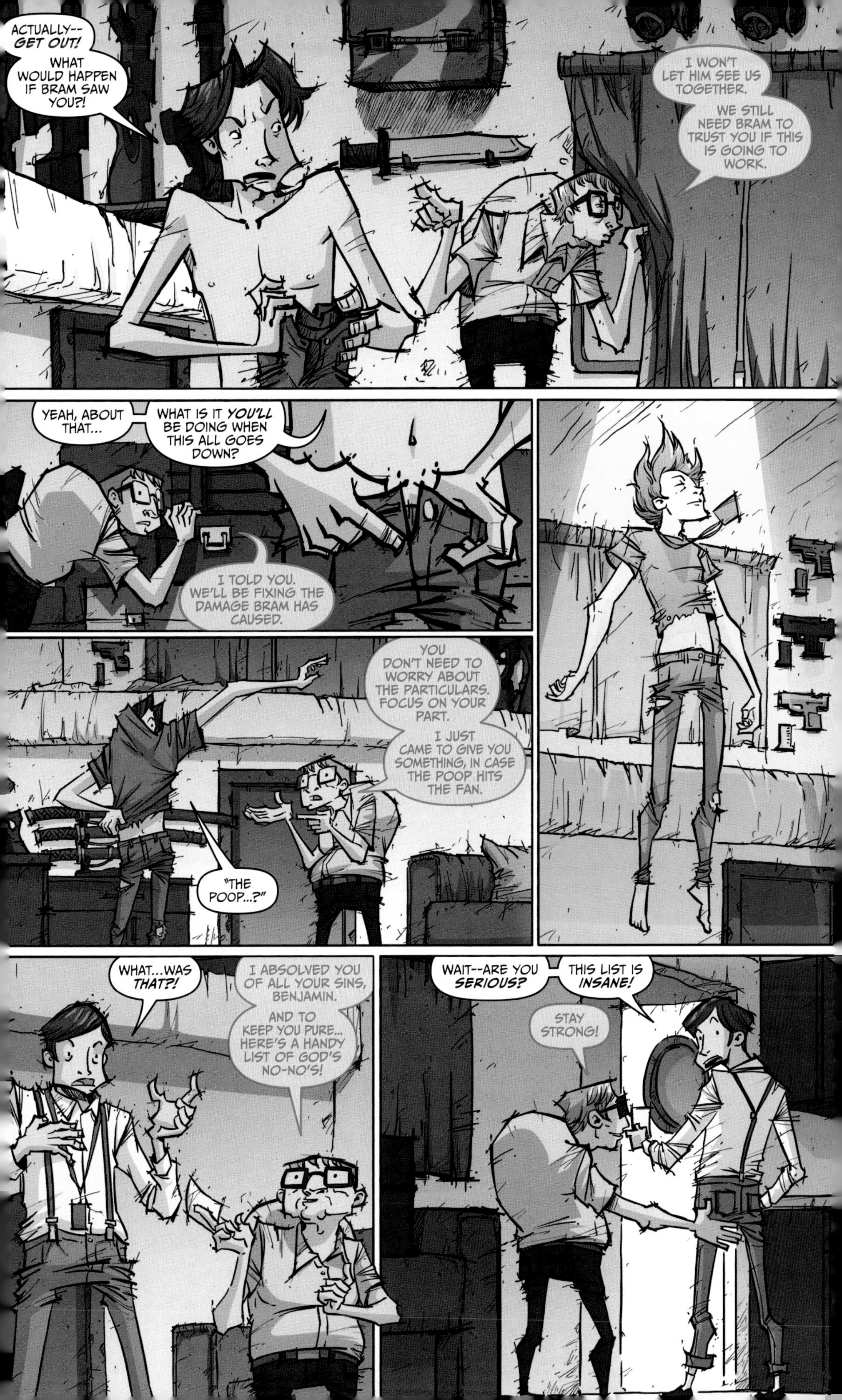
ACTUALLY-- GET OUT!
WHAT WOULD HAPPEN IF BRAM SAW YOU?!
I WON'T LET HIM SEE US TOGETHER.
WE STILL NEED BRAM TO TRUST YOU IF THIS IS GOING TO WORK.
YEAH, ABOUT THAT...
WHAT IS IT YOU'LL BE DOING WHEN THIS ALL GOES DOWN?
I TOLD YOU. WE'LL BE FIXING THE DAMAGE BRAM HAS CAUSED.
YOU DON'T NEED TO WORRY ABOUT THE PARTICULARS. FOCUS ON YOUR PART.
I JUST CAME TO GIVE YOU SOMETHING, IN CASE THE POOP HITS THE FAN.
"THE POOP...?"
WHAT...WAS THAT?!
I ABSOLVED YOU OF ALL YOUR SINS, BENJAMIN.
AND TO KEEP YOU PURE... HERE'S A HANDY LIST OF GOD'S NO-NO'S!
WAIT--ARE YOU SERIOUS?
THIS LIST IS INSANE!
STAY STRONG!

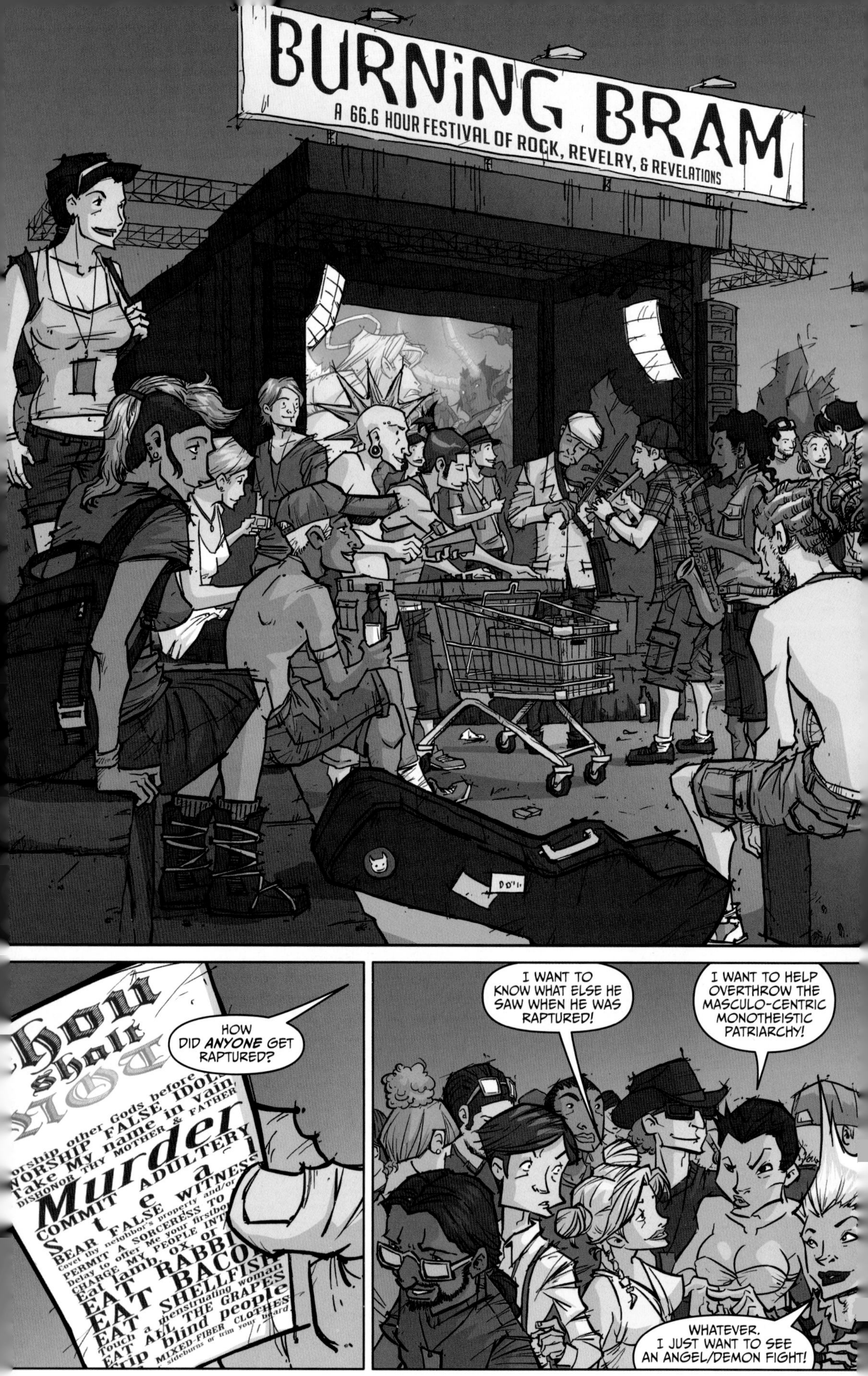
BURNING BRAM
A 66.6 HOUR FESTIVAL OF ROCK, REVELRY, & REVELATIONS
HOW DID ANYONE GET RAPTURED?
I WANT TO KNOW WHAT ELSE HE SAW WHEN HE WAS RAPTURED!
I WANT TO HELP OVERTHROW THE MASCULO-CENTRIC MONOTHEISTIC PATRIARCHY!
WHATEVER. I JUST WANT TO SEE AN ANGEL/DEMON FIGHT!

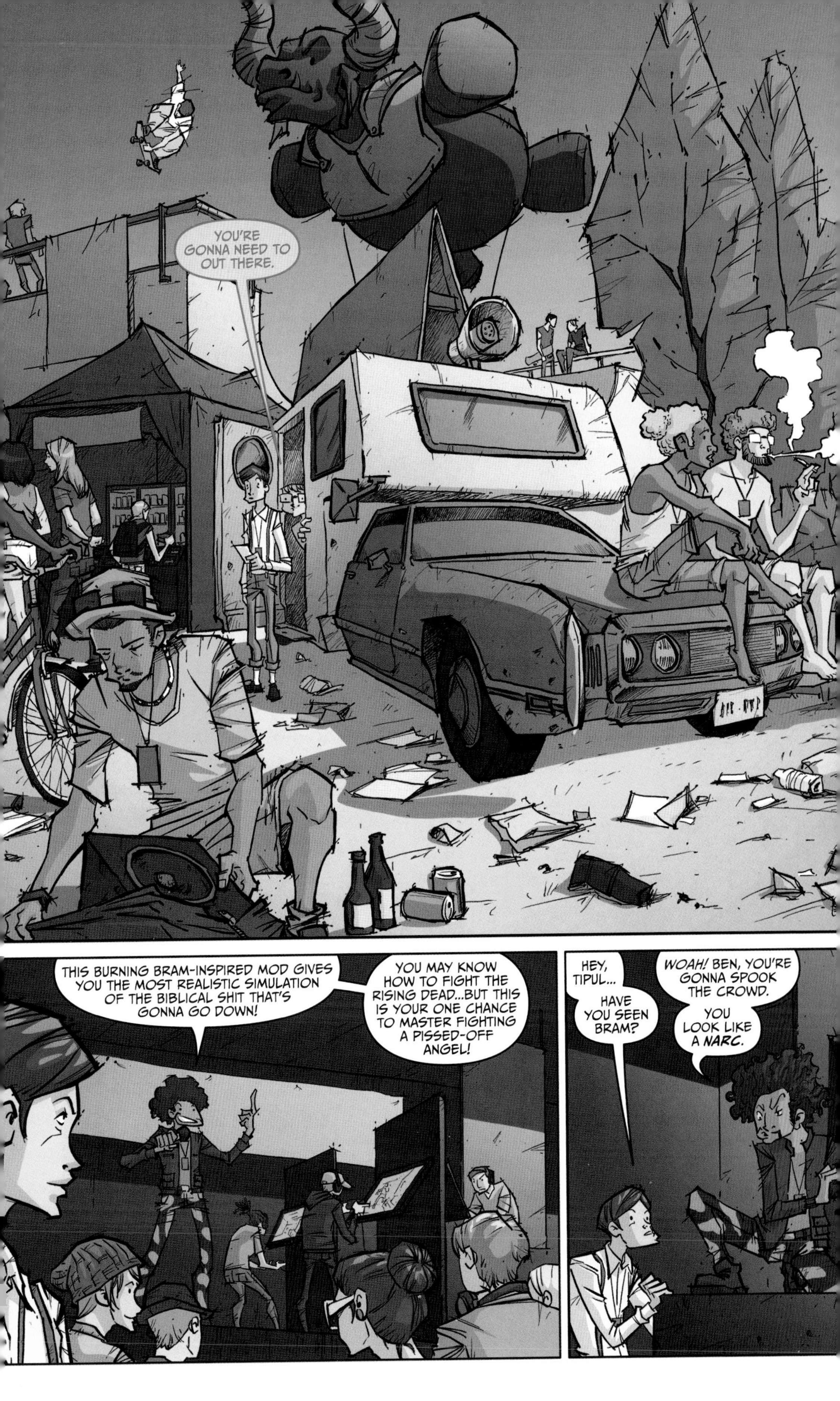
YOU'RE GONNA NEED TO OUT THERE.
THIS BURNING BRAM-INSPIRED MOD GIVES YOU THE MOST REALISTIC SIMULATION OF THE BIBLICAL SHIT THAT'S GONNA GO DOWN!
YOU MAY KNOW HOW TO FIGHT THE RISING DEAD...BUT THIS IS YOUR ONE CHANCE TO MASTER FIGHTING A PISSED-OFF ANGEL!
HEY, TIPUL...
HAVE YOU SEEN BRAM?
*WOAH!* BEN, YOU'RE GONNA SPOOK THE CROWD.
YOU LOOK LIKE A ***NARC***.

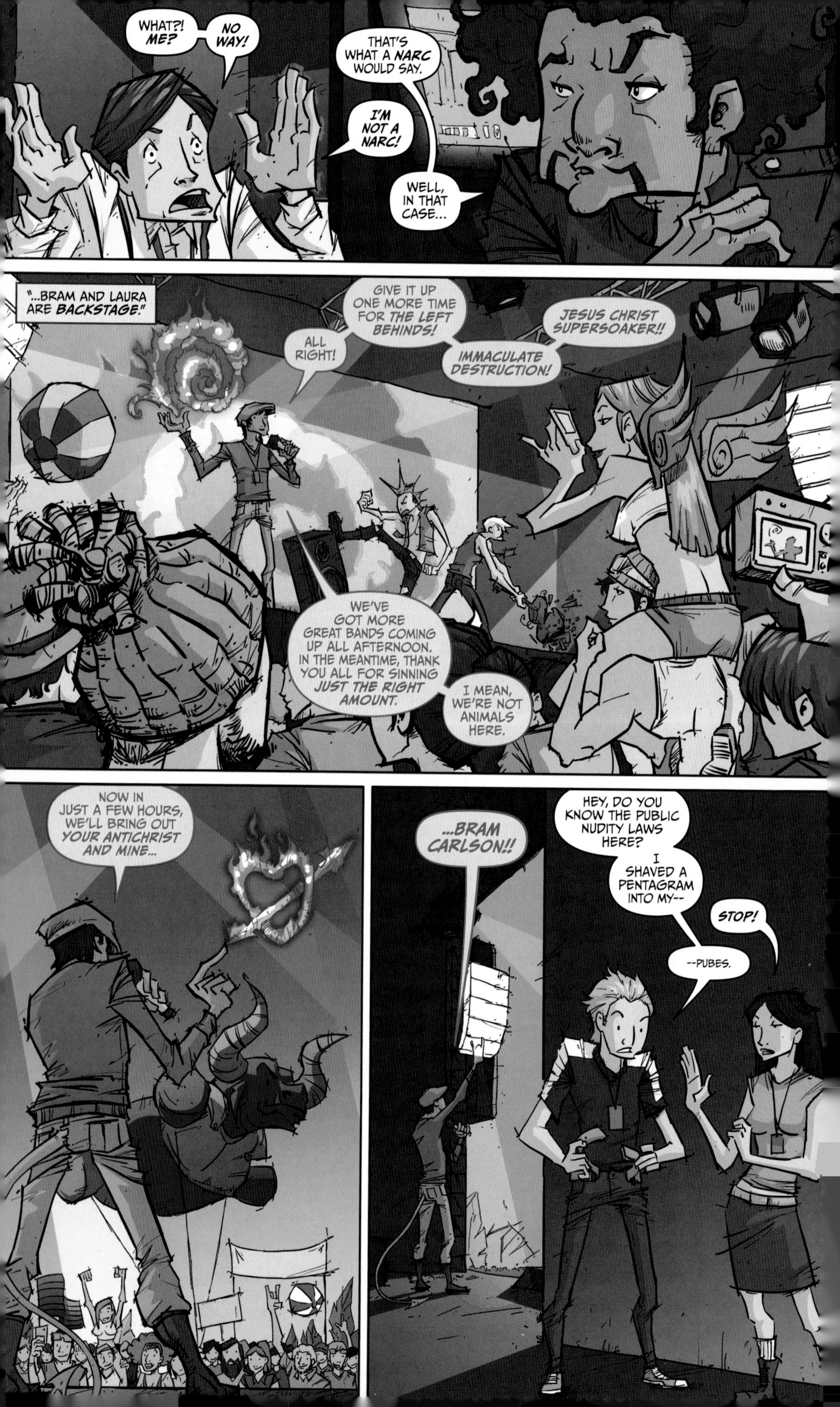
WHAT?! ME?
NO WAY!
THAT'S WHAT A NARC WOULD SAY.
I'M NOT A NARC!
WELL, IN THAT CASE...
"...BRAM AND LAURA ARE BACKSTAGE."
ALL RIGHT!
GIVE IT UP ONE MORE TIME FOR THE LEFT BEHINDS!
JESUS CHRIST SUPERSOAKER!!
IMMACULATE DESTRUCTION!
WE'VE GOT MORE GREAT BANDS COMING UP ALL AFTERNOON. IN THE MEANTIME, THANK YOU ALL FOR SINNING JUST THE RIGHT AMOUNT.
I MEAN, WE'RE NOT ANIMALS HERE.
NOW IN JUST A FEW HOURS, WE'LL BRING OUT YOUR ANTICHRIST AND MINE...
...BRAM CARLSON!!
HEY, DO YOU KNOW THE PUBLIC NUDITY LAWS HERE?
I SHAVED A PENTAGRAM INTO MY--
STOP!
--PUBES.

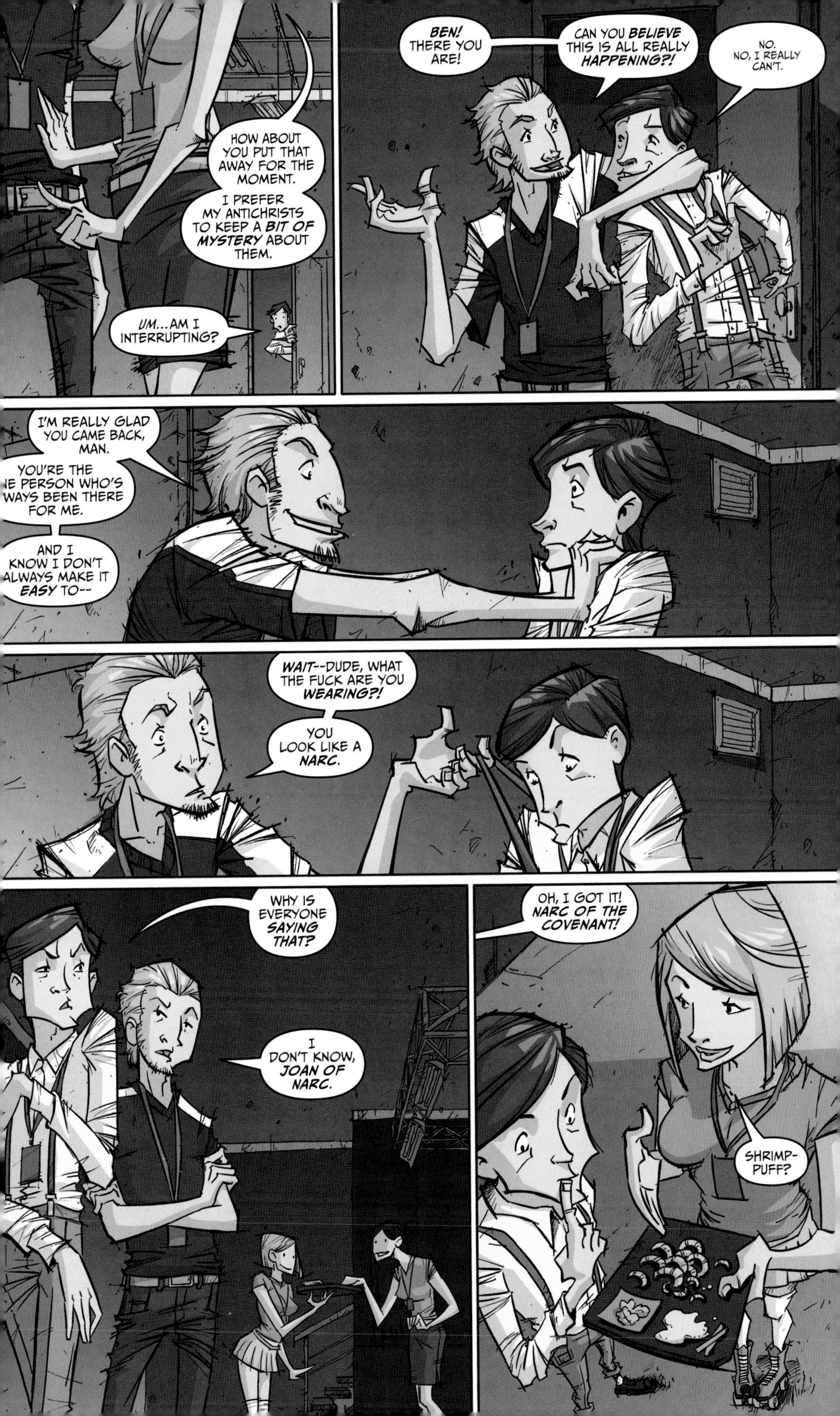
HOW ABOUT YOU PUT THAT AWAY FOR THE MOMENT.
I PREFER MY ANTICHRISTS TO KEEP A BIT OF MYSTERY ABOUT THEM.
UM...AM I INTERRUPTING?
BEN! THERE YOU ARE!
CAN YOU BELIEVE THIS IS ALL REALLY HAPPENING?!
NO. NO, I REALLY CAN'T.
I'M REALLY GLAD YOU CAME BACK, MAN.
YOU'RE THE
E PERSON WHO'S
WAYS BEEN THERE FOR ME.
AND I KNOW I DON'T ALWAYS MAKE IT EASY TO--
WAIT--DUDE, WHAT THE FUCK ARE YOU WEARING?!
YOU LOOK LIKE A NARC.
WHY IS EVERYONE SAYING THAT?
I DON'T KNOW, JOAN OF NARC.
OH, I GOT IT! NARC OF THE COVENANT!
SHRIMP-PUFF?

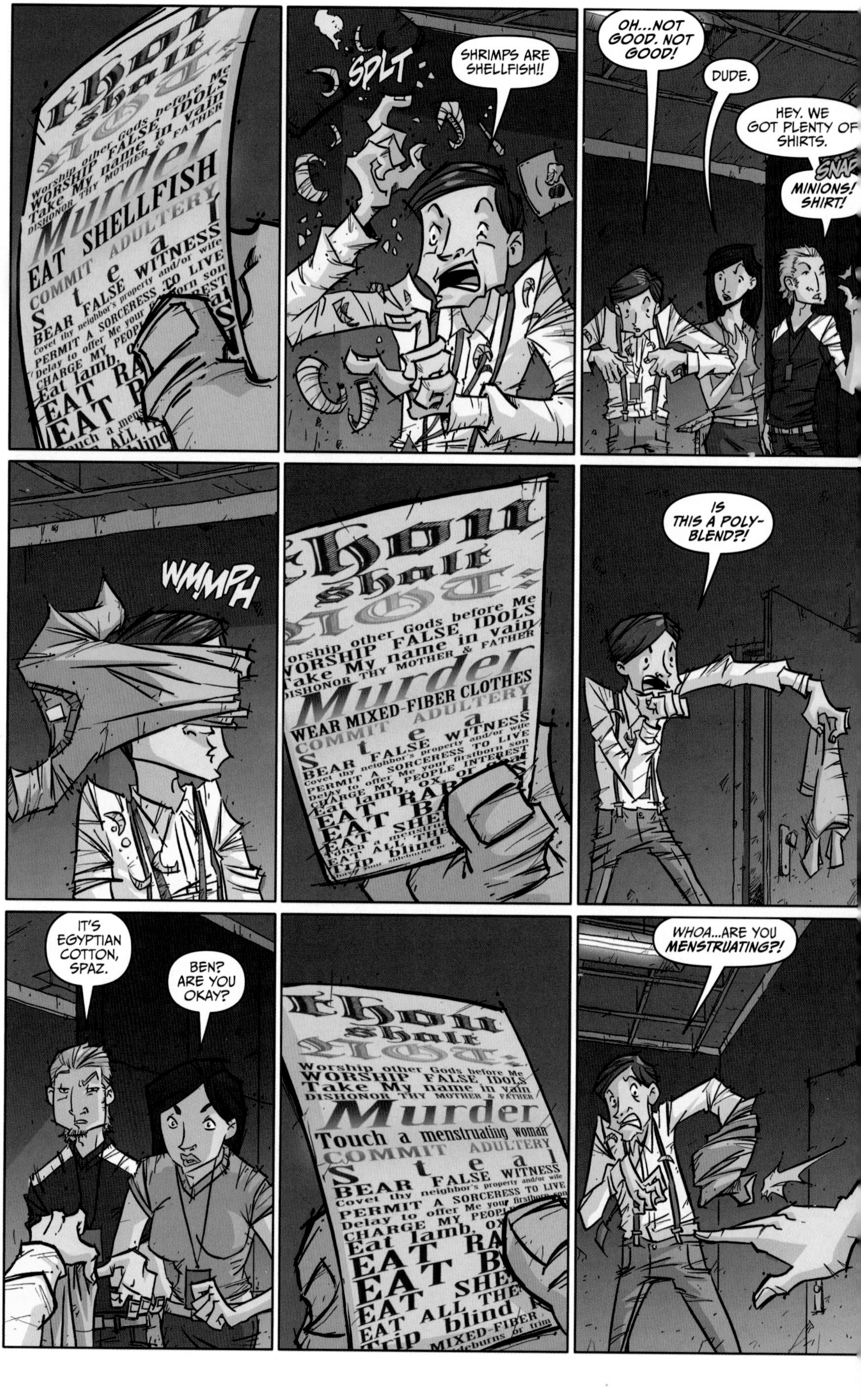
Thou shalt NOT:
Worship other Gods before Me
WORSHIP FALSE IDOLS
Take My name in vain
DISHONOR THY MOTHER & FATHER
Murder
EAT SHELLFISH
COMMIT ADULTERY
S t e a l
BEAR FALSE WITNESS
SPLT
SHRIMPS ARE SHELLFISH!!
OH...NOT GOOD. NOT GOOD!
DUDE.
HEY. WE GOT PLENTY OF SHIRTS.
MINIONS! SHIRT!
WMMPH
Thou shalt NOT:
Worship other Gods before Me
WORSHIP FALSE IDOLS
Take My name in vain
DISHONOR THY MOTHER & FATHER
Murder
WEAR MIXED-FIBER CLOTHES
COMMIT ADULTERY
S t e a l
BEAR FALSE WITNESS
Covet thy neighbor's property and/or wife
PERMIT A SORCERESS TO LIVE
IS THIS A POLY-BLEND?!
IT'S EGYPTIAN COTTON, SPAZ.
BEN? ARE YOU OKAY?
Thou shalt NOT:
Worship other Gods before Me
WORSHIP FALSE IDOLS
Take My name in vain
DISHONOR THY MOTHER & FATHER
Murder
Touch a menstruating woman
COMMIT ADULTERY
S t e a l
BEAR FALSE WITNESS
Covet thy neighbor's property and/or wife
PERMIT A SORCERESS TO LIVE
WHOA...ARE YOU MENSTRUATING?!

**I NEED SOME AIR.**

**LAURA, WAIT—**

**YOU SHOULD PROBABLY LET HER GO.**

**(ESPECIALLY IF SHE *IS* ON THE RAG.)**

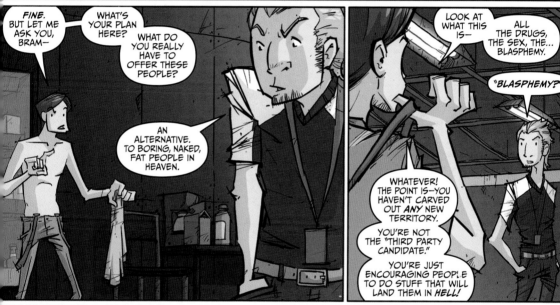

**FINE. BUT LET ME ASK YOU, BRAM—**

**WHAT'S YOUR PLAN HERE? WHAT DO YOU REALLY HAVE TO OFFER THESE PEOPLE?**

**AN ALTERNATIVE. TO BORING, NAKED, FAT PEOPLE IN HEAVEN.**

**LOOK AT WHAT THIS IS—**

**ALL THE DRUGS, THE SEX, THE... BLASPHEMY.**

**"BLASPHEMY?"**

**WHATEVER! THE POINT IS—YOU HAVEN'T CARVED OUT *ANY* NEW TERRITORY.**

**YOU'RE NOT THE "THIRD PARTY CANDIDATE."**

**YOU'RE JUST ENCOURAGING PEOPLE TO DO STUFF THAT WILL LAND THEM IN *HELL!***

**IF YOU KEEP THIS UP—YOU COULD REALLY SCREW OVER ALL THESE INNOCENT, CONFUSED PEOPLE!**

**AND YOURSELF... AND *LAURA*.**

**BEN... *RELAX*. TIPUL SAID THE APOCALYPSE TAKES *SEVEN YEARS*.**

**I'LL FIGURE SOMETHING OUT EVENTUALLY!**

**BUT I DON'T THINK YOU'VE CONSIDERED THE CONSEQUENCES.**

**THAT'S DISAPPOINTING, BRAM.**

**I THINK YOU JUST WANT TO *REJECT HEAVEN* THE WAY THEY REJECTED *YOU*...**

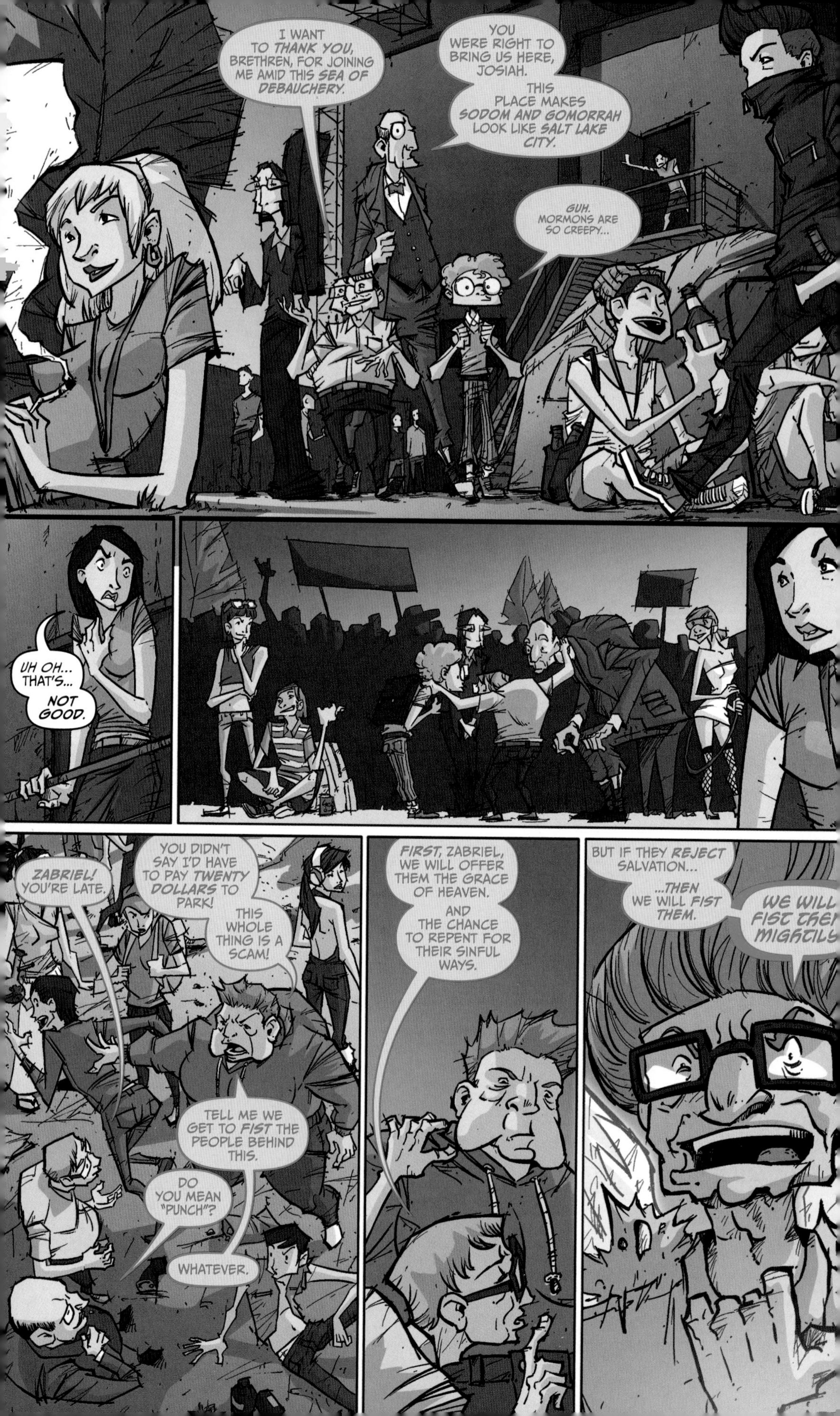
I WANT TO THANK YOU, BRETHREN, FOR JOINING ME AMID THIS SEA OF DEBAUCHERY.
YOU WERE RIGHT TO BRING US HERE, JOSIAH.
THIS PLACE MAKES SODOM AND GOMORRAH LOOK LIKE SALT LAKE CITY.
GUH. MORMONS ARE SO CREEPY...
UH OH... THAT'S... NOT GOOD.
ZABRIEL! YOU'RE LATE.
YOU DIDN'T SAY I'D HAVE TO PAY TWENTY DOLLARS TO PARK!
THIS WHOLE THING IS A SCAM!
TELL ME WE GET TO FIST THE PEOPLE BEHIND THIS.
DO YOU MEAN "PUNCH"?
WHATEVER.
FIRST, ZABRIEL, WE WILL OFFER THEM THE GRACE OF HEAVEN.
AND THE CHANCE TO REPENT FOR THEIR SINFUL WAYS.
BUT IF THEY REJECT SALVATION...
...THEN WE WILL FIST THEM.

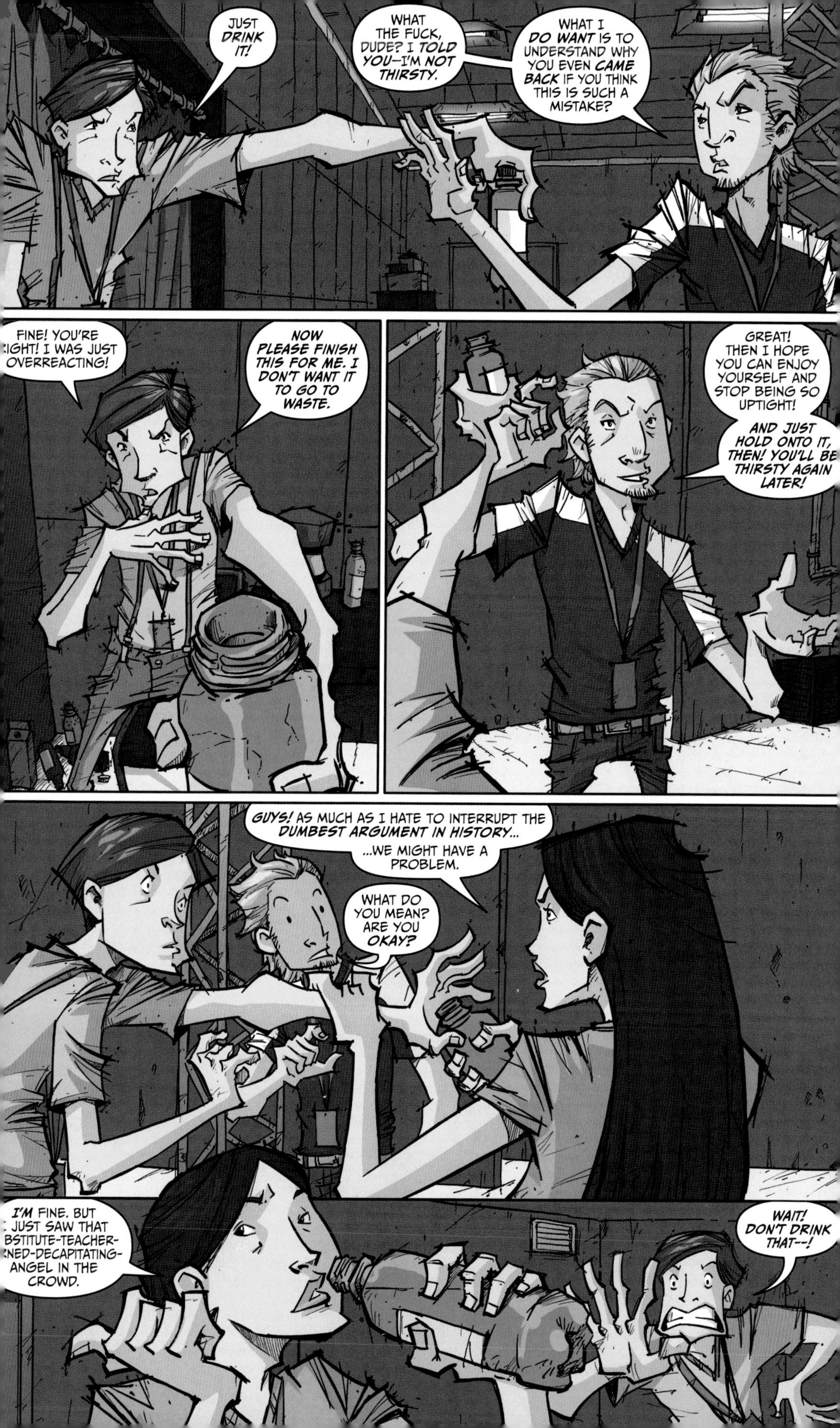
JUST DRINK IT!
WHAT THE FUCK, DUDE? I TOLD YOU—I'M NOT THIRSTY.
WHAT I DO WANT IS TO UNDERSTAND WHY YOU EVEN CAME BACK IF YOU THINK THIS IS SUCH A MISTAKE?
FINE! YOU'RE IGHT! I WAS JUST OVERREACTING!
NOW PLEASE FINISH THIS FOR ME. I DON'T WANT IT TO GO TO WASTE.
GREAT! THEN I HOPE YOU CAN ENJOY YOURSELF AND STOP BEING SO UPTIGHT!
AND JUST HOLD ONTO IT, THEN! YOU'LL BE THIRSTY AGAIN LATER!
GUYS! AS MUCH AS I HATE TO INTERRUPT THE DUMBEST ARGUMENT IN HISTORY...
...WE MIGHT HAVE A PROBLEM.
WHAT DO YOU MEAN? ARE YOU OKAY?
I'M FINE. BUT JUST SAW THAT BSTITUTE-TEACHER-RNED-DECAPITATING-ANGEL IN THE CROWD.
WAIT! DON'T DRINK THAT--!

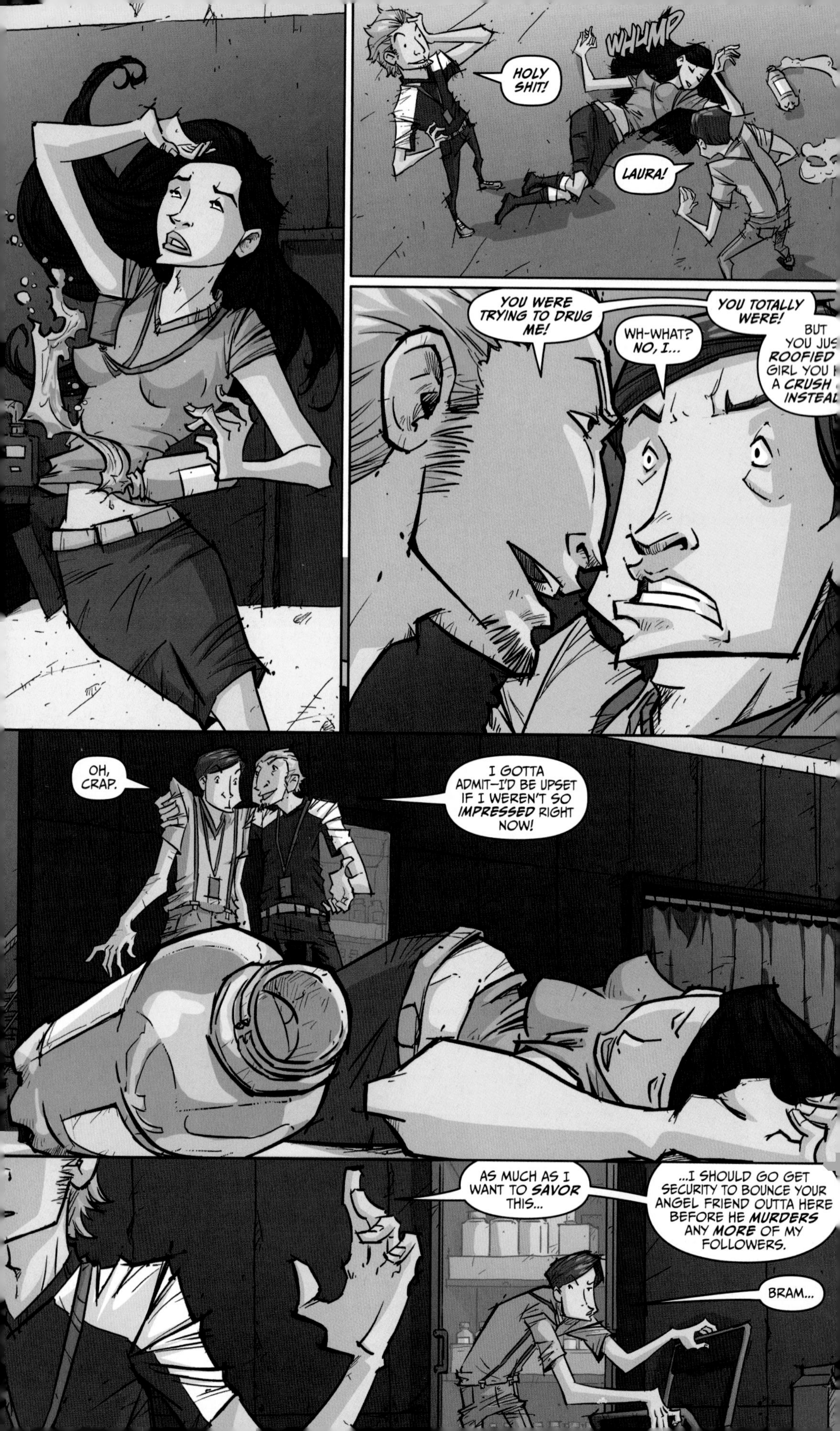
WHUMP
HOLY SHIT!
LAURA!
YOU WERE TRYING TO DRUG ME!
WH-WHAT? NO, I...
YOU TOTALLY WERE!
BUT YOU JUS ROOFIED GIRL YOU A CRUSH INSTEA
OH, CRAP.
I GOTTA ADMIT—I'D BE UPSET IF I WEREN'T SO IMPRESSED RIGHT NOW!
AS MUCH AS I WANT TO SAVOR THIS...
...I SHOULD GO GET SECURITY TO BOUNCE YOUR ANGEL FRIEND OUTTA HERE BEFORE HE MURDERS ANY MORE OF MY FOLLOWERS.
BRAM...

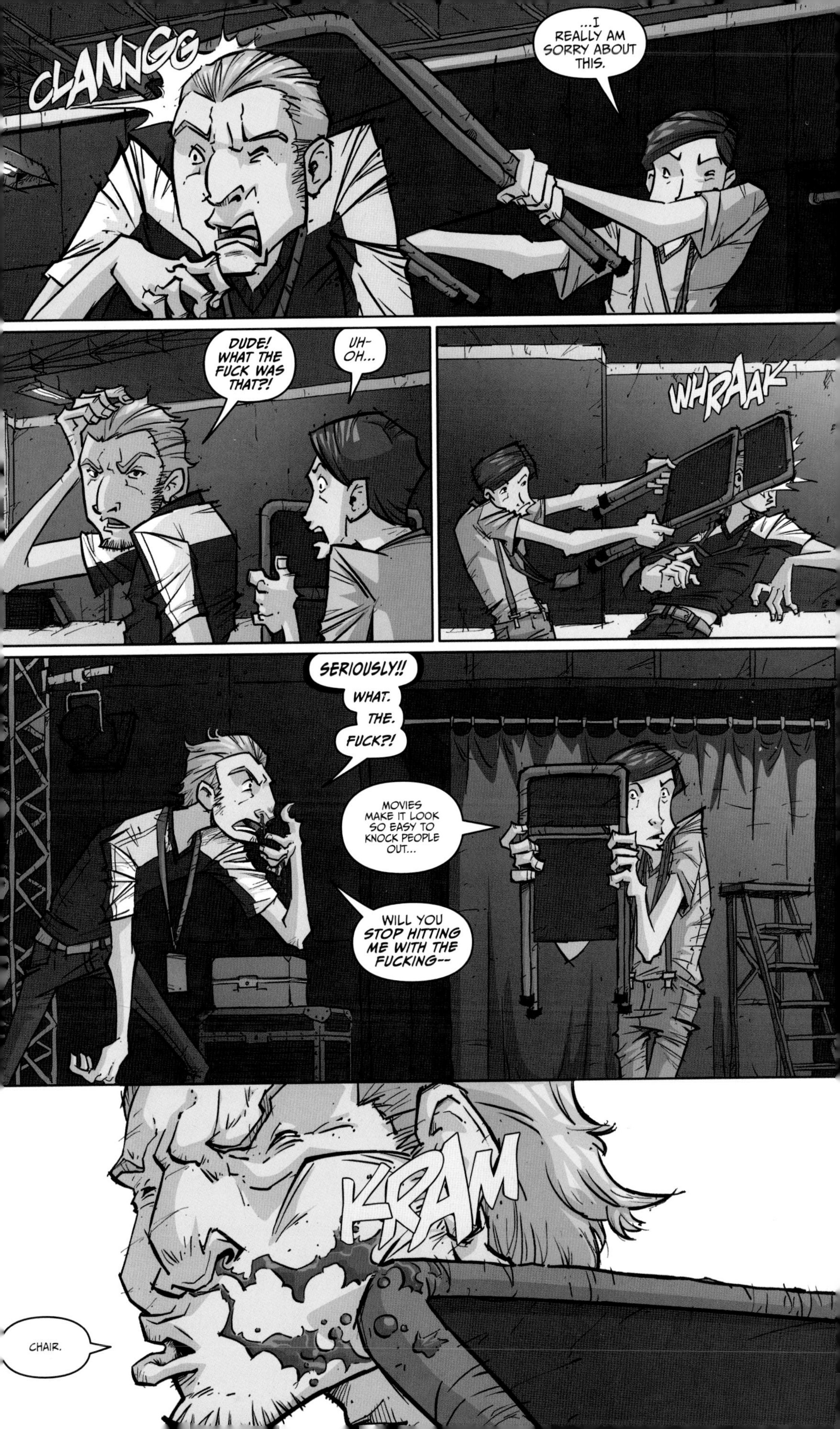
CLANNGG
...I REALLY AM SORRY ABOUT THIS.
DUDE! WHAT THE FUCK WAS THAT?!
UH-OH...
WHRAAK
SERIOUSLY!!
WHAT.
THE.
FUCK?!
MOVIES MAKE IT LOOK SO EASY TO KNOCK PEOPLE OUT...
WILL YOU STOP HITTING ME WITH THE FUCKING--
KRAM
CHAIR.

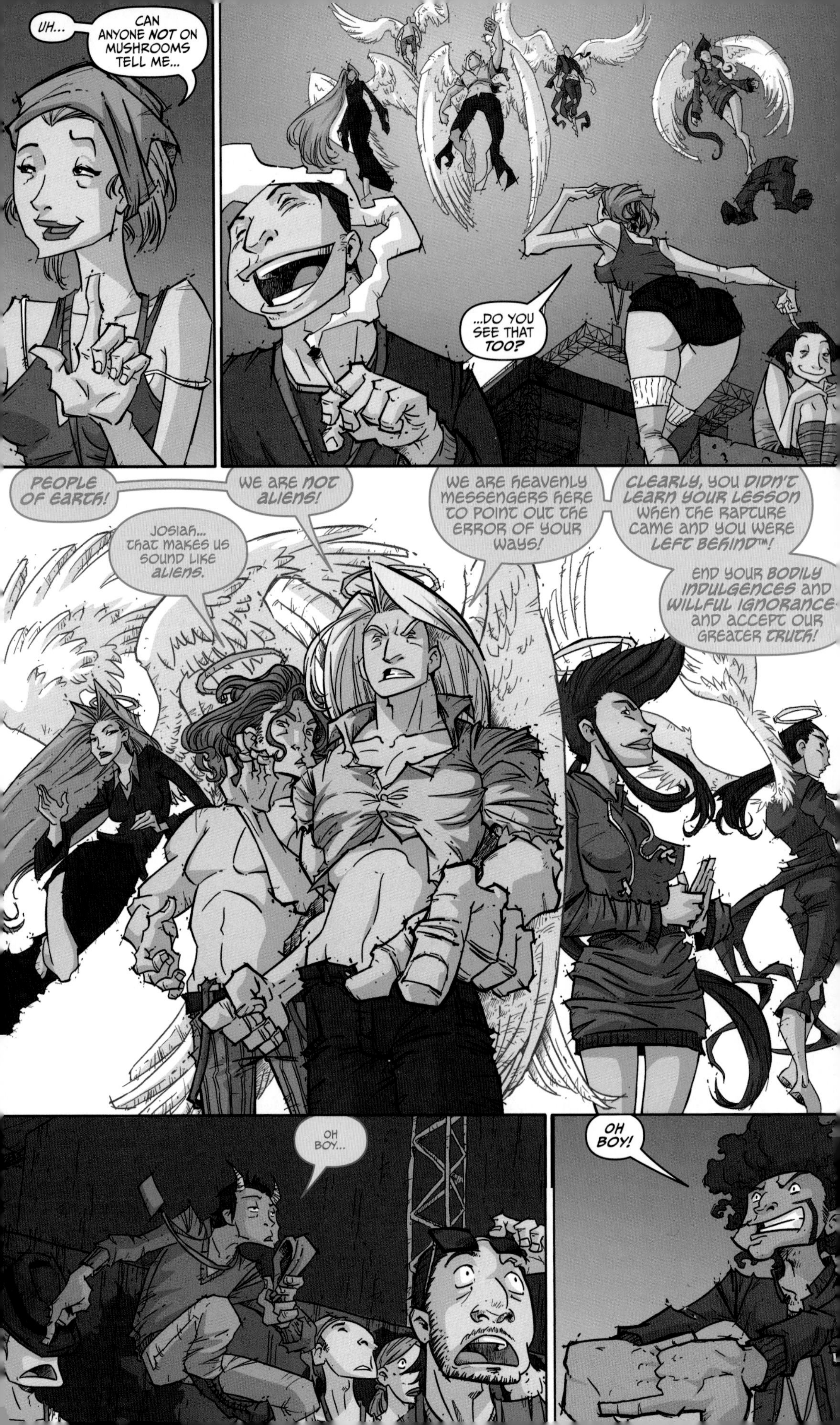
UH...
CAN ANYONE NOT ON MUSHROOMS TELL ME...
...DO YOU SEE THAT TOO?
PEOPLE OF EARTH!
WE ARE NOT ALIENS!
JOSIAH... THAT MAKES US SOUND LIKE ALIENS.
WE ARE HEAVENLY MESSENGERS HERE TO POINT OUT THE ERROR OF YOUR WAYS!
CLEARLY, YOU DIDN'T LEARN YOUR LESSON WHEN THE RAPTURE CAME AND YOU WERE LEFT BEHIND™!
END YOUR BODILY INDULGENCES AND WILLFUL IGNORANCE AND ACCEPT OUR GREATER TRUTH!
OH BOY...
OH BOY!

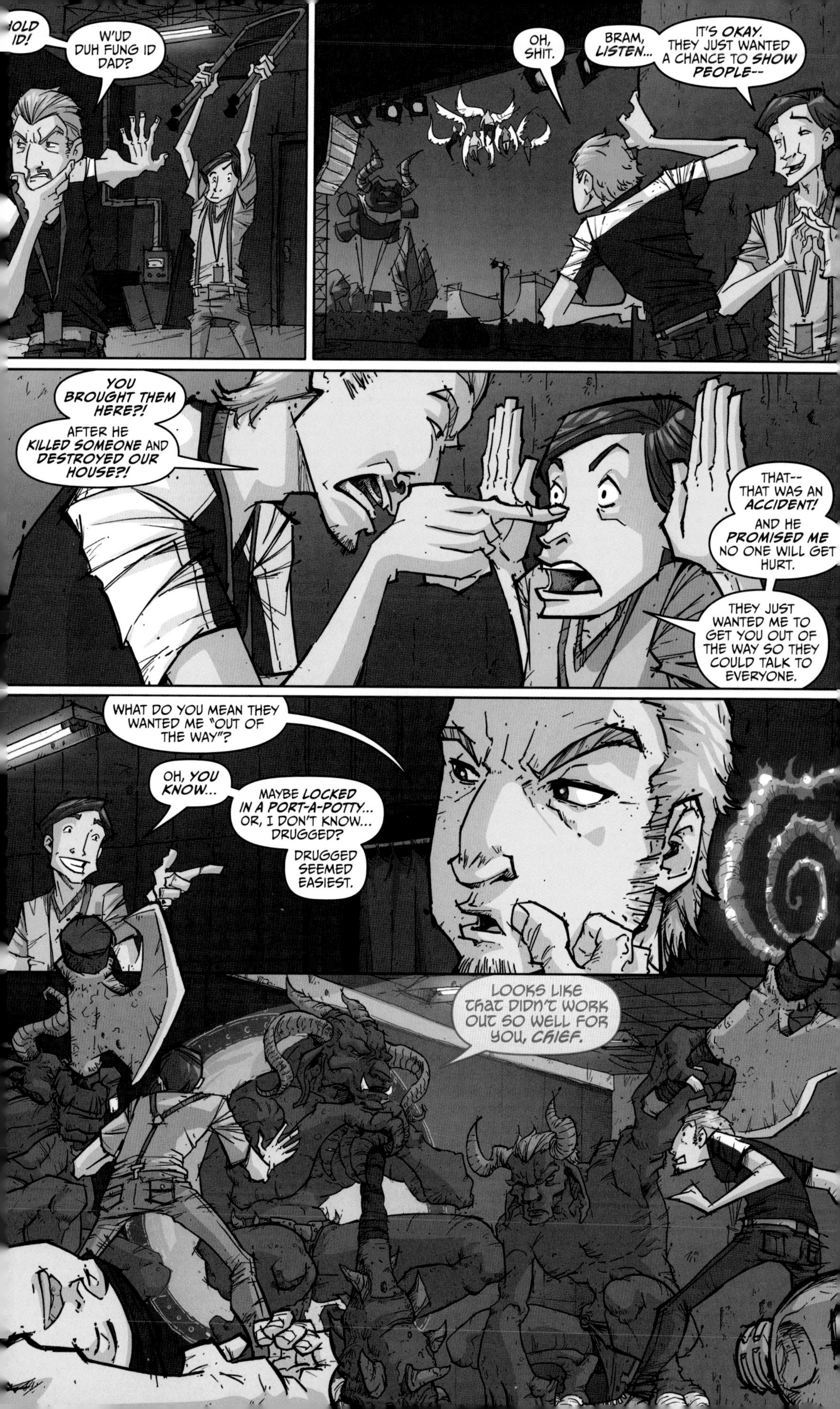
HOLD ID!
W'UD DUH FUNG ID DAD?
OH, SHIT.
BRAM, LISTEN...
IT'S OKAY. THEY JUST WANTED A CHANCE TO SHOW PEOPLE--
YOU BROUGHT THEM HERE?!
AFTER HE KILLED SOMEONE AND DESTROYED OUR HOUSE?!
THAT-- THAT WAS AN ACCIDENT!
AND HE PROMISED ME NO ONE WILL GET HURT.
THEY JUST WANTED ME TO GET YOU OUT OF THE WAY SO THEY COULD TALK TO EVERYONE.
WHAT DO YOU MEAN THEY WANTED ME "OUT OF THE WAY"?
OH, YOU KNOW...
MAYBE LOCKED IN A PORT-A-POTTY... OR, I DON'T KNOW... DRUGGED?
DRUGGED SEEMED EASIEST.
LOOKS LIKE THAT DIDN'T WORK OUT SO WELL FOR YOU, CHIEF.

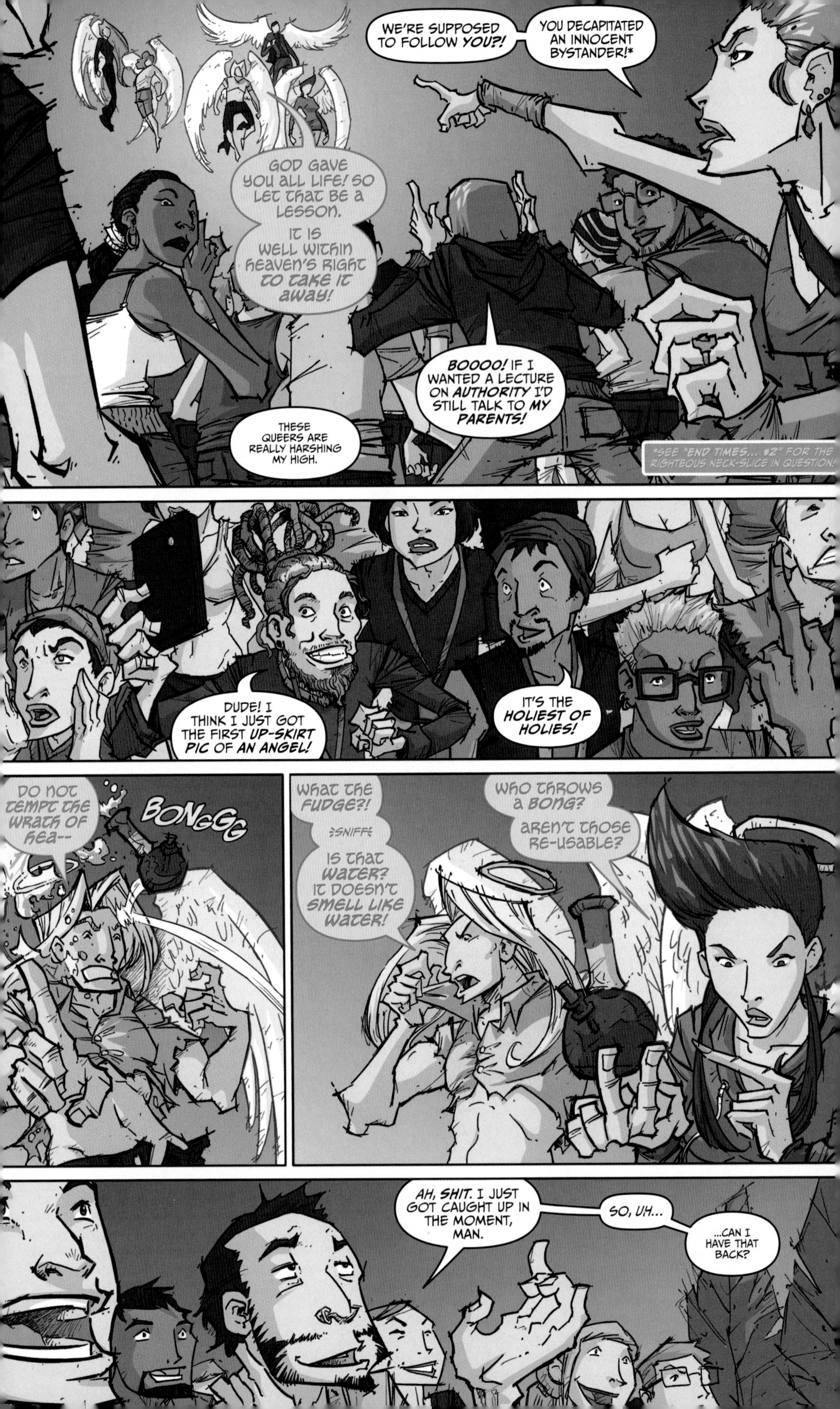
WE'RE SUPPOSED TO FOLLOW YOU?!
YOU DECAPITATED AN INNOCENT BYSTANDER!*
GOD GAVE YOU ALL LIFE! SO LET THAT BE A LESSON.
IT IS WELL WITHIN HEAVEN'S RIGHT TO TAKE IT AWAY!
BOOOO! IF I WANTED A LECTURE ON AUTHORITY I'D STILL TALK TO MY PARENTS!
THESE QUEERS ARE REALLY HARSHING MY HIGH.
*SEE "END TIMES... #2" FOR THE RIGHTEOUS NECK-SLICE IN QUESTION!
DUDE! I THINK I JUST GOT THE FIRST UP-SKIRT PIC OF AN ANGEL!
IT'S THE HOLIEST OF HOLIES!
DO NOT TEMPT THE WRATH OF HEA--
BONGGG
WHAT THE FUDGE?!
SNIFF
IS THAT WATER? IT DOESN'T SMELL LIKE WATER!
WHO THROWS A BONG?
AREN'T THOSE RE-USABLE?
AH, SHIT. I JUST GOT CAUGHT UP IN THE MOMENT, MAN.
SO, UH...
...CAN I HAVE THAT BACK?

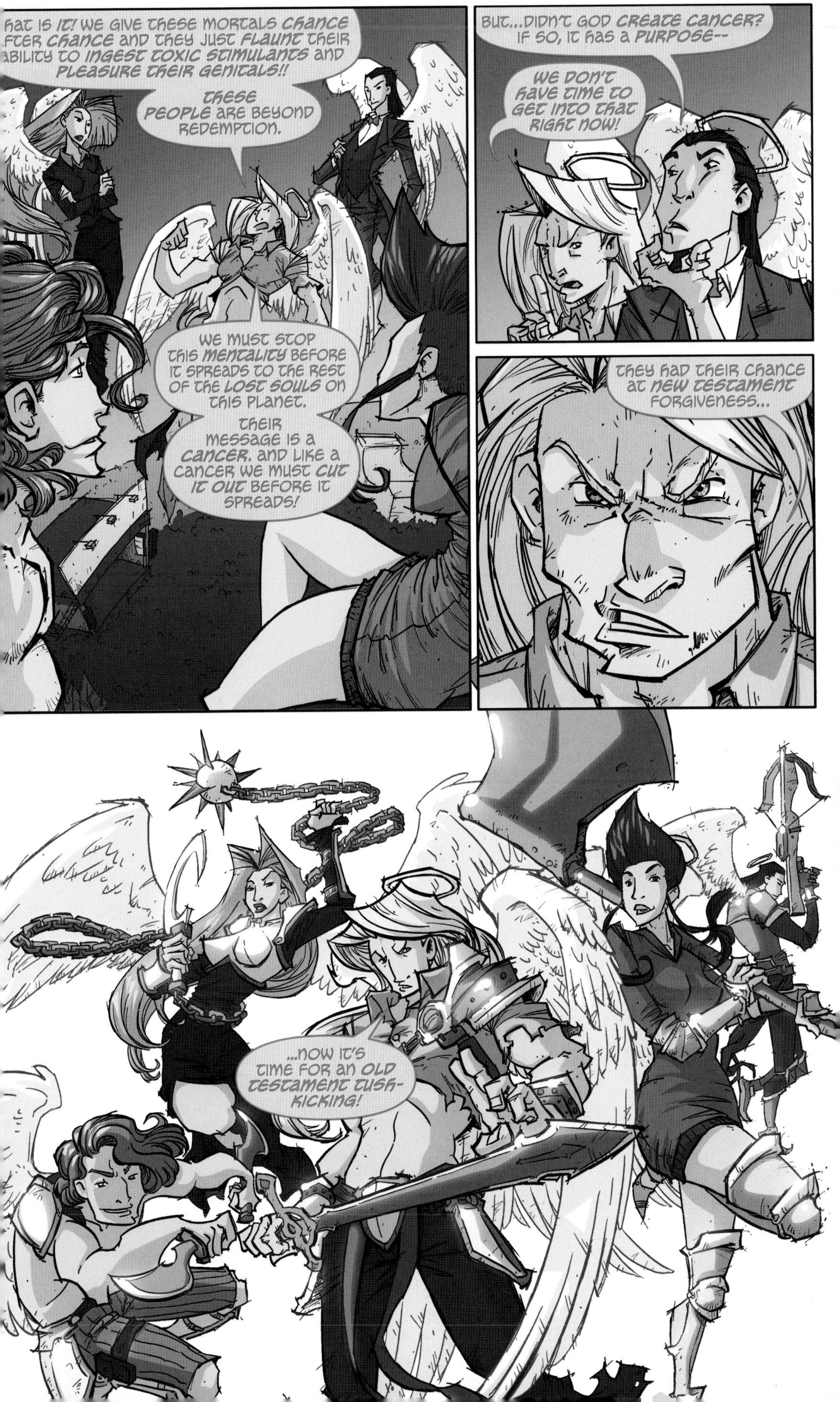
hat is it! We give these mortals chance
fter chance and they just flaunt their
ability to ingest toxic stimulants and
pleasure their genitals!!
These people are beyond redemption.
We must stop this mentality before it spreads to the rest of the lost souls on this planet.
Their message is a cancer. And like a cancer we must cut it out before it spreads!
But...didn't God create cancer? If so, it has a purpose--
We don't have time to get into that right now!
They had their chance at new testament forgiveness...
...now it's time for an old testament tush-kicking!

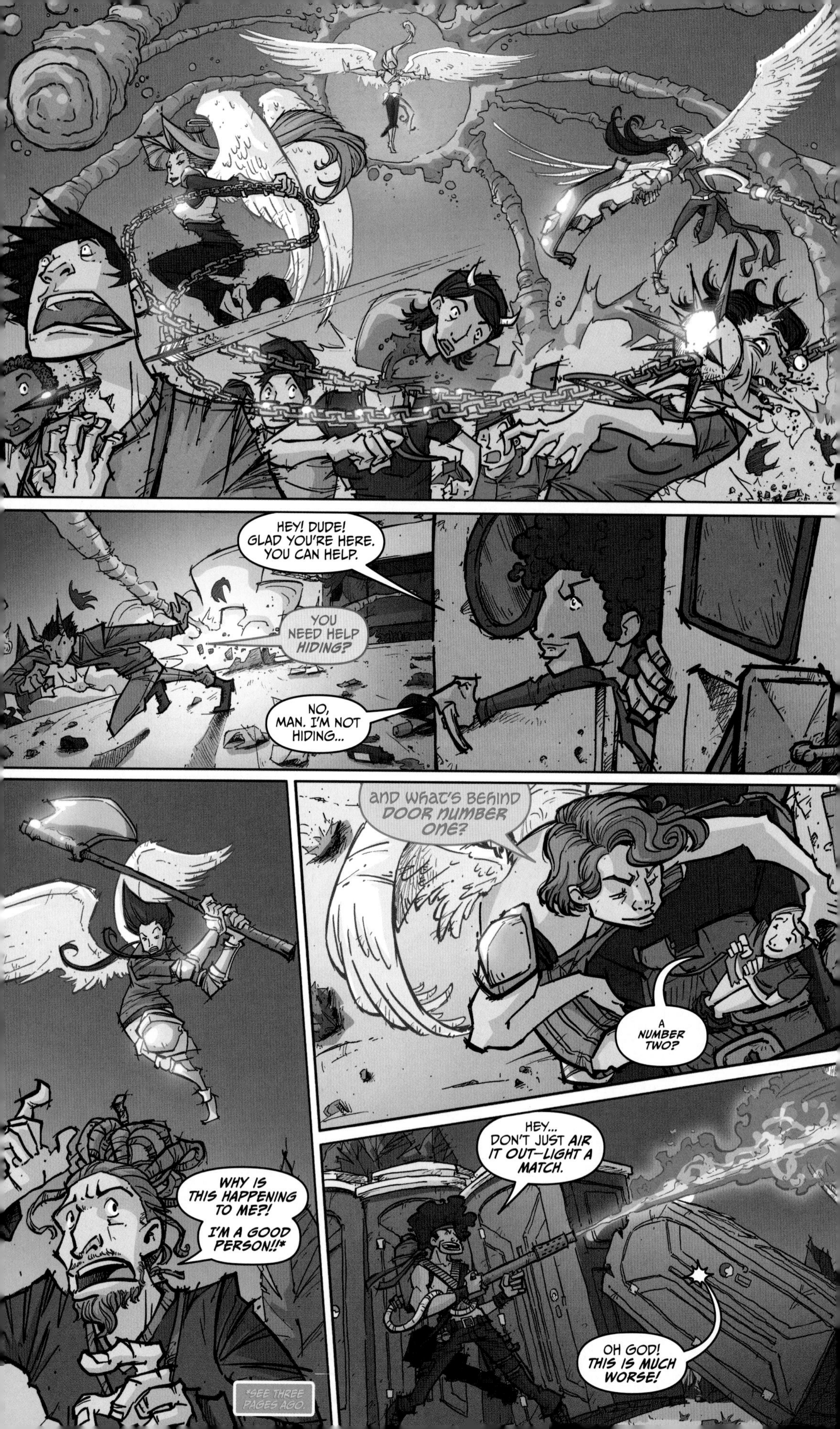

HEY! DUDE! GLAD YOU'RE HERE. YOU CAN HELP.
YOU NEED HELP HIDING?
NO, MAN. I'M NOT HIDING...
AND WHAT'S BEHIND DOOR NUMBER ONE?
A NUMBER TWO?
WHY IS THIS HAPPENING TO ME?!
I'M A GOOD PERSON!!*
HEY... DON'T JUST AIR IT OUT—LIGHT A MATCH.
OH GOD! THIS IS MUCH WORSE!
*SEE THREE PAGES AGO

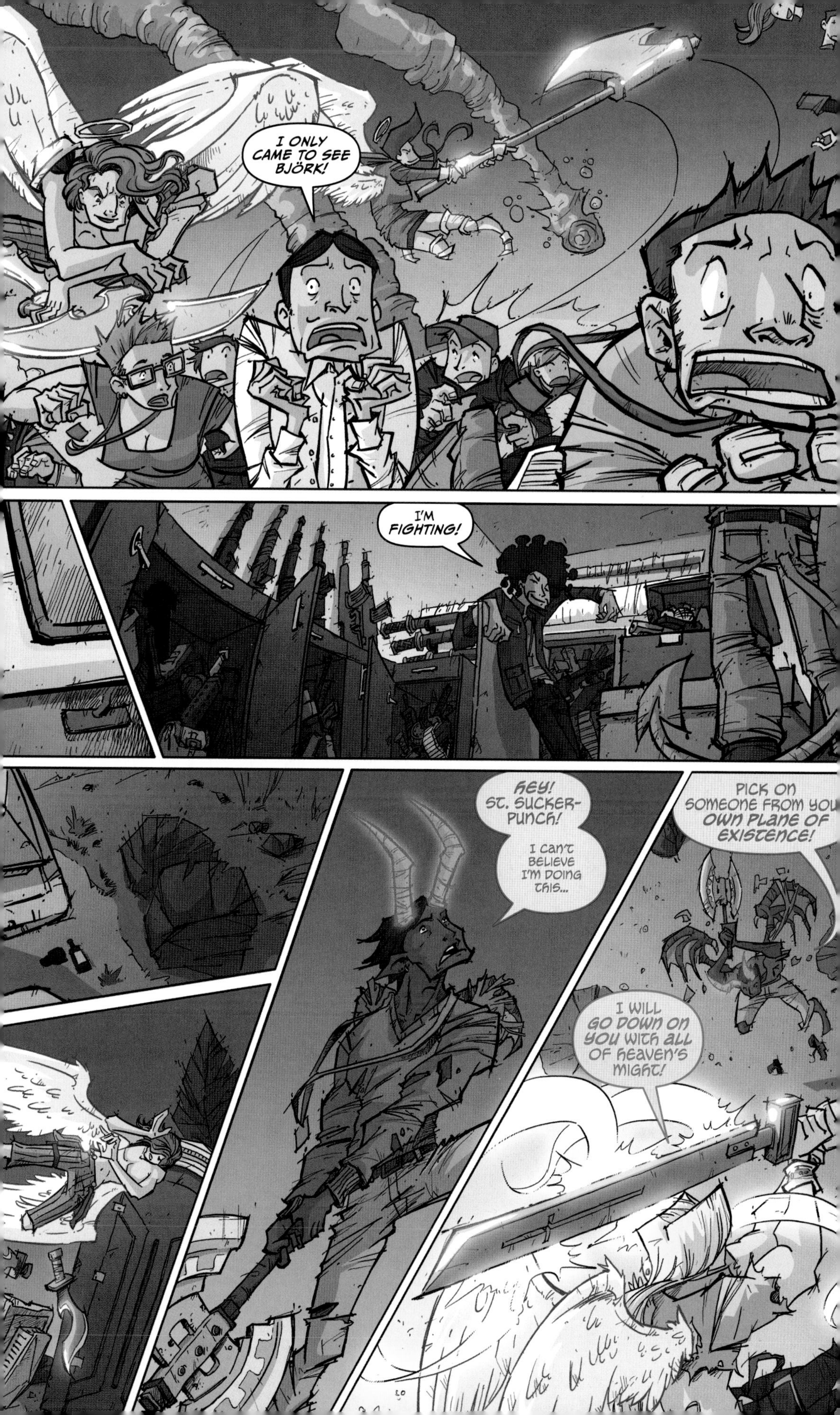
I ONLY CAME TO SEE BJÖRK!
I'M FIGHTING!
HEY! ST. SUCKER-PUNCH!
I CAN'T BELIEVE I'M DOING THIS...
PICK ON SOMEONE FROM YOU OWN PLANE OF EXISTENCE!
I WILL GO DOWN ON YOU WITH ALL OF HEAVEN'S MIGHT!

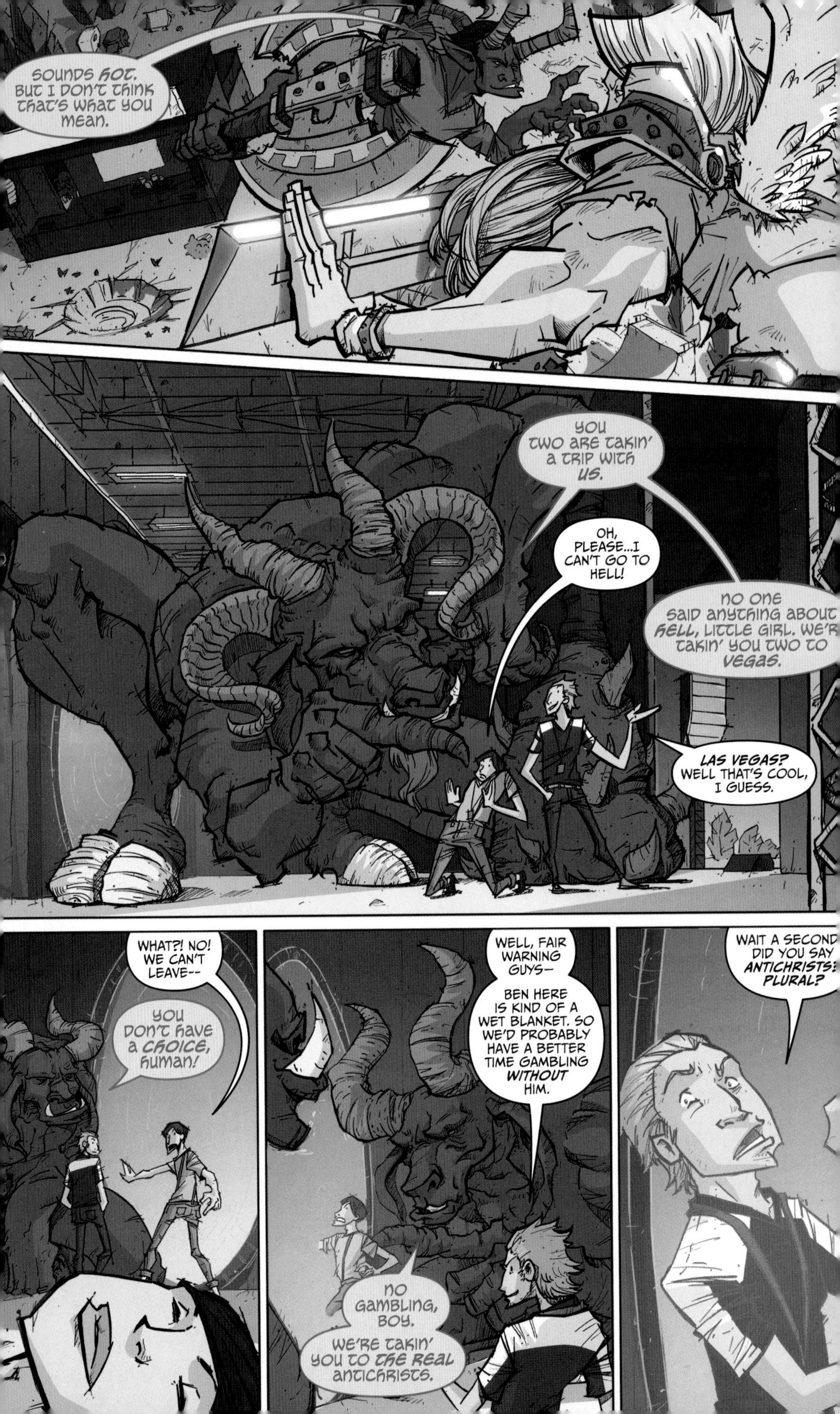
SOUNDS HOT. BUT I DON'T THINK THAT'S WHAT YOU MEAN.
YOU TWO ARE TAKIN' A TRIP WITH US.
OH, PLEASE...I CAN'T GO TO HELL!
NO ONE SAID ANYTHING ABOUT HELL, LITTLE GIRL. WE'R TAKIN' YOU TWO TO VEGAS.
LAS VEGAS? WELL THAT'S COOL, I GUESS.
WHAT?! NO! WE CAN'T LEAVE--
YOU DON'T HAVE A CHOICE, HUMAN!
WELL, FAIR WARNING GUYS—
BEN HERE IS KIND OF A WET BLANKET. SO WE'D PROBABLY HAVE A BETTER TIME GAMBLING WITHOUT HIM.
NO GAMBLING, BOY.
WE'RE TAKIN' YOU TO THE REAL ANTICHRISTS.
WAIT A SECOND DID YOU SAY ANTICHRISTS PLURAL?

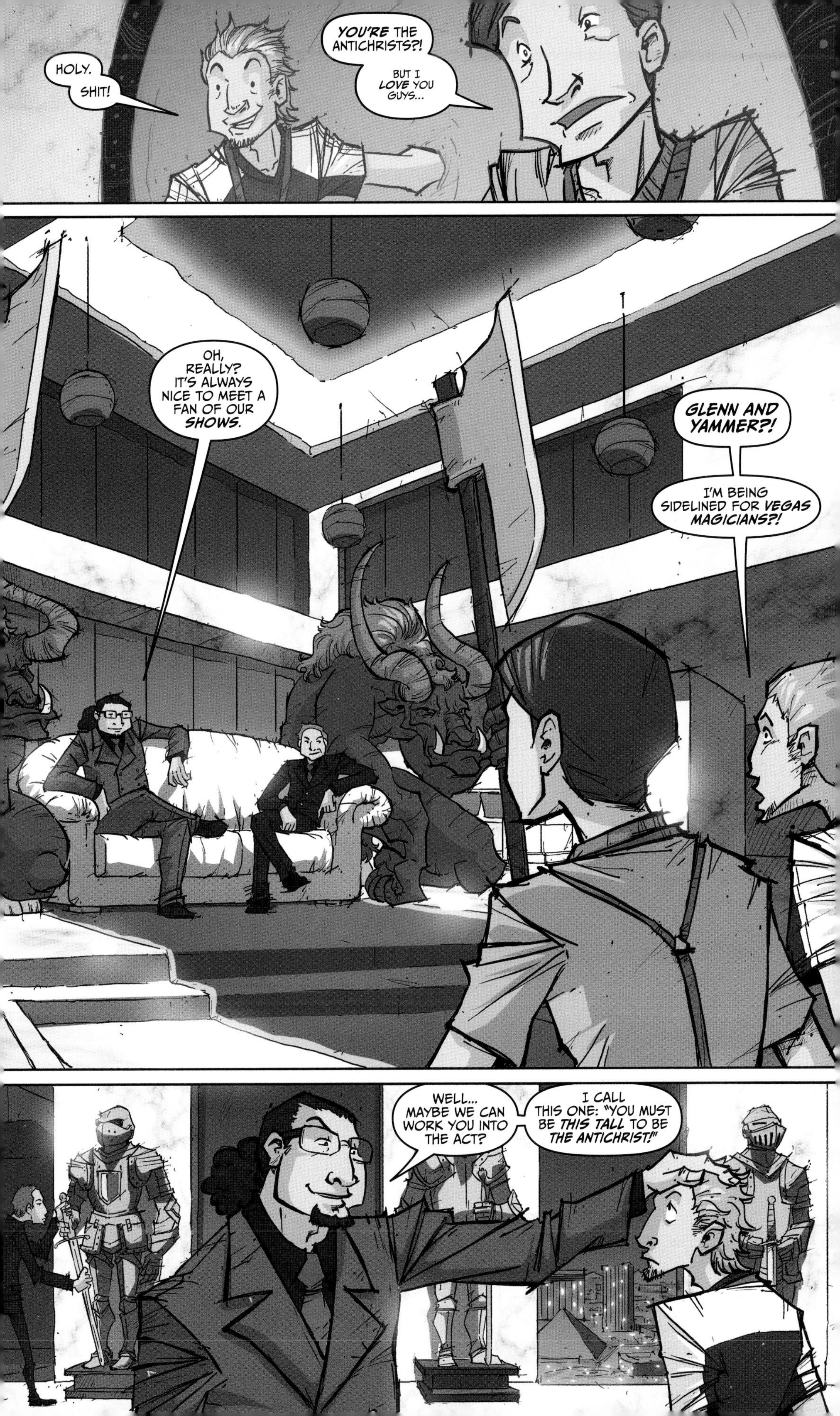
HOLY.
SHIT!
YOU'RE THE ANTICHRISTS?!
BUT I LOVE YOU GUYS...
OH, REALLY? IT'S ALWAYS NICE TO MEET A FAN OF OUR SHOWS.
GLENN AND YAMMER?!
I'M BEING SIDELINED FOR VEGAS MAGICIANS?!
WELL... MAYBE WE CAN WORK YOU INTO THE ACT?
I CALL THIS ONE: "YOU MUST BE THIS TALL TO BE THE ANTICHRIST!"

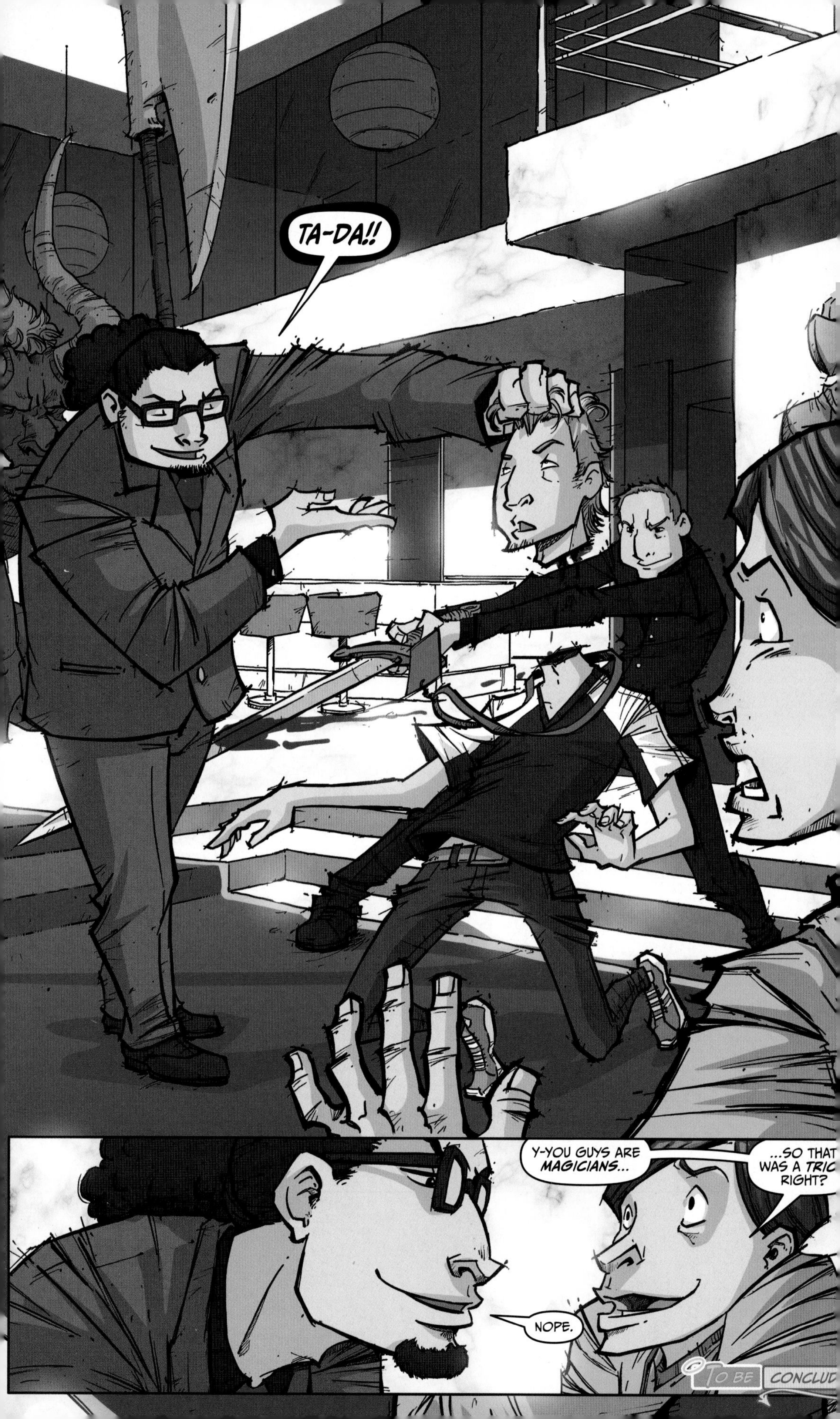
TA-DA!!
Y-YOU GUYS ARE *MAGICIANS*...
...SO THAT WAS A *TRIC*
RIGHT?
NOPE.
TO BE CONCLUD

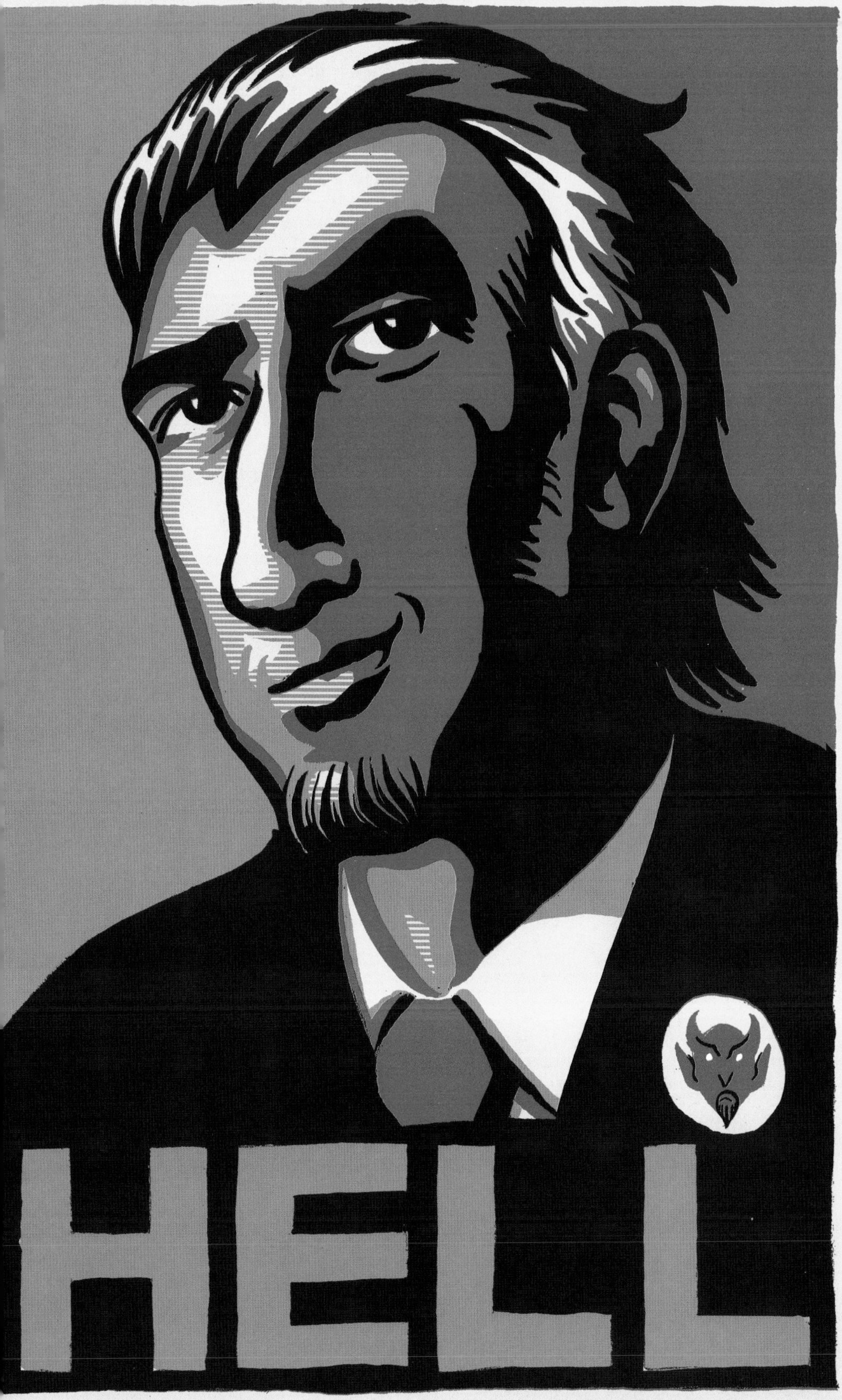
HELL

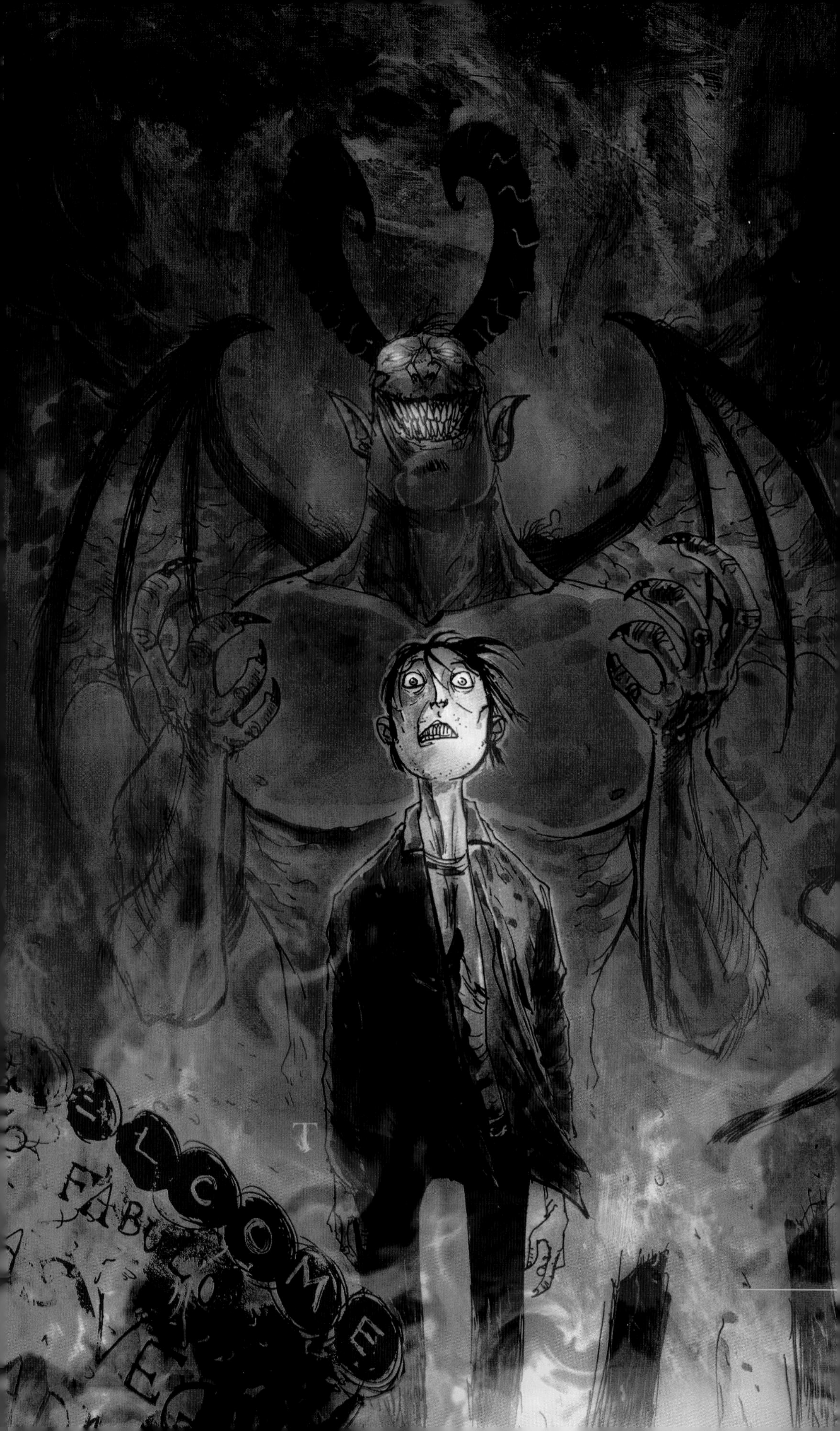

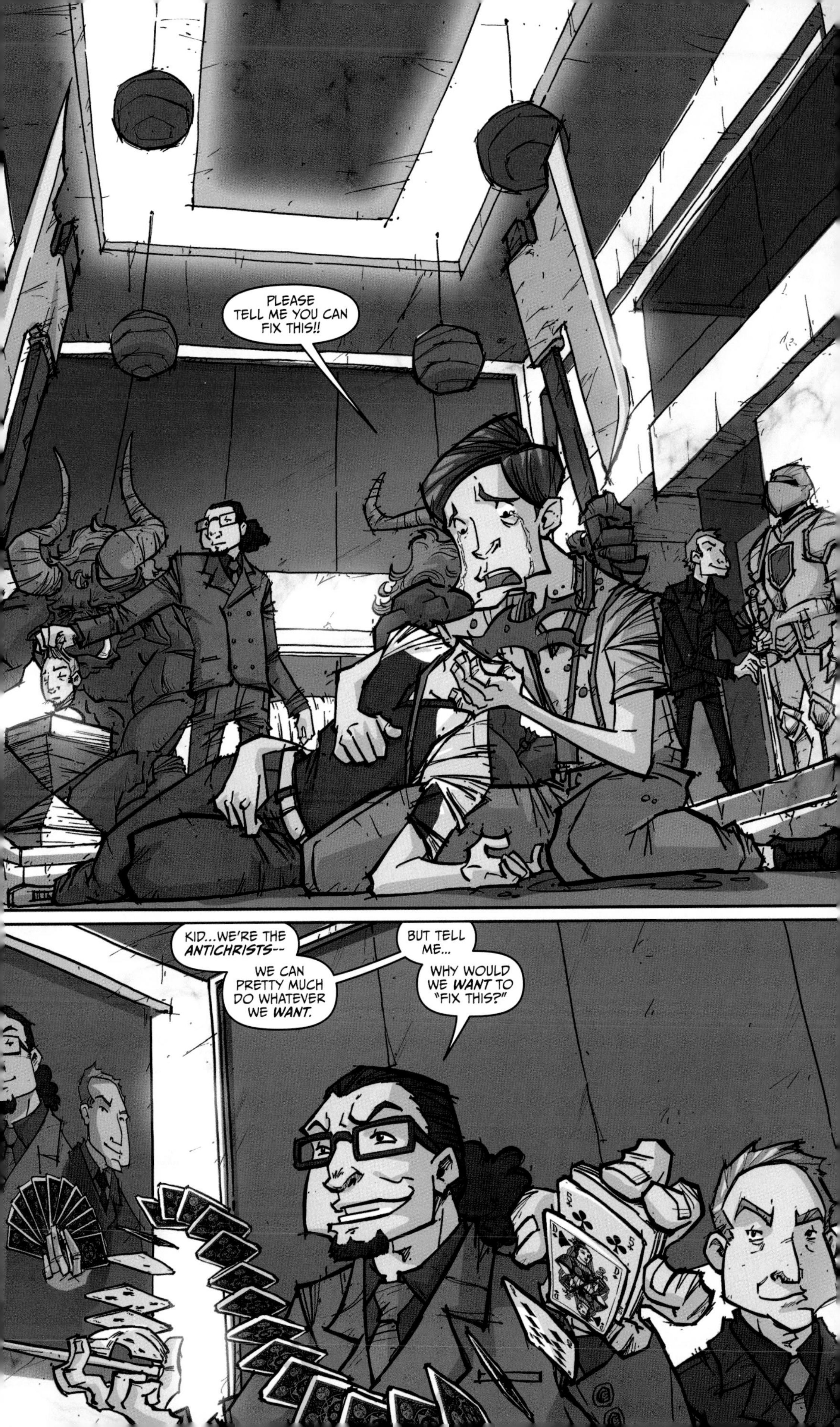
PLEASE TELL ME YOU CAN FIX THIS!!
KID...WE'RE THE ANTICHRISTS--
WE CAN PRETTY MUCH DO WHATEVER WE WANT.
BUT TELL ME...
WHY WOULD WE WANT TO "FIX THIS?"

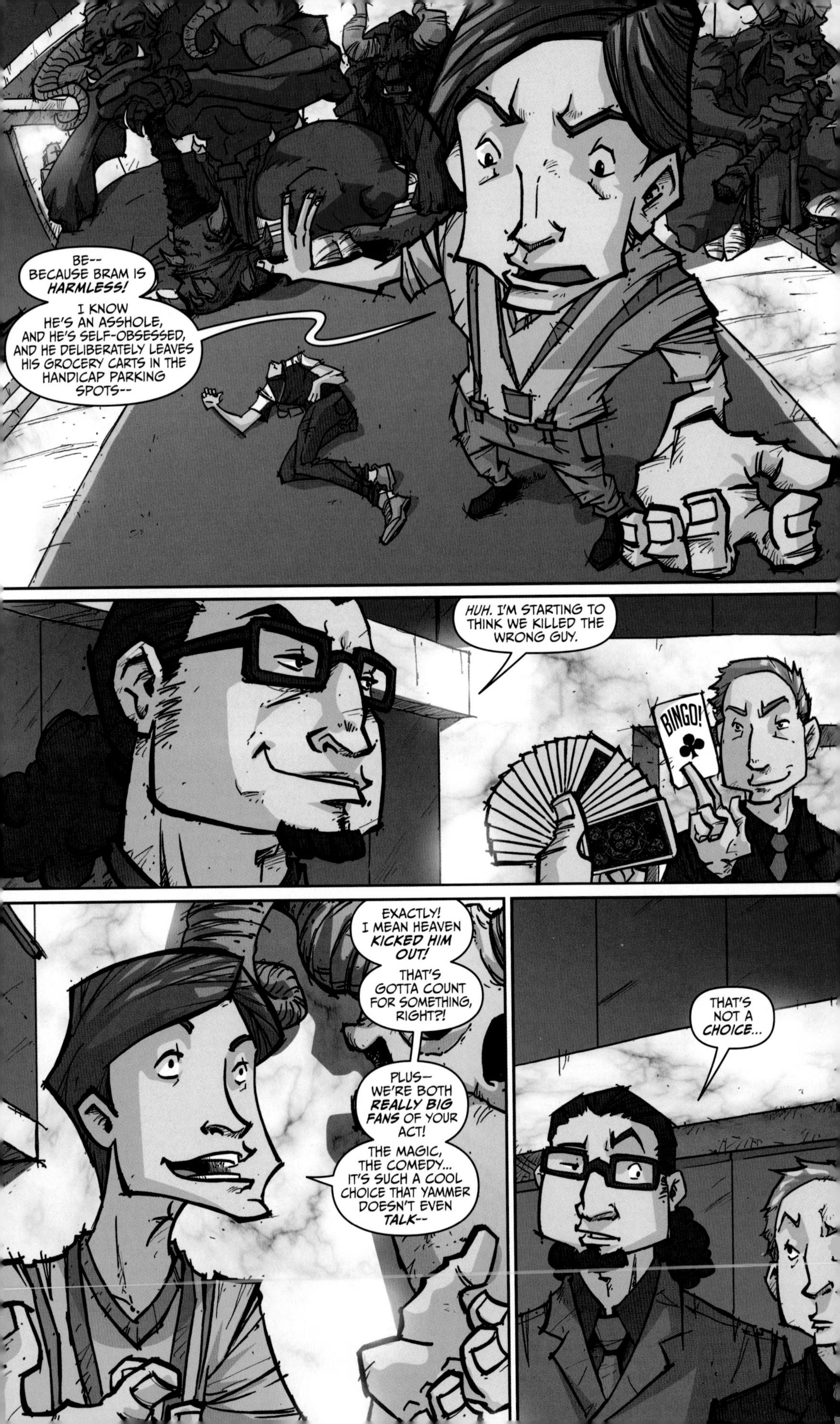
BE-- BECAUSE BRAM IS ***HARMLESS!***
I KNOW HE'S AN ASSHOLE, AND HE'S SELF-OBSESSED, AND HE DELIBERATELY LEAVES HIS GROCERY CARTS IN THE HANDICAP PARKING SPOTS--
*HUH.* I'M STARTING TO THINK WE KILLED THE WRONG GUY.
BINGO!
EXACTLY! I MEAN HEAVEN ***KICKED HIM OUT!***
THAT'S GOTTA COUNT FOR SOMETHING, RIGHT?!
PLUS— WE'RE BOTH ***REALLY BIG FANS*** OF YOUR ACT!
THE MAGIC, THE COMEDY... IT'S SUCH A COOL CHOICE THAT YAMMER DOESN'T EVEN *TALK--*
THAT'S NOT A ***CHOICE...***

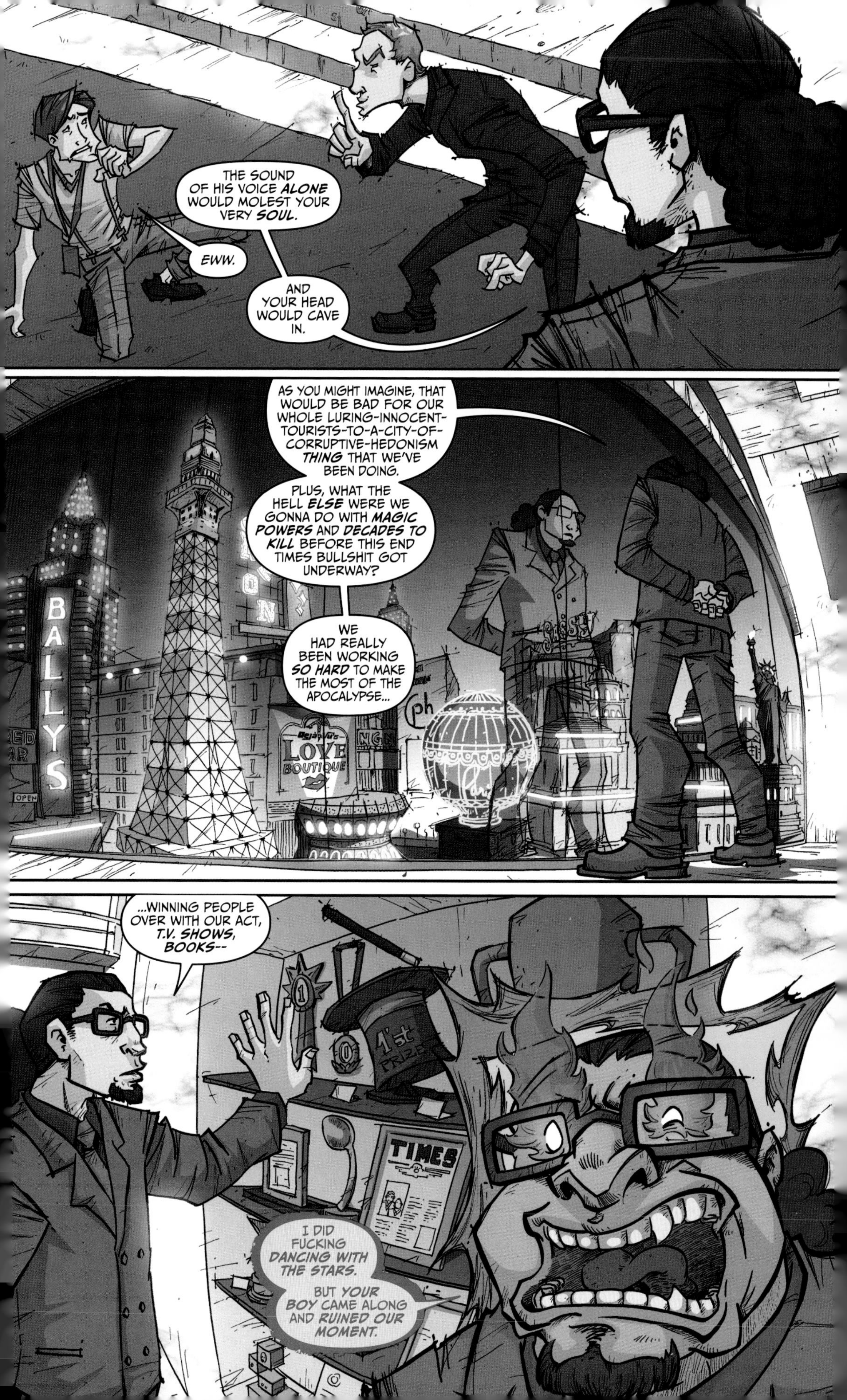
THE SOUND OF HIS VOICE *ALONE* WOULD MOLEST YOUR VERY *SOUL.*
*EWW.*
AND YOUR HEAD WOULD CAVE IN.
AS YOU MIGHT IMAGINE, THAT WOULD BE BAD FOR OUR WHOLE LURING-INNOCENT-TOURISTS-TO-A-CITY-OF-CORRUPTIVE-HEDONISM *THING* THAT WE'VE BEEN DOING.
PLUS, WHAT THE HELL *ELSE* WERE WE GONNA DO WITH *MAGIC POWERS* AND *DECADES TO KILL* BEFORE THIS END TIMES BULLSHIT GOT UNDERWAY?
WE HAD REALLY BEEN WORKING *SO HARD* TO MAKE THE MOST OF THE APOCALYPSE...
BALLYS
OPEN
LOVE BOUTIQUE
...WINNING PEOPLE OVER WITH OUR ACT, *T.V. SHOWS, BOOKS--*
1st PRIZE
TIMES
I DID FUCKING *DANCING WITH THE STARS.*
BUT *YOUR BOY* CAME ALONG AND *RUINED OUR MOMENT.*

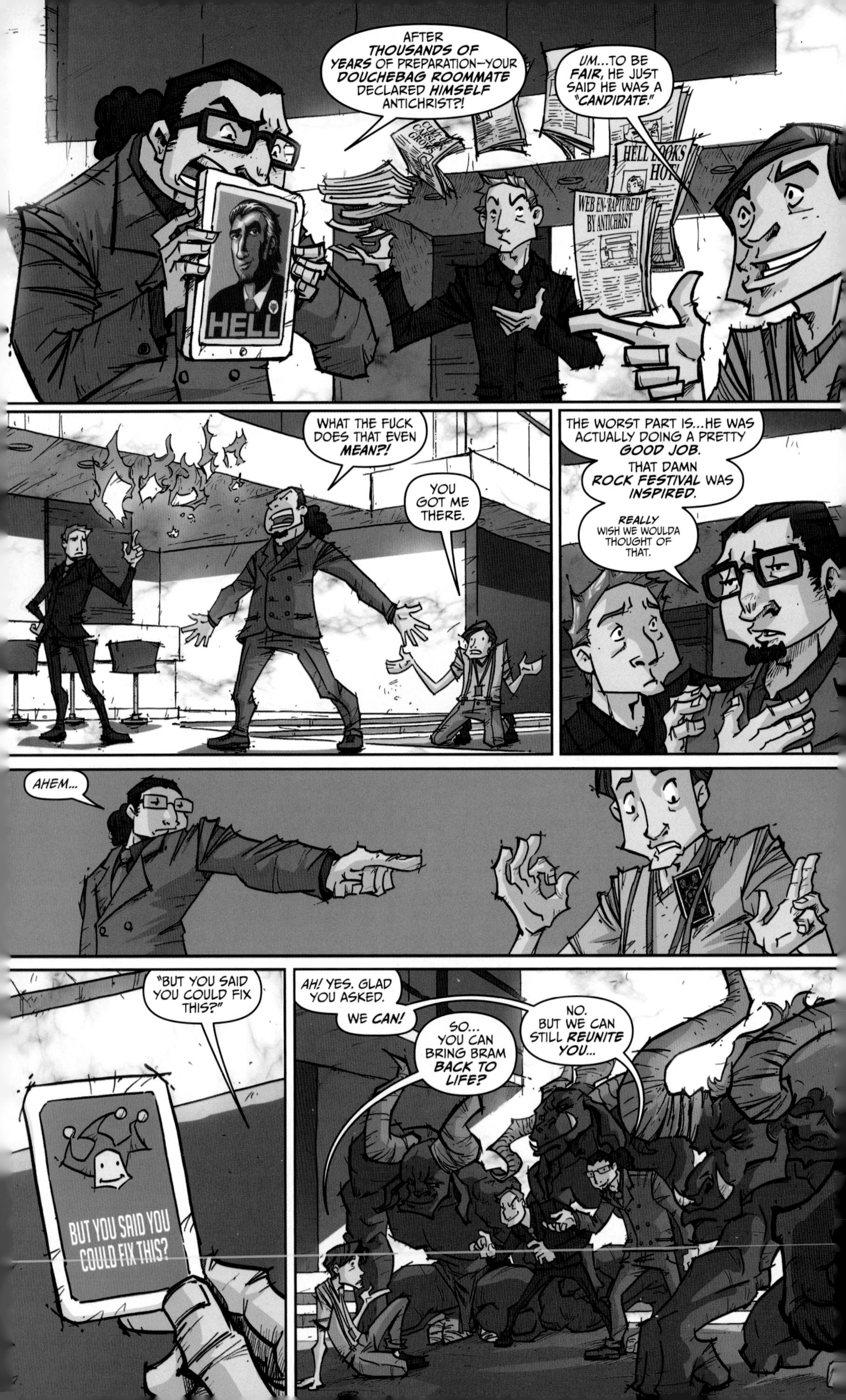
AFTER THOUSANDS OF YEARS OF PREPARATION—YOUR DOUCHEBAG ROOMMATE DECLARED HIMSELF ANTICHRIST?!
UM...TO BE FAIR, HE JUST SAID HE WAS A "CANDIDATE."
HELL
HELL LOOKS HOT!
WEB EN-'RAPTURED' BY ANTICHRIST
WHAT THE FUCK DOES THAT EVEN MEAN?!
YOU GOT ME THERE.
THE WORST PART IS...HE WAS ACTUALLY DOING A PRETTY GOOD JOB.
THAT DAMN ROCK FESTIVAL WAS INSPIRED.
REALLY WISH WE WOULDA THOUGHT OF THAT.
AHEM...
"BUT YOU SAID YOU COULD FIX THIS?"
BUT YOU SAID YOU COULD FIX THIS?
AH! YES. GLAD YOU ASKED.
WE CAN!
SO... YOU CAN BRING BRAM BACK TO LIFE?
NO. BUT WE CAN STILL REUNITE YOU...

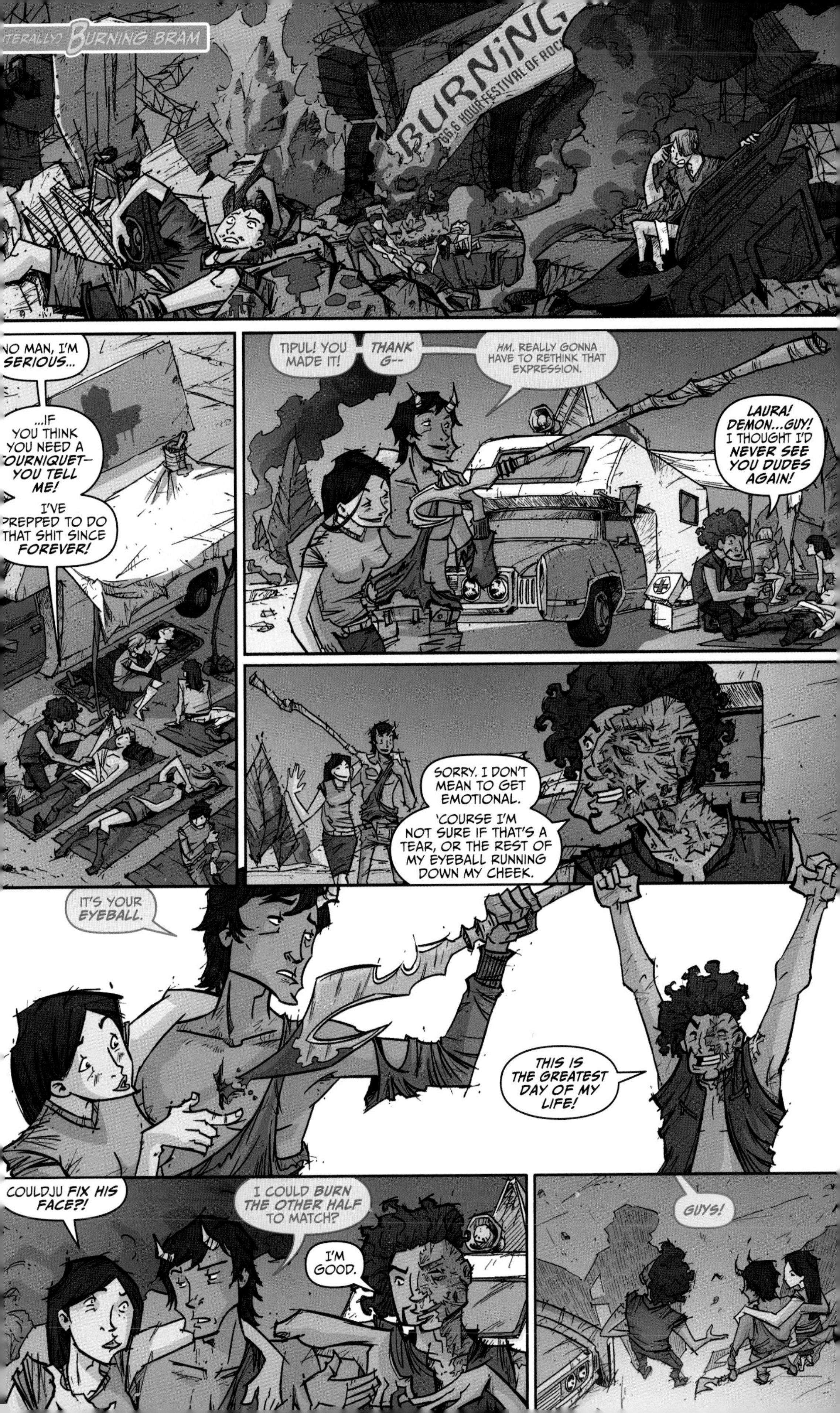
(LITERALLY) BURNING BRAM
BURNING
66.6 HOUR FESTIVAL OF ROCK
NO MAN, I'M SERIOUS...
...IF YOU THINK YOU NEED A TOURNIQUET— YOU TELL ME!
I'VE PREPPED TO DO THAT SHIT SINCE FOREVER!
TIPUL! YOU MADE IT!
THANK G--
HM. REALLY GONNA HAVE TO RETHINK THAT EXPRESSION.
LAURA! DEMON...GUY! I THOUGHT I'D NEVER SEE YOU DUDES AGAIN!
SORRY. I DON'T MEAN TO GET EMOTIONAL.
'COURSE I'M NOT SURE IF THAT'S A TEAR, OR THE REST OF MY EYEBALL RUNNING DOWN MY CHEEK.
IT'S YOUR EYEBALL.
THIS IS THE GREATEST DAY OF MY LIFE!
COULDJU FIX HIS FACE?!
I COULD BURN THE OTHER HALF TO MATCH?
I'M GOOD.
GUYS!

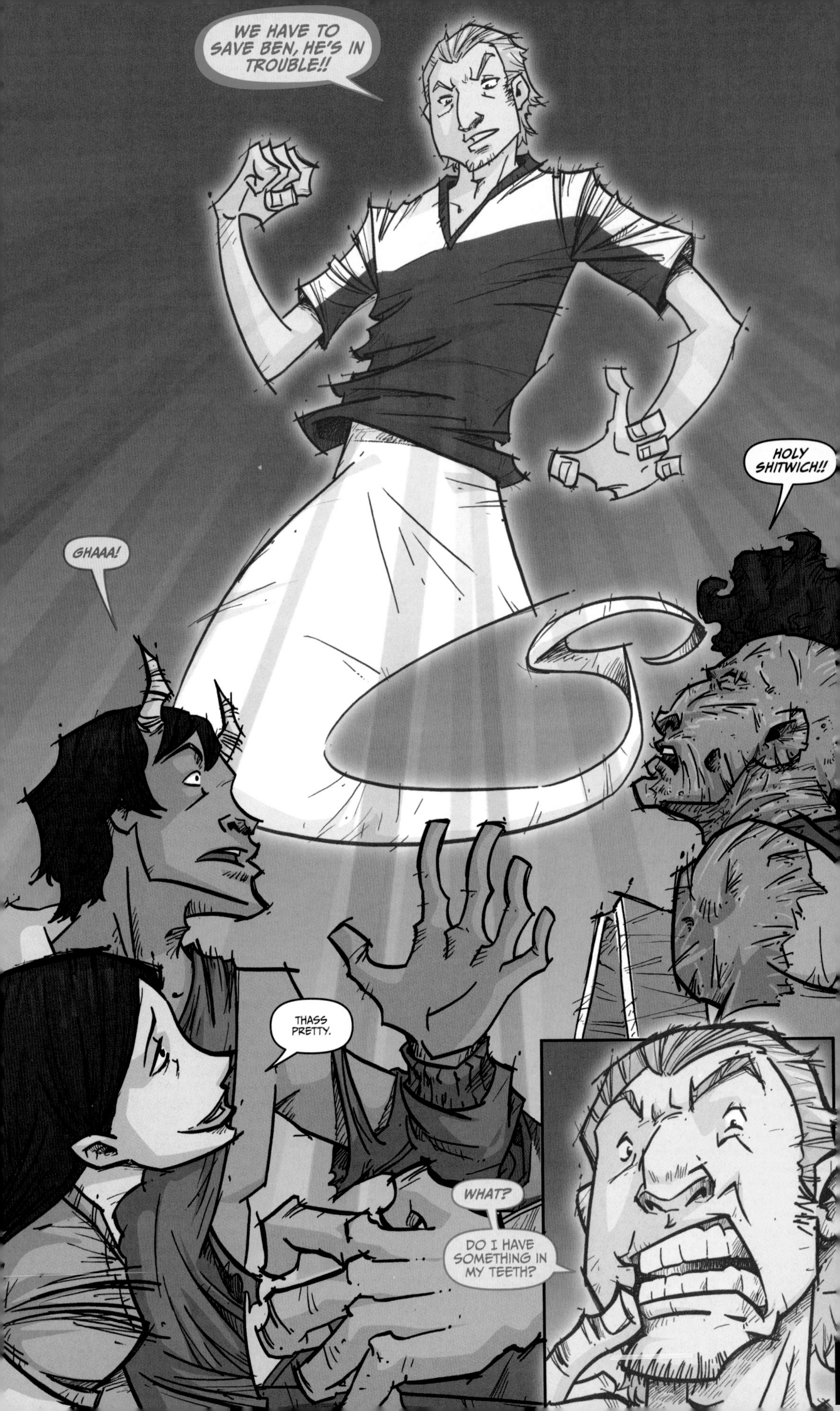
WE HAVE TO SAVE BEN, HE'S IN TROUBLE!!
HOLY SHITWICH!!
GHAAA!
THASS PRETTY.
WHAT?
DO I HAVE SOMETHING IN MY TEETH?

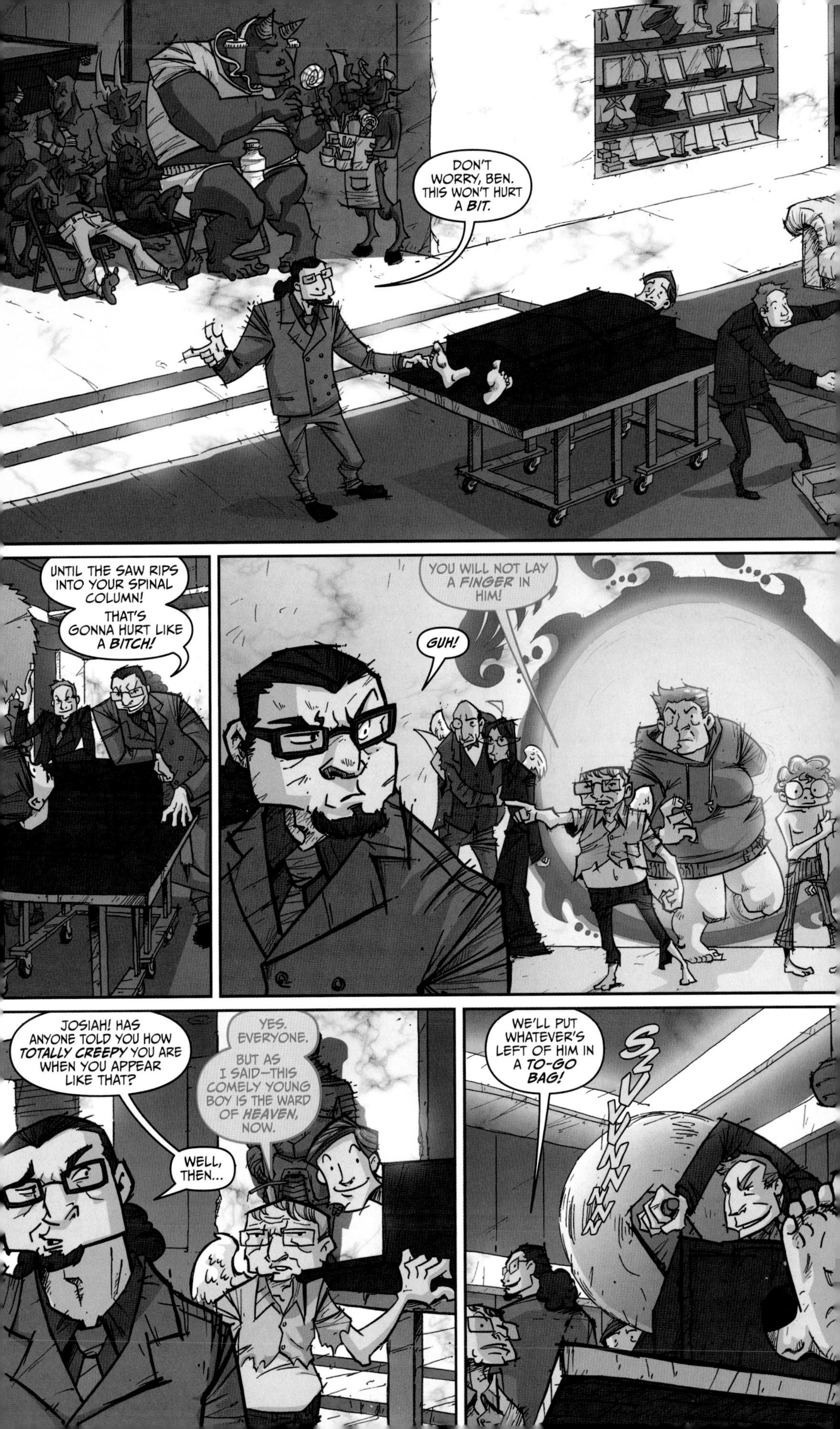
DON'T WORRY, BEN. THIS WON'T HURT A *BIT.*
UNTIL THE SAW RIPS INTO YOUR SPINAL COLUMN!
THAT'S GONNA HURT LIKE A *BITCH!*
YOU WILL NOT LAY A *FINGER* IN HIM!
*GUH!*
JOSIAH! HAS ANYONE TOLD YOU HOW *TOTALLY CREEPY* YOU ARE WHEN YOU APPEAR LIKE THAT?
YES. EVERYONE.
BUT AS I SAID—THIS COMELY YOUNG BOY IS THE WARD OF *HEAVEN,* NOW.
WELL, THEN...
WE'LL PUT WHATEVER'S LEFT OF HIM IN A *TO-GO BAG!*
SZVUNNNN

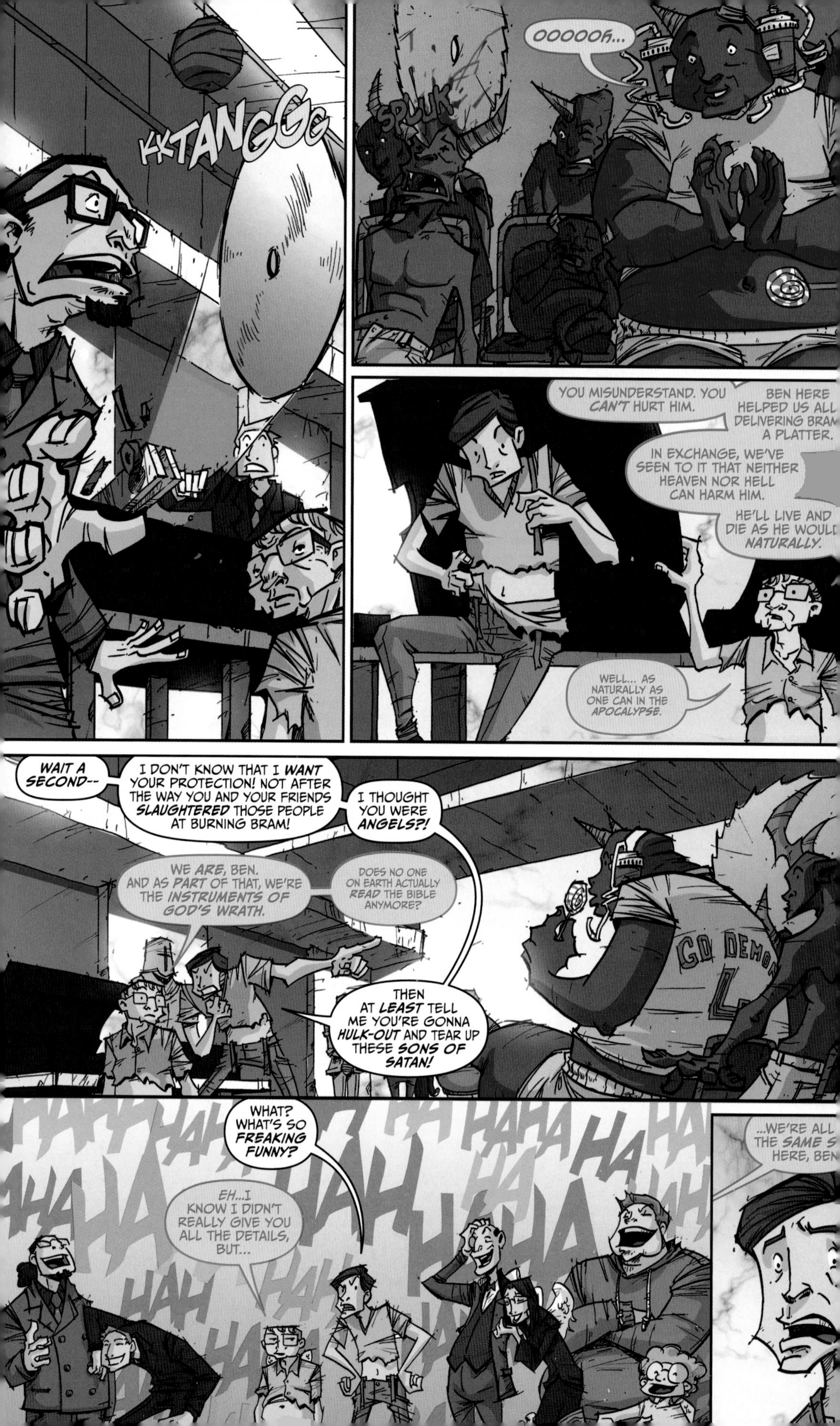
KKTANGGG
SPLUK
OOOOOH...
YOU MISUNDERSTAND. YOU CAN'T HURT HIM.
BEN HERE HELPED US ALL
DELIVERING BRAM
A PLATTER.
IN EXCHANGE, WE'VE SEEN TO IT THAT NEITHER HEAVEN NOR HELL CAN HARM HIM.
HE'LL LIVE AND DIE AS HE WOULD NATURALLY.
WELL... AS NATURALLY AS ONE CAN IN THE APOCALYPSE.
WAIT A SECOND--
I DON'T KNOW THAT I WANT YOUR PROTECTION! NOT AFTER THE WAY YOU AND YOUR FRIENDS SLAUGHTERED THOSE PEOPLE AT BURNING BRAM!
I THOUGHT YOU WERE ANGELS?!
WE ARE, BEN. AND AS PART OF THAT, WE'RE THE INSTRUMENTS OF GOD'S WRATH.
DOES NO ONE ON EARTH ACTUALLY READ THE BIBLE ANYMORE?
THEN AT LEAST TELL ME YOU'RE GONNA HULK-OUT AND TEAR UP THESE SONS OF SATAN!
GO DEMON
HAHAHA HAHA HAH HA HAH
WHAT? WHAT'S SO FREAKING FUNNY?
EH...I KNOW I DIDN'T REALLY GIVE YOU ALL THE DETAILS, BUT...
...WE'RE ALL THE SAME S
HERE, BEN

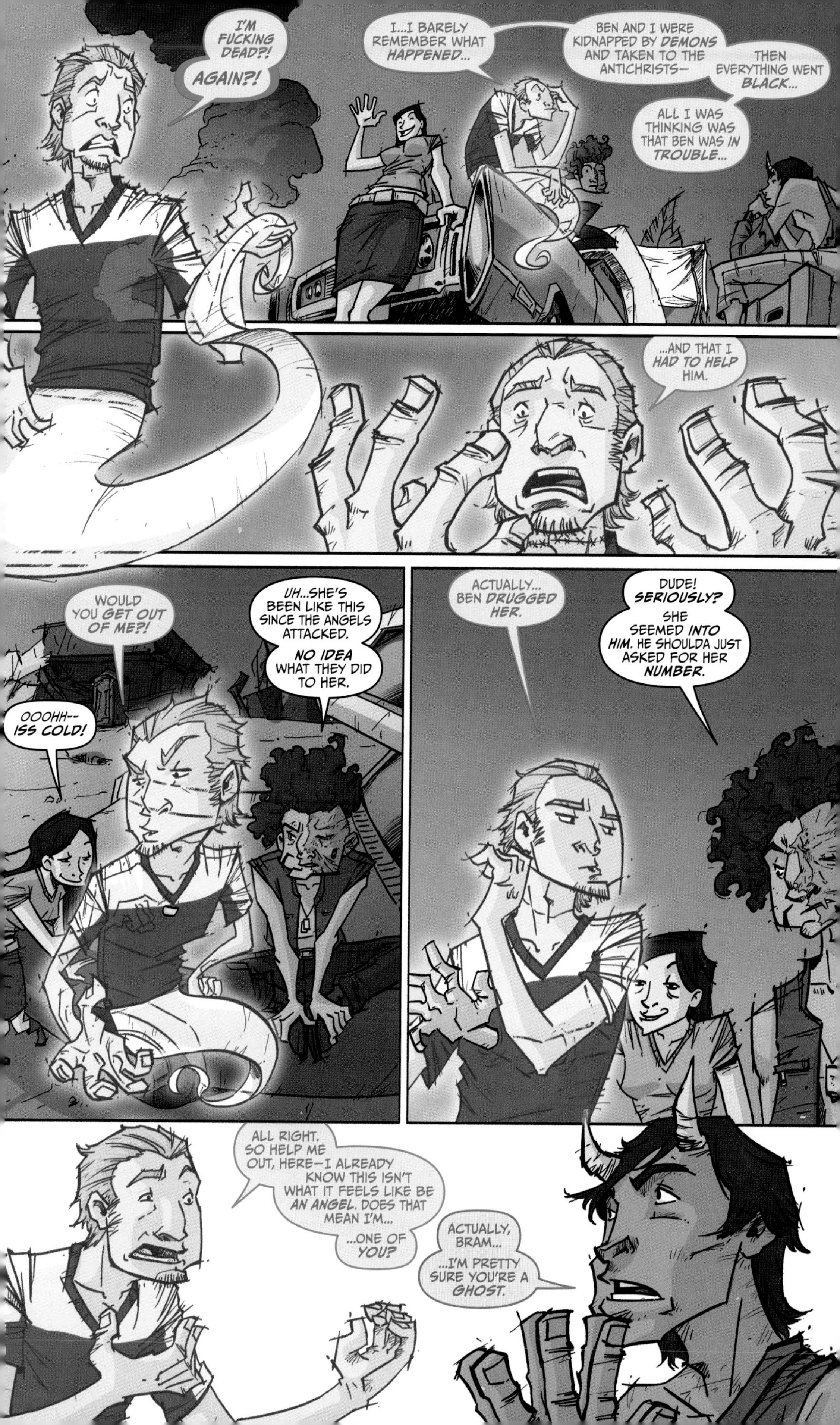
I'M FUCKING DEAD?! AGAIN?!
I...I BARELY REMEMBER WHAT HAPPENED...
BEN AND I WERE KIDNAPPED BY DEMONS AND TAKEN TO THE ANTICHRISTS—
THEN EVERYTHING WENT BLACK...
ALL I WAS THINKING WAS THAT BEN WAS IN TROUBLE...
...AND THAT I HAD TO HELP HIM.
WOULD YOU GET OUT OF ME?!
UH...SHE'S BEEN LIKE THIS SINCE THE ANGELS ATTACKED.
NO IDEA WHAT THEY DID TO HER.
OOOHH-- ISS COLD!
ACTUALLY... BEN DRUGGED HER.
DUDE! SERIOUSLY?
SHE SEEMED INTO HIM. HE SHOULDA JUST ASKED FOR HER NUMBER.
ALL RIGHT. SO HELP ME OUT, HERE—I ALREADY KNOW THIS ISN'T WHAT IT FEELS LIKE BE AN ANGEL. DOES THAT MEAN I'M...
...ONE OF YOU?
ACTUALLY, BRAM...
...I'M PRETTY SURE YOU'RE A GHOST.

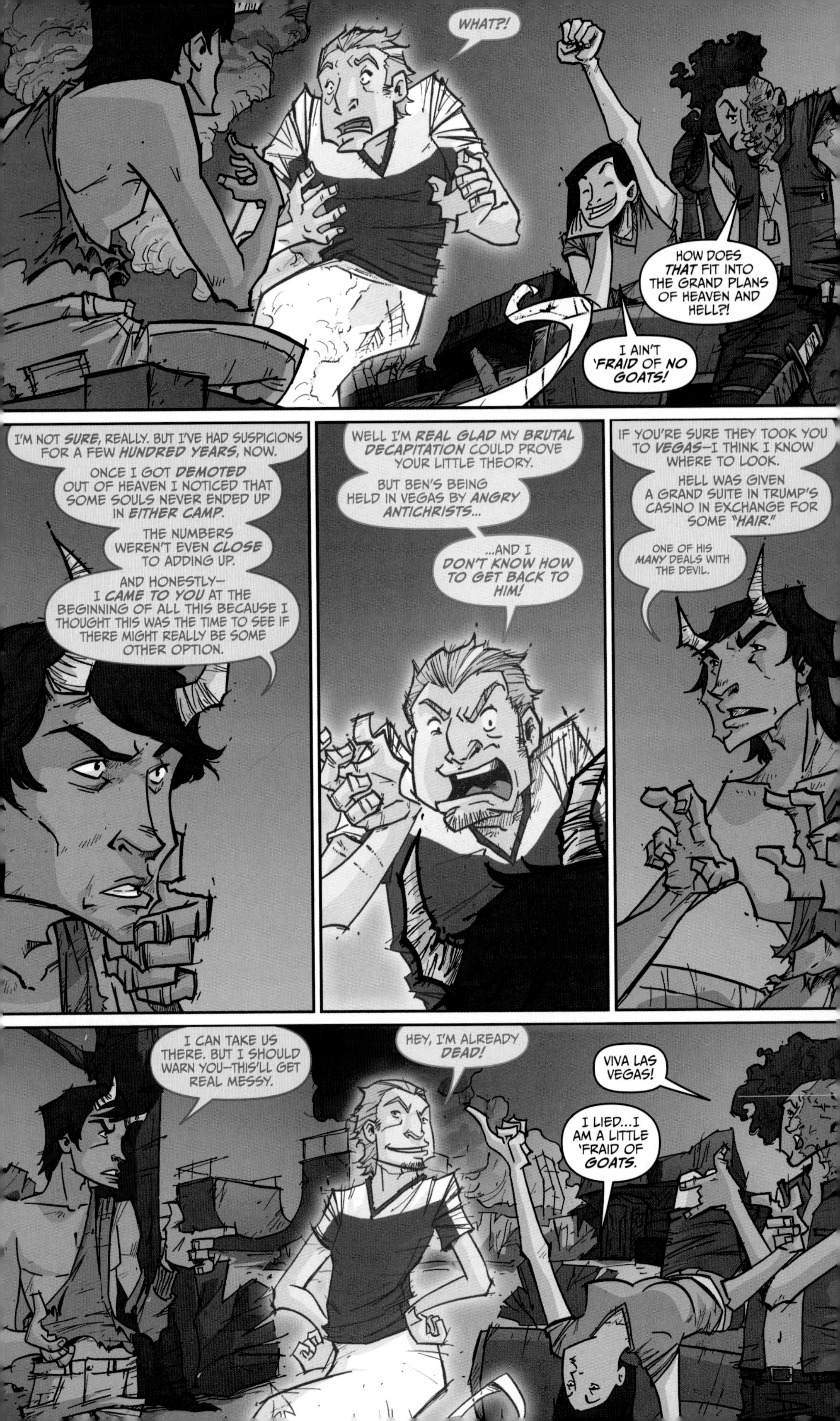
WHAT?!
HOW DOES THAT FIT INTO THE GRAND PLANS OF HEAVEN AND HELL?!
I AIN'T 'FRAID OF NO GOATS!
I'M NOT SURE, REALLY. BUT I'VE HAD SUSPICIONS FOR A FEW HUNDRED YEARS, NOW.
ONCE I GOT DEMOTED OUT OF HEAVEN I NOTICED THAT SOME SOULS NEVER ENDED UP IN EITHER CAMP.
THE NUMBERS WEREN'T EVEN CLOSE TO ADDING UP.
AND HONESTLY— I CAME TO YOU AT THE BEGINNING OF ALL THIS BECAUSE I THOUGHT THIS WAS THE TIME TO SEE IF THERE MIGHT REALLY BE SOME OTHER OPTION.
WELL I'M REAL GLAD MY BRUTAL DECAPITATION COULD PROVE YOUR LITTLE THEORY.
BUT BEN'S BEING HELD IN VEGAS BY ANGRY ANTICHRISTS...
...AND I DON'T KNOW HOW TO GET BACK TO HIM!
IF YOU'RE SURE THEY TOOK YOU TO VEGAS—I THINK I KNOW WHERE TO LOOK.
HELL WAS GIVEN A GRAND SUITE IN TRUMP'S CASINO IN EXCHANGE FOR SOME "HAIR."
ONE OF HIS MANY DEALS WITH THE DEVIL.
I CAN TAKE US THERE. BUT I SHOULD WARN YOU—THIS'LL GET REAL MESSY.
HEY, I'M ALREADY DEAD!
VIVA LAS VEGAS!
I LIED...I AM A LITTLE 'FRAID OF GOATS.

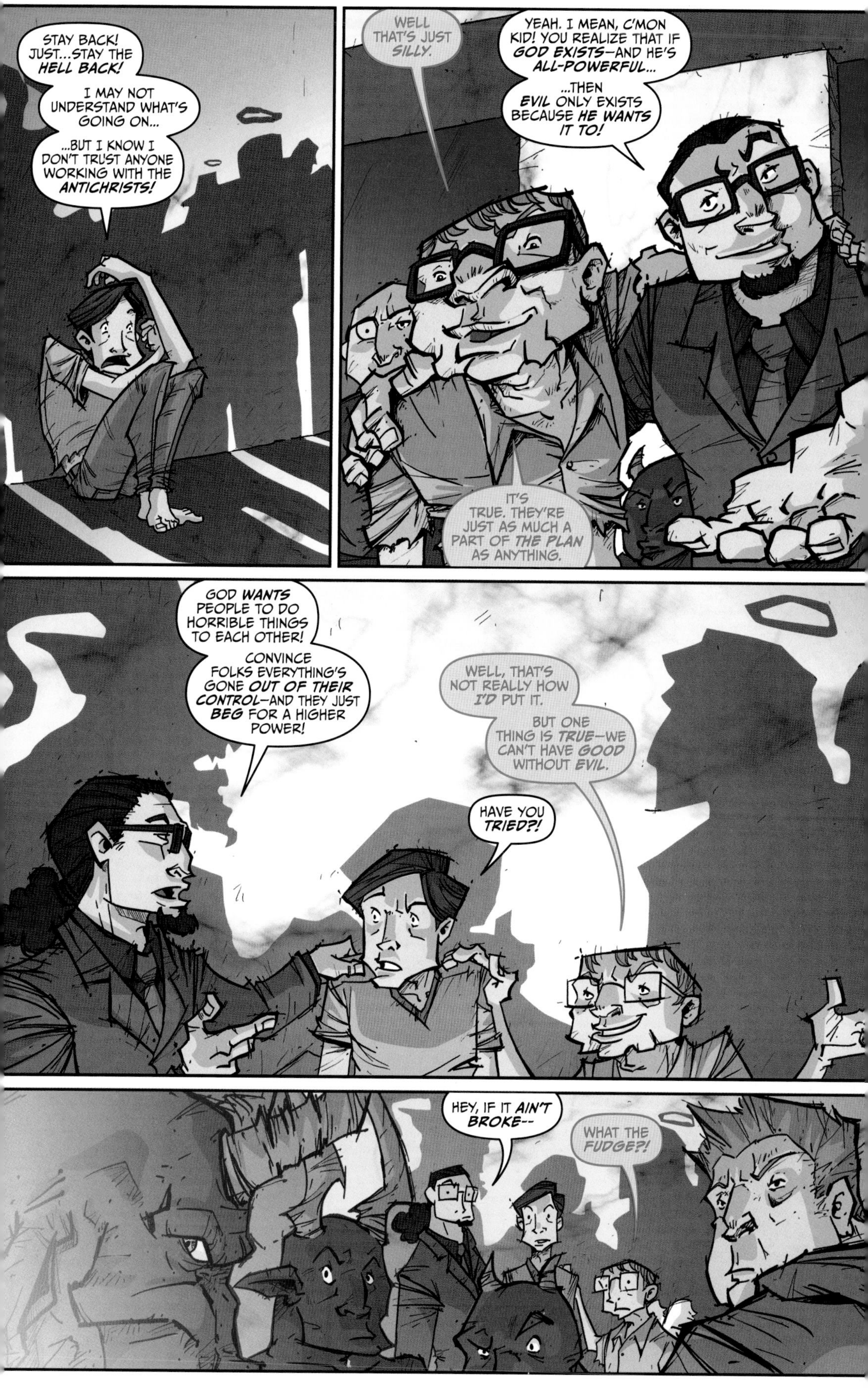
STAY BACK! JUST...STAY THE HELL BACK!
I MAY NOT UNDERSTAND WHAT'S GOING ON...
...BUT I KNOW I DON'T TRUST ANYONE WORKING WITH THE ANTICHRISTS!
WELL THAT'S JUST SILLY.
YEAH. I MEAN, C'MON KID! YOU REALIZE THAT IF GOD EXISTS—AND HE'S ALL-POWERFUL...
...THEN EVIL ONLY EXISTS BECAUSE HE WANTS IT TO!
IT'S TRUE. THEY'RE JUST AS MUCH A PART OF THE PLAN AS ANYTHING.
GOD WANTS PEOPLE TO DO HORRIBLE THINGS TO EACH OTHER!
CONVINCE FOLKS EVERYTHING'S GONE OUT OF THEIR CONTROL—AND THEY JUST BEG FOR A HIGHER POWER!
WELL, THAT'S NOT REALLY HOW I'D PUT IT.
BUT ONE THING IS TRUE—WE CAN'T HAVE GOOD WITHOUT EVIL.
HAVE YOU TRIED?!
HEY, IF IT AIN'T BROKE--
WHAT THE FUDGE?!

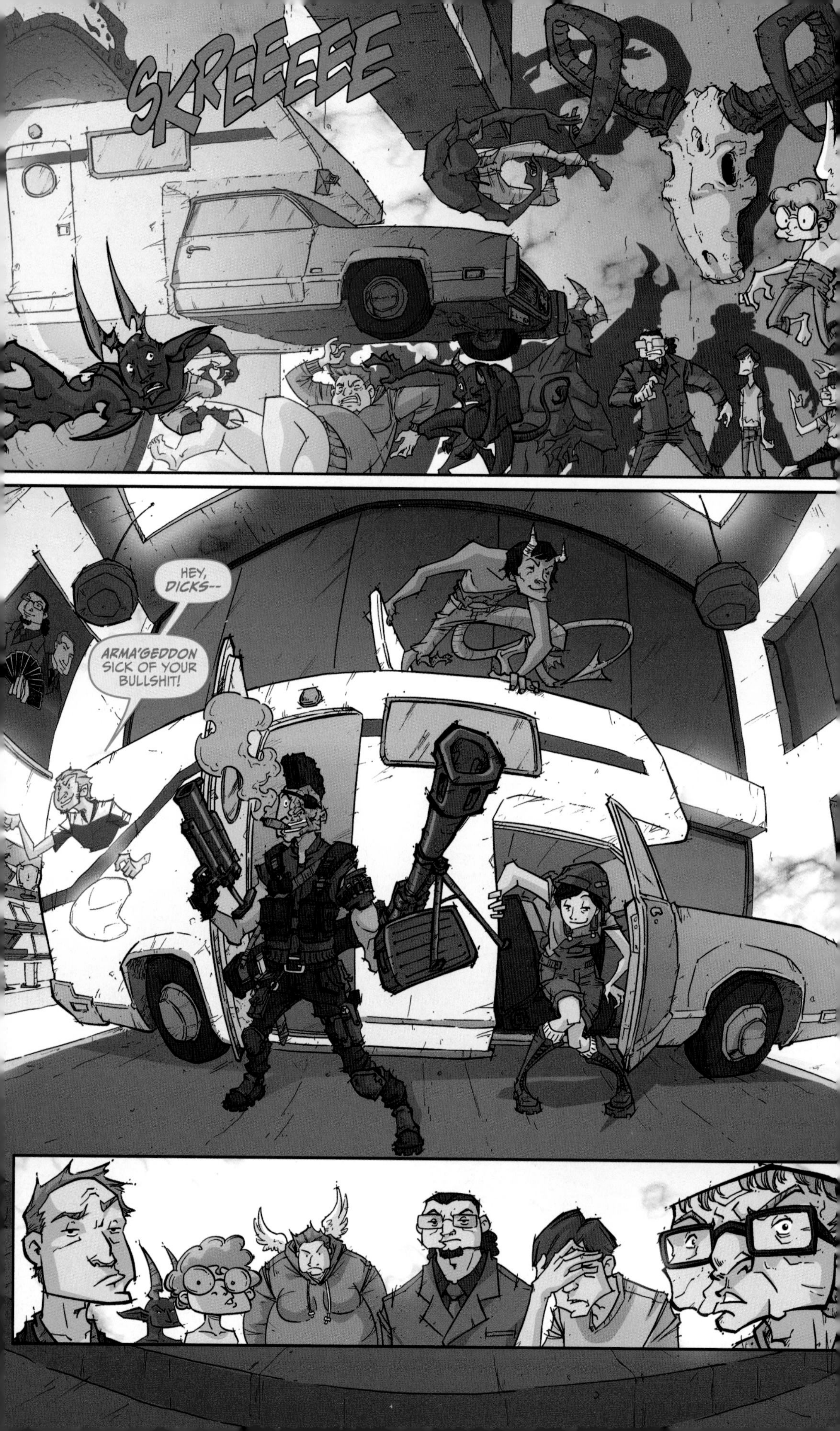
SKREEEEEE
HEY, DICKS--
ARMA'GEDDON SICK OF YOUR BULLSHIT!

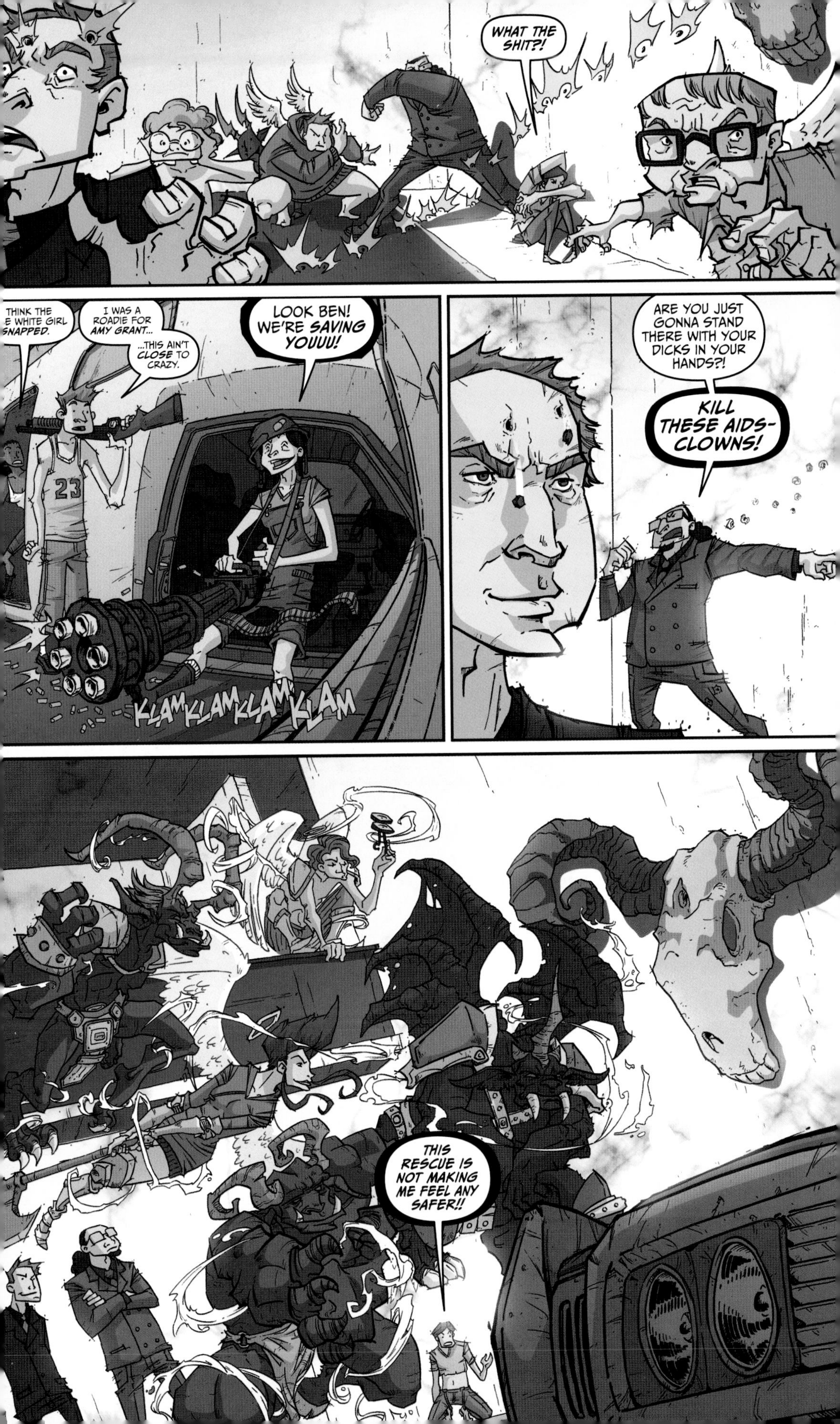
WHAT THE SHIT?!
THINK THE E WHITE GIRL SNAPPED.
I WAS A ROADIE FOR AMY GRANT...
...THIS AIN'T CLOSE TO CRAZY.
LOOK BEN! WE'RE SAVING YOUUU!
KLAMKLAMKLAMKLAM
ARE YOU JUST GONNA STAND THERE WITH YOUR DICKS IN YOUR HANDS?!
KILL THESE AIDS-CLOWNS!
THIS RESCUE IS NOT MAKING ME FEEL ANY SAFER!!

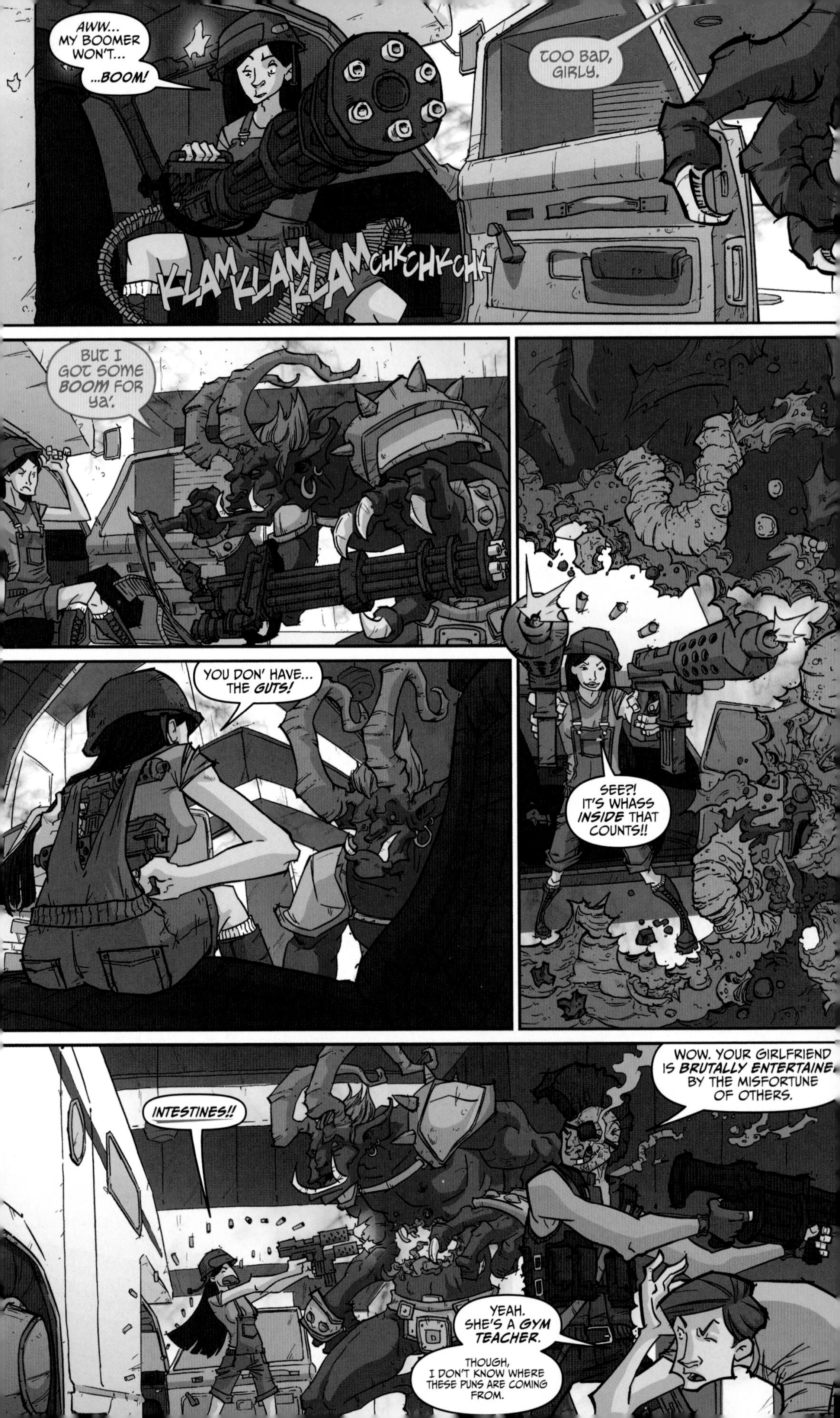
AWW... MY BOOMER WON'T... ...BOOM!
TOO BAD, GIRLY.
KLAM KLAM KLAM CHK CHK CHK
BUT I GOT SOME BOOM FOR YA'.
YOU DON' HAVE... THE GUTS!
SEE?! IT'S WHASS INSIDE THAT COUNTS!!
INTESTINES!!
WOW. YOUR GIRLFRIEND IS BRUTALLY ENTERTAINED BY THE MISFORTUNE OF OTHERS.
YEAH. SHE'S A GYM TEACHER.
THOUGH, I DON'T KNOW WHERE THESE PUNS ARE COMING FROM.

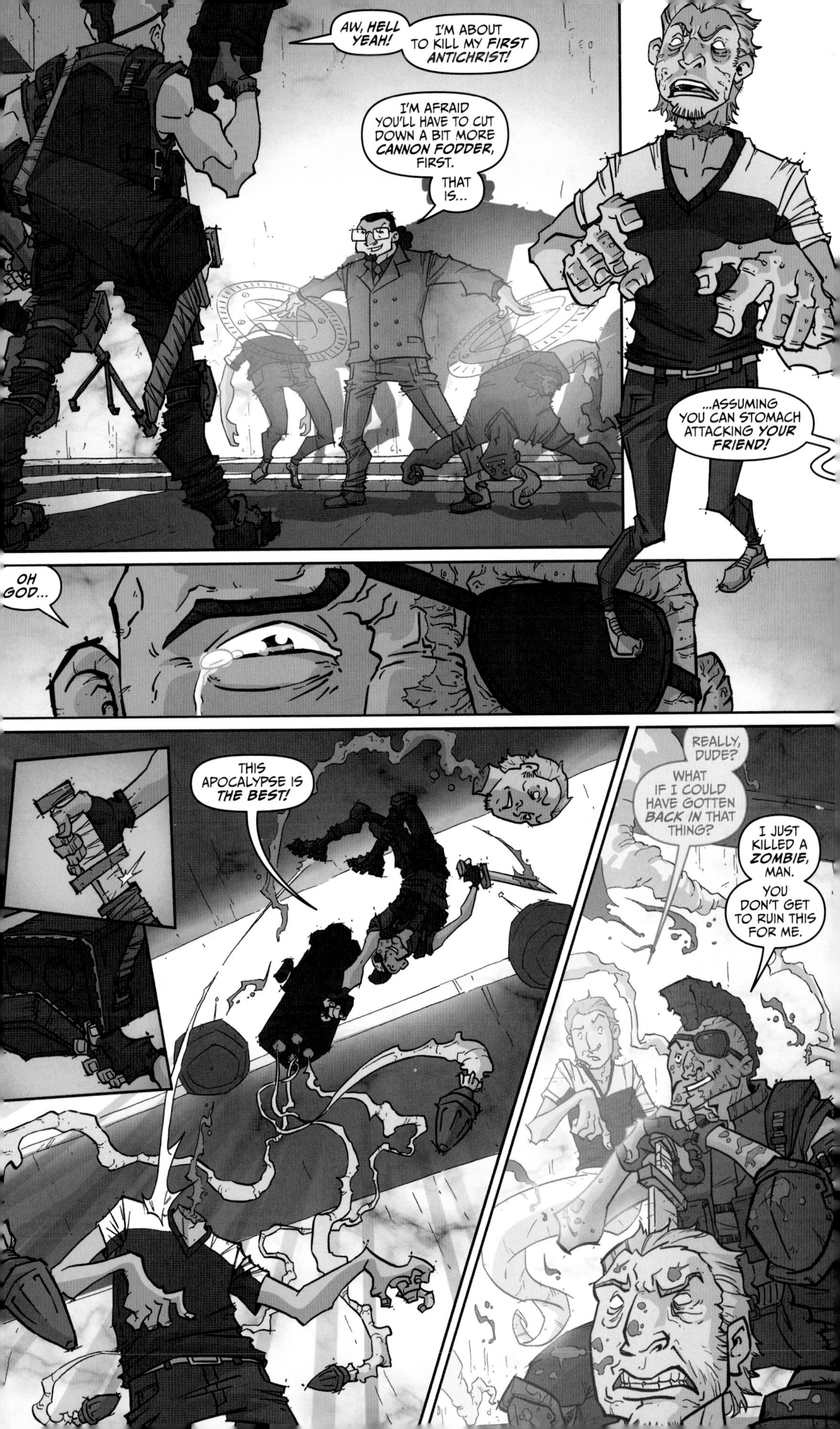
AW, HELL YEAH!
I'M ABOUT TO KILL MY FIRST ANTICHRIST!
I'M AFRAID YOU'LL HAVE TO CUT DOWN A BIT MORE CANNON FODDER, FIRST.
THAT IS...
...ASSUMING YOU CAN STOMACH ATTACKING YOUR FRIEND!
OH GOD...
THIS APOCALYPSE IS THE BEST!
REALLY, DUDE?
WHAT IF I COULD HAVE GOTTEN BACK IN THAT THING?
I JUST KILLED A ZOMBIE, MAN.
YOU DON'T GET TO RUIN THIS FOR ME.

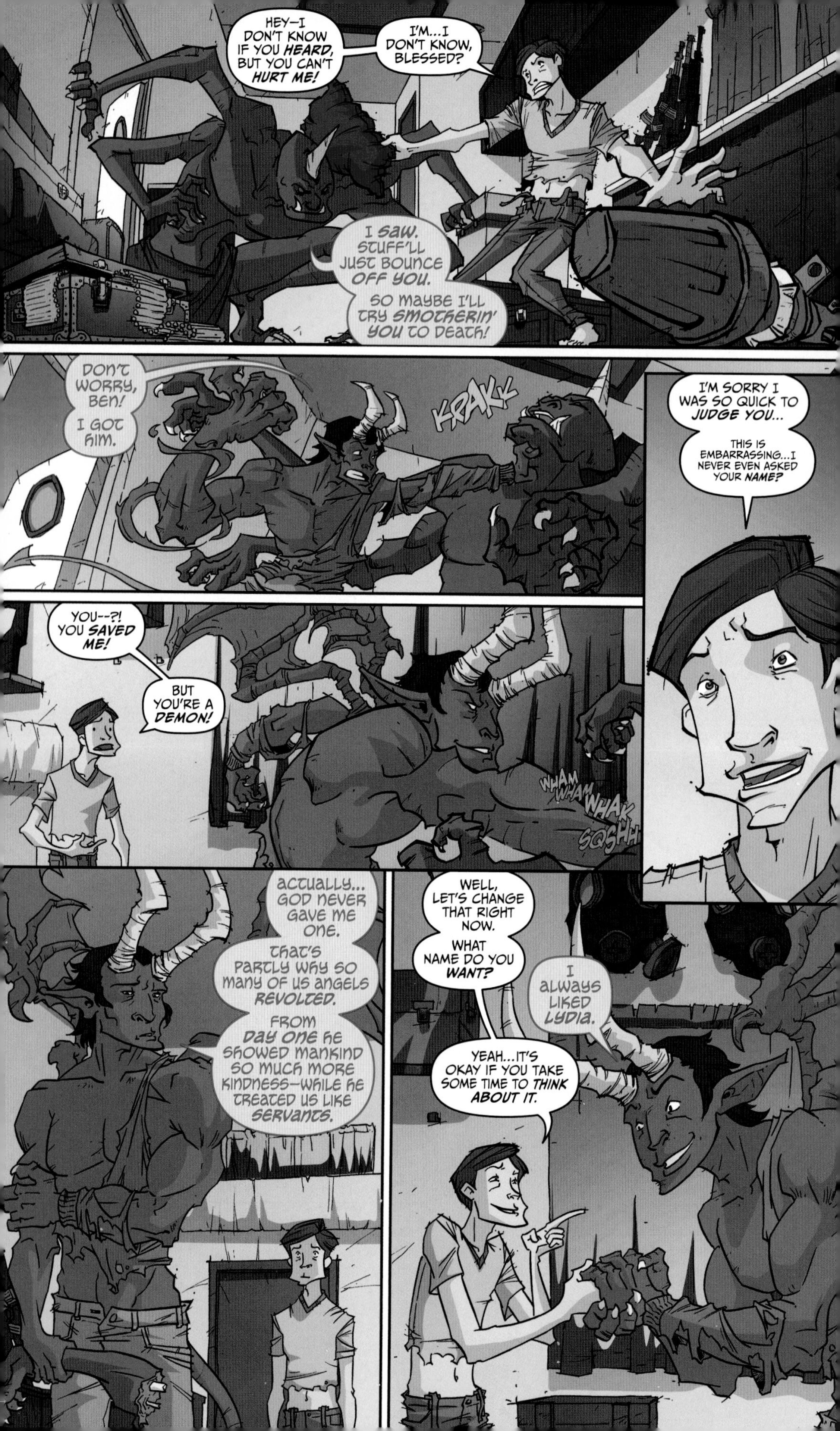
HEY—I DON'T KNOW IF YOU HEARD, BUT YOU CAN'T HURT ME!
I'M...I DON'T KNOW, BLESSED?
I SAW. STUFF'LL JUST BOUNCE OFF YOU.
SO MAYBE I'LL TRY SMOTHERIN' YOU TO DEATH!
DON'T WORRY, BEN!
I GOT HIM.
KRAKK
YOU--?! YOU SAVED ME!
BUT YOU'RE A DEMON!
WHAM WHAM WHAK SQSHH
I'M SORRY I WAS SO QUICK TO JUDGE YOU...
THIS IS EMBARRASSING...I NEVER EVEN ASKED YOUR NAME?
ACTUALLY... GOD NEVER GAVE ME ONE.
THAT'S PARTLY WHY SO MANY OF US ANGELS REVOLTED.
FROM DAY ONE HE SHOWED MANKIND SO MUCH MORE KINDNESS—WHILE HE TREATED US LIKE SERVANTS.
WELL, LET'S CHANGE THAT RIGHT NOW.
WHAT NAME DO YOU WANT?
I ALWAYS LIKED LYDIA.
YEAH...IT'S OKAY IF YOU TAKE SOME TIME TO THINK ABOUT IT.

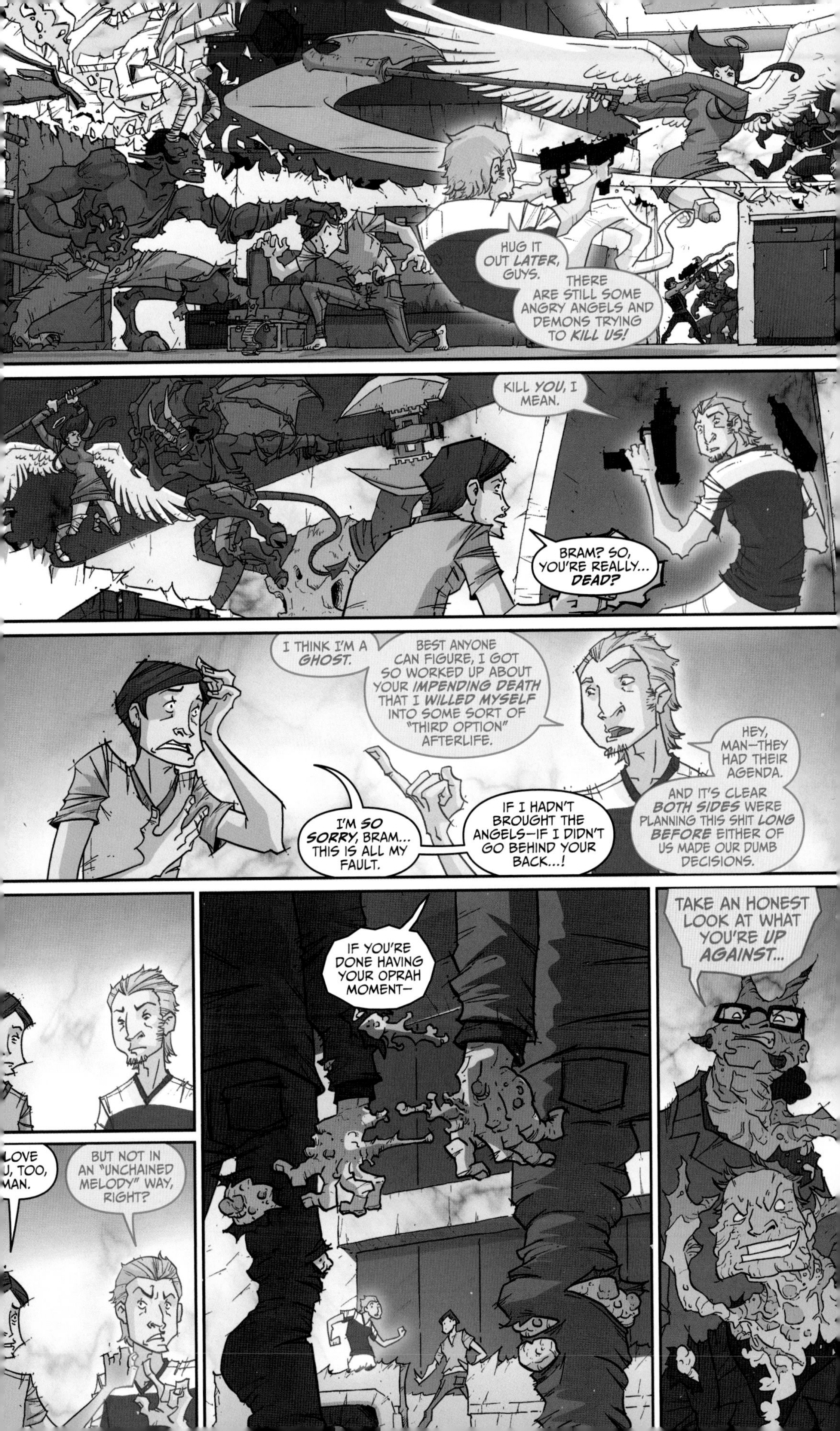
HUG IT OUT LATER, GUYS.
THERE ARE STILL SOME ANGRY ANGELS AND DEMONS TRYING TO KILL US!
KILL YOU, I MEAN.
BRAM? SO, YOU'RE REALLY... DEAD?
I THINK I'M A GHOST.
BEST ANYONE CAN FIGURE, I GOT SO WORKED UP ABOUT YOUR IMPENDING DEATH THAT I WILLED MYSELF INTO SOME SORT OF "THIRD OPTION" AFTERLIFE.
I'M SO SORRY, BRAM... THIS IS ALL MY FAULT.
IF I HADN'T BROUGHT THE ANGELS—IF I DIDN'T GO BEHIND YOUR BACK...!
HEY, MAN—THEY HAD THEIR AGENDA.
AND IT'S CLEAR BOTH SIDES WERE PLANNING THIS SHIT LONG BEFORE EITHER OF US MADE OUR DUMB DECISIONS.
LOVE U, TOO, MAN.
BUT NOT IN AN "UNCHAINED MELODY" WAY, RIGHT?
IF YOU'RE DONE HAVING YOUR OPRAH MOMENT—
TAKE AN HONEST LOOK AT WHAT YOU'RE UP AGAINST...

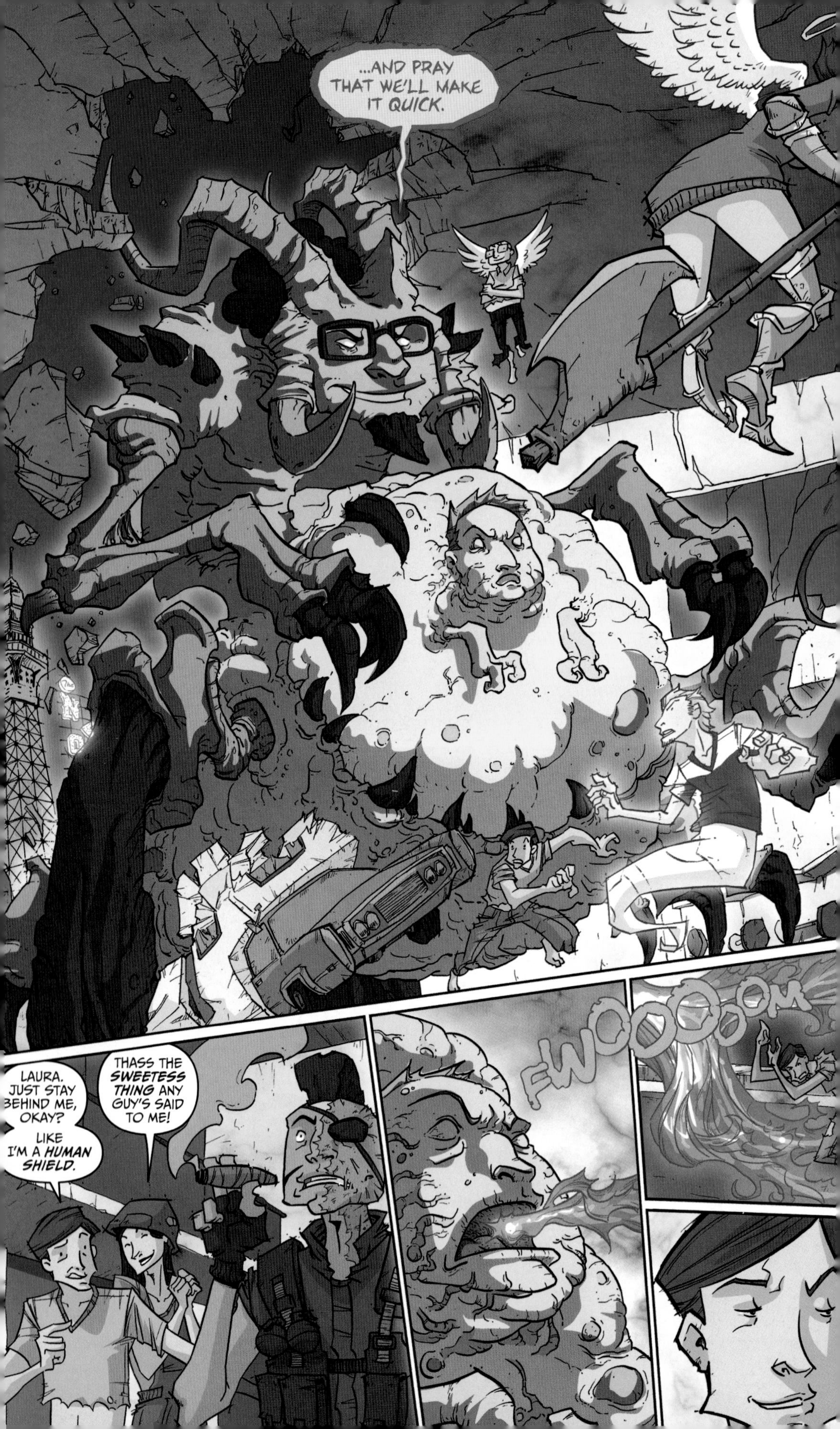
...AND PRAY THAT WE'LL MAKE IT QUICK.
LAURA. JUST STAY BEHIND ME, OKAY?
LIKE I'M A HUMAN SHIELD.
THASS THE SWEETESS THING ANY GUY'S SAID TO ME!
FWOOOOOOM

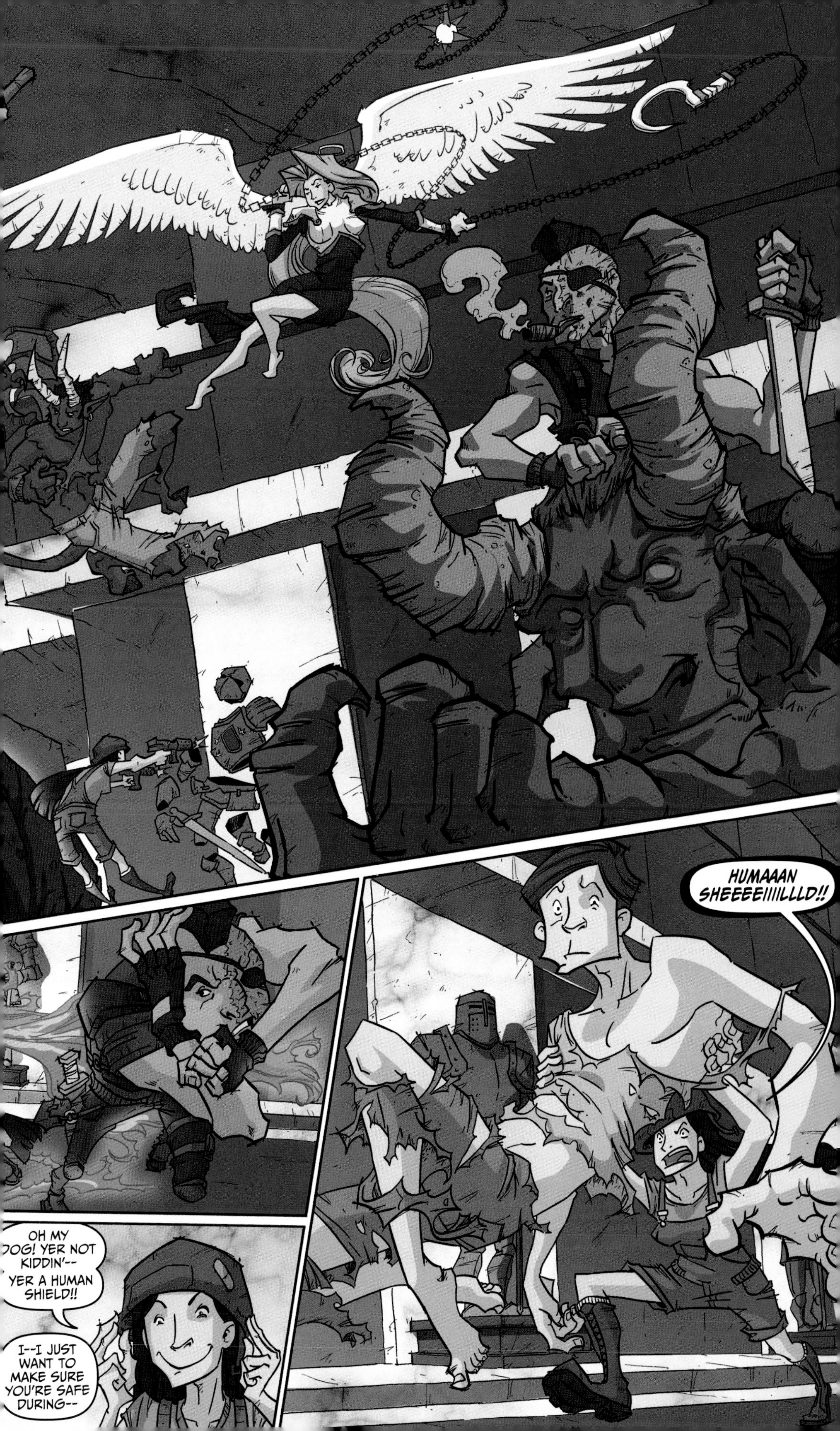
HUMAAAN SHEEEEIIIILLLD!!
OH MY DOG! YER NOT KIDDIN'-- YER A HUMAN SHIELD!!
I--I JUST WANT TO MAKE SURE YOU'RE SAFE DURING--

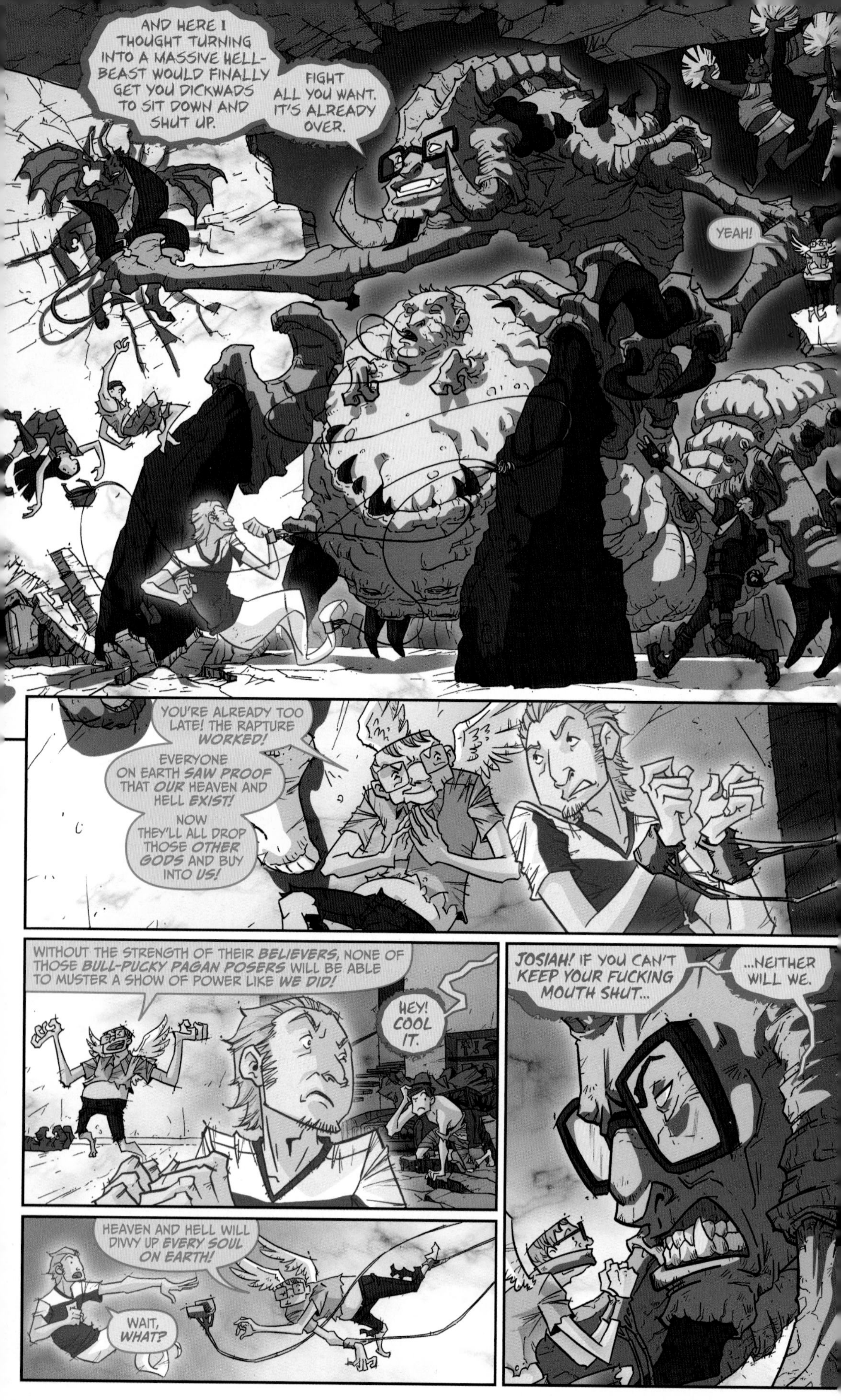
AND HERE I THOUGHT TURNING INTO A MASSIVE HELL-BEAST WOULD FINALLY GET YOU DICKWADS TO SIT DOWN AND SHUT UP.
FIGHT ALL YOU WANT. IT'S ALREADY OVER.
YEAH!
YOU'RE ALREADY TOO LATE! THE RAPTURE WORKED!
EVERYONE ON EARTH SAW PROOF THAT OUR HEAVEN AND HELL EXIST!
NOW THEY'LL ALL DROP THOSE OTHER GODS AND BUY INTO US!
WITHOUT THE STRENGTH OF THEIR BELIEVERS, NONE OF THOSE BULL-PUCKY PAGAN POSERS WILL BE ABLE TO MUSTER A SHOW OF POWER LIKE WE DID!
HEY! COOL IT.
HEAVEN AND HELL WILL DIVVY UP EVERY SOUL ON EARTH!
WAIT, WHAT?
JOSIAH! IF YOU CAN'T KEEP YOUR FUCKING MOUTH SHUT...
...NEITHER WILL WE.

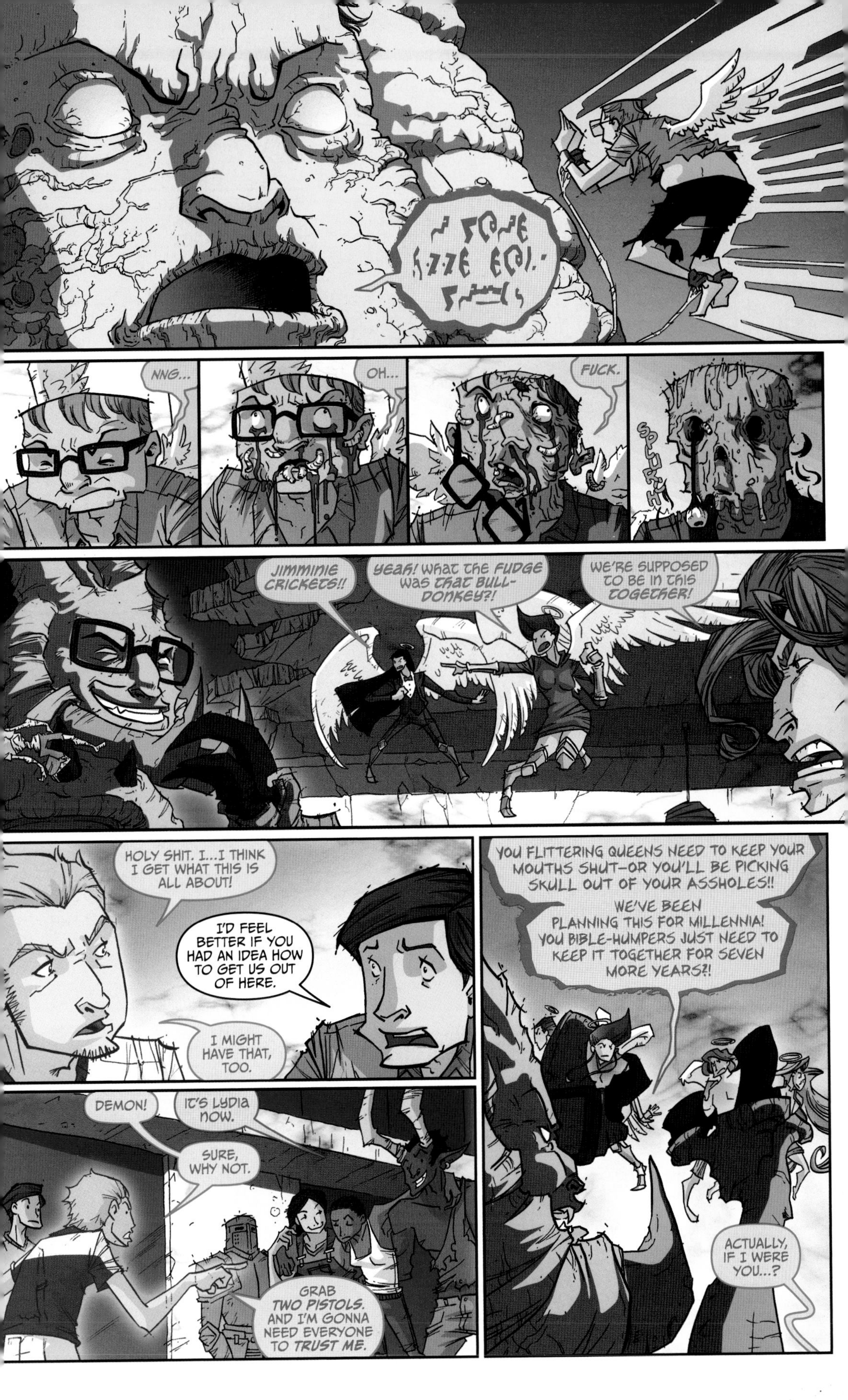
NNG...
OH...
FUCK.
SPLURCH
JIMMINIE CRICKETS!!
YEAH! WHAT THE FUDGE WAS THAT BULL-DONKEY?!
WE'RE SUPPOSED TO BE IN THIS TOGETHER!
HOLY SHIT. I...I THINK I GET WHAT THIS IS ALL ABOUT!
I'D FEEL BETTER IF YOU HAD AN IDEA HOW TO GET US OUT OF HERE.
I MIGHT HAVE THAT, TOO.
DEMON!
IT'S LYDIA NOW.
SURE, WHY NOT.
GRAB TWO PISTOLS. AND I'M GONNA NEED EVERYONE TO TRUST ME.
YOU FLITTERING QUEENS NEED TO KEEP YOUR MOUTHS SHUT—OR YOU'LL BE PICKING SKULL OUT OF YOUR ASSHOLES!!
WE'VE BEEN PLANNING THIS FOR MILLENNIA! YOU BIBLE-HUMPERS JUST NEED TO KEEP IT TOGETHER FOR SEVEN MORE YEARS?!
ACTUALLY, IF I WERE YOU...?

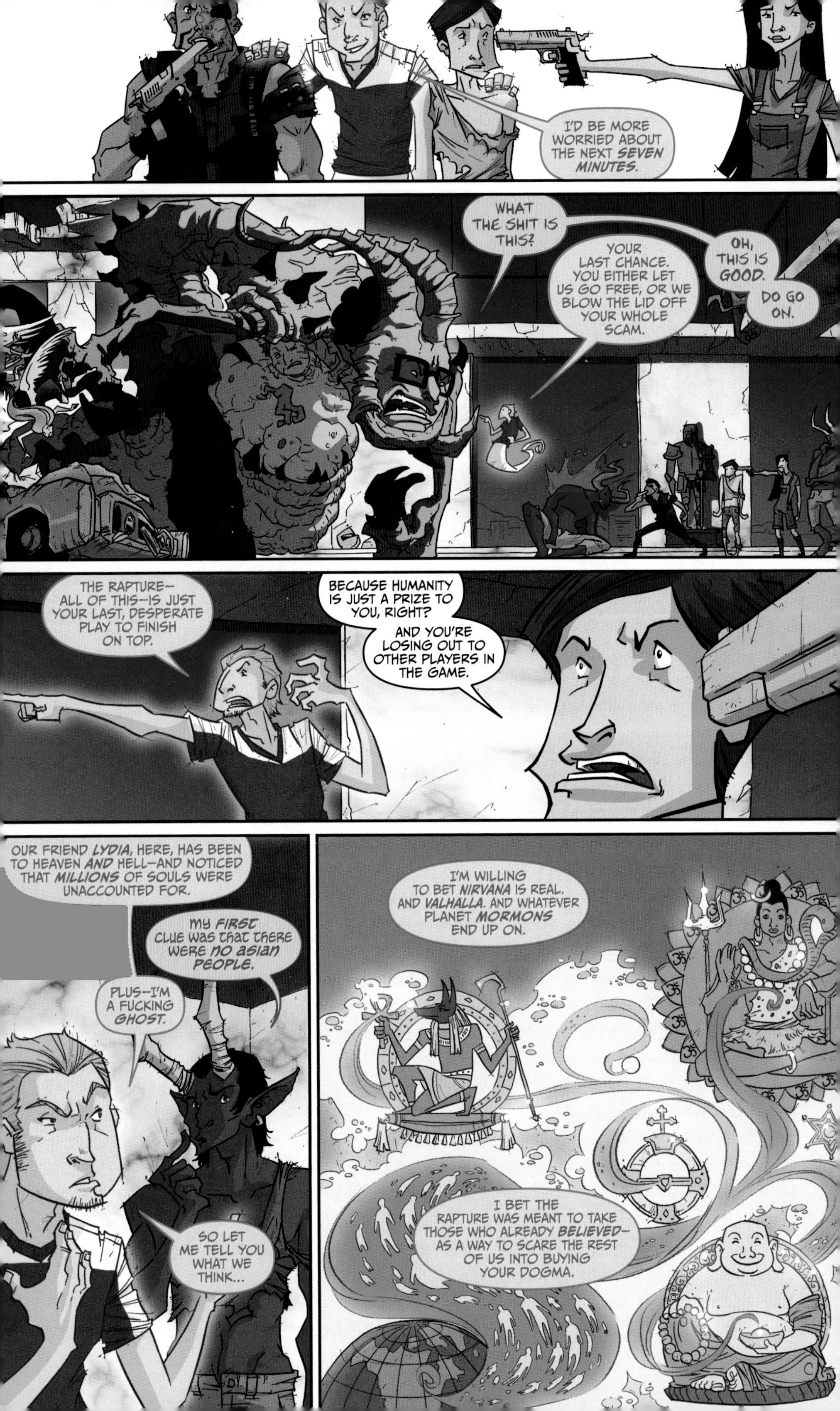
I'D BE MORE WORRIED ABOUT THE NEXT SEVEN MINUTES.
WHAT THE SHIT IS THIS?
YOUR LAST CHANCE. YOU EITHER LET US GO FREE, OR WE BLOW THE LID OFF YOUR WHOLE SCAM.
OH, THIS IS GOOD.
DO GO ON.
THE RAPTURE—ALL OF THIS—IS JUST YOUR LAST, DESPERATE PLAY TO FINISH ON TOP.
BECAUSE HUMANITY IS JUST A PRIZE TO YOU, RIGHT?
AND YOU'RE LOSING OUT TO OTHER PLAYERS IN THE GAME.
OUR FRIEND LYDIA, HERE, HAS BEEN TO HEAVEN AND HELL—AND NOTICED THAT MILLIONS OF SOULS WERE UNACCOUNTED FOR.
MY FIRST CLUE WAS THAT THERE WERE NO ASIAN PEOPLE.
PLUS—I'M A FUCKING GHOST.
SO LET ME TELL YOU WHAT WE THINK...
I'M WILLING TO BET NIRVANA IS REAL. AND VALHALLA. AND WHATEVER PLANET MORMONS END UP ON.
I BET THE RAPTURE WAS MEANT TO TAKE THOSE WHO ALREADY BELIEVED—AS A WAY TO SCARE THE REST OF US INTO BUYING YOUR DOGMA.

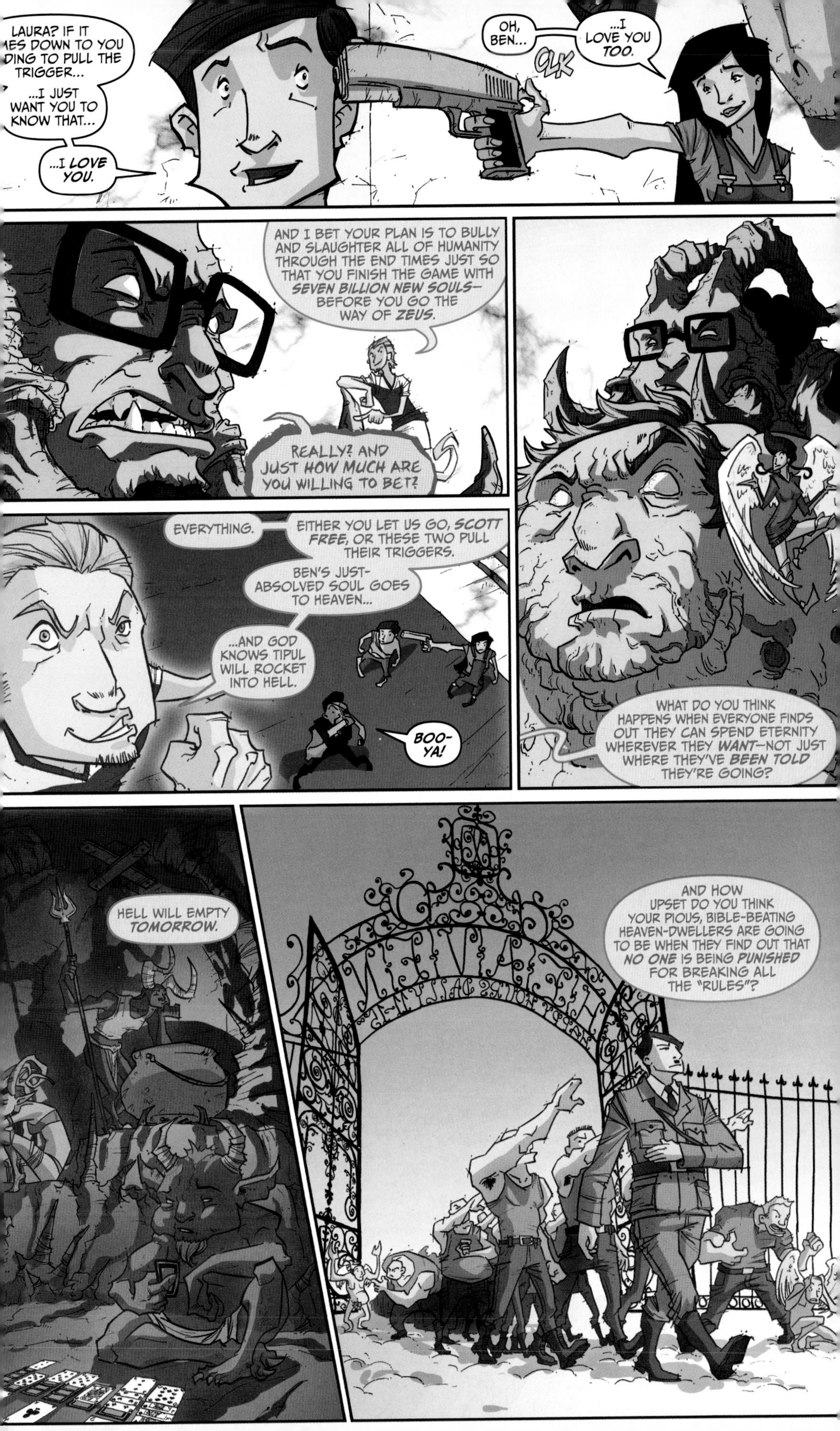
LAURA? IF IT
...ES DOWN TO YOU
...DING TO PULL THE TRIGGER...
...I JUST WANT YOU TO KNOW THAT...
...I LOVE YOU.
OH, BEN...
...I LOVE YOU TOO.
CLK
AND I BET YOUR PLAN IS TO BULLY AND SLAUGHTER ALL OF HUMANITY THROUGH THE END TIMES JUST SO THAT YOU FINISH THE GAME WITH SEVEN BILLION NEW SOULS—BEFORE YOU GO THE WAY OF ZEUS.
REALLY? AND JUST HOW MUCH ARE YOU WILLING TO BET?
EVERYTHING.
EITHER YOU LET US GO, SCOTT FREE, OR THESE TWO PULL THEIR TRIGGERS.
BEN'S JUST-ABSOLVED SOUL GOES TO HEAVEN...
...AND GOD KNOWS TIPUL WILL ROCKET INTO HELL.
BOO-YA!
WHAT DO YOU THINK HAPPENS WHEN EVERYONE FINDS OUT THEY CAN SPEND ETERNITY WHEREVER THEY WANT—NOT JUST WHERE THEY'VE BEEN TOLD THEY'RE GOING?
HELL WILL EMPTY TOMORROW.
AND HOW UPSET DO YOU THINK YOUR PIOUS, BIBLE-BEATING HEAVEN-DWELLERS ARE GOING TO BE WHEN THEY FIND OUT THAT NO ONE IS BEING PUNISHED FOR BREAKING ALL THE "RULES"?

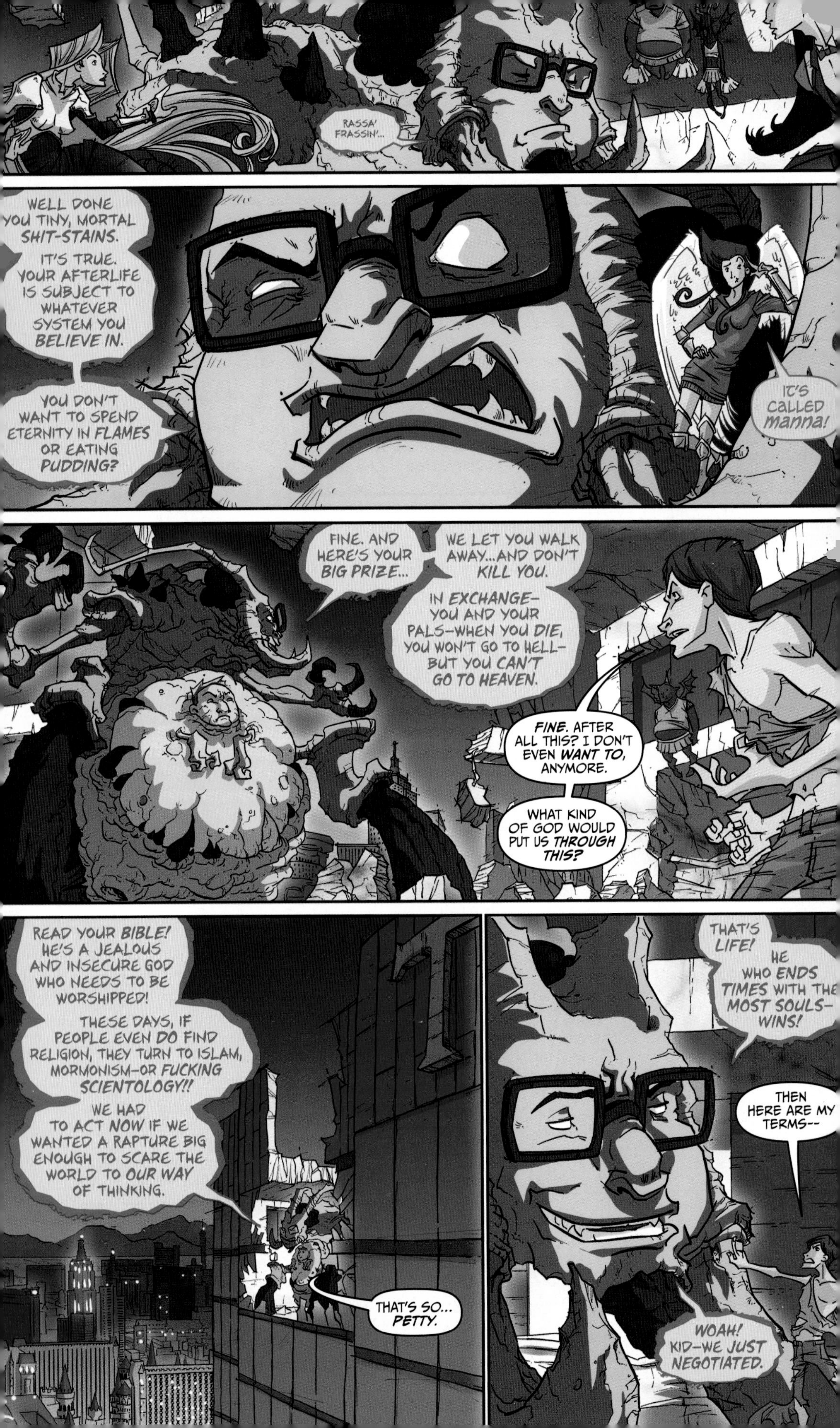
RASSA' FRASSIN'...
WELL DONE YOU TINY, MORTAL SHIT-STAINS.
IT'S TRUE. YOUR AFTERLIFE IS SUBJECT TO WHATEVER SYSTEM YOU BELIEVE IN.
YOU DON'T WANT TO SPEND ETERNITY IN FLAMES OR EATING PUDDING?
IT'S CALLED manna!
FINE. AND HERE'S YOUR BIG PRIZE...
WE LET YOU WALK AWAY...AND DON'T KILL YOU.
IN EXCHANGE— YOU AND YOUR PALS—WHEN YOU DIE, YOU WON'T GO TO HELL— BUT YOU CAN'T GO TO HEAVEN.
FINE. AFTER ALL THIS? I DON'T EVEN WANT TO, ANYMORE.
WHAT KIND OF GOD WOULD PUT US THROUGH THIS?
READ YOUR BIBLE! HE'S A JEALOUS AND INSECURE GOD WHO NEEDS TO BE WORSHIPPED!
THESE DAYS, IF PEOPLE EVEN DO FIND RELIGION, THEY TURN TO ISLAM, MORMONISM—OR FUCKING SCIENTOLOGY!!
WE HAD TO ACT NOW IF WE WANTED A RAPTURE BIG ENOUGH TO SCARE THE WORLD TO OUR WAY OF THINKING.
THAT'S SO... PETTY.
THAT'S LIFE!
HE WHO ENDS TIMES WITH THE MOST SOULS— WINS!
THEN HERE ARE MY TERMS--
WOAH! KID—WE JUST NEGOTIATED.

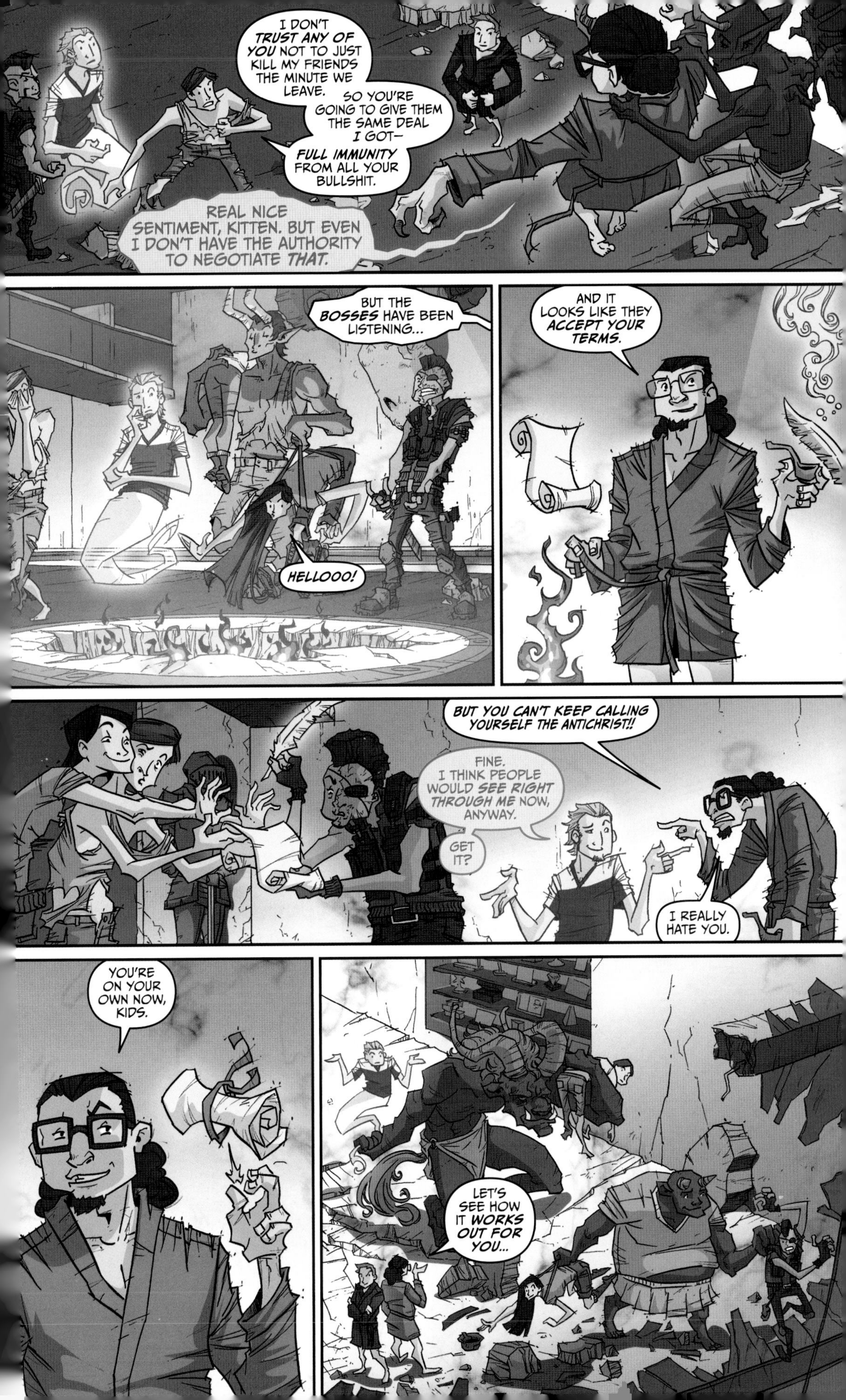

I DON'T TRUST ANY OF YOU NOT TO JUST KILL MY FRIENDS THE MINUTE WE LEAVE.
SO YOU'RE GOING TO GIVE THEM THE SAME DEAL I GOT—
FULL IMMUNITY FROM ALL YOUR BULLSHIT.
REAL NICE SENTIMENT, KITTEN. BUT EVEN I DON'T HAVE THE AUTHORITY TO NEGOTIATE THAT.
BUT THE BOSSES HAVE BEEN LISTENING...
HELLOOO!
AND IT LOOKS LIKE THEY ACCEPT YOUR TERMS.
BUT YOU CAN'T KEEP CALLING YOURSELF THE ANTICHRIST!!
FINE. I THINK PEOPLE WOULD SEE RIGHT THROUGH ME NOW, ANYWAY.
GET IT?
I REALLY HATE YOU.
YOU'RE ON YOUR OWN NOW, KIDS.
LET'S SEE HOW IT WORKS OUT FOR YOU...

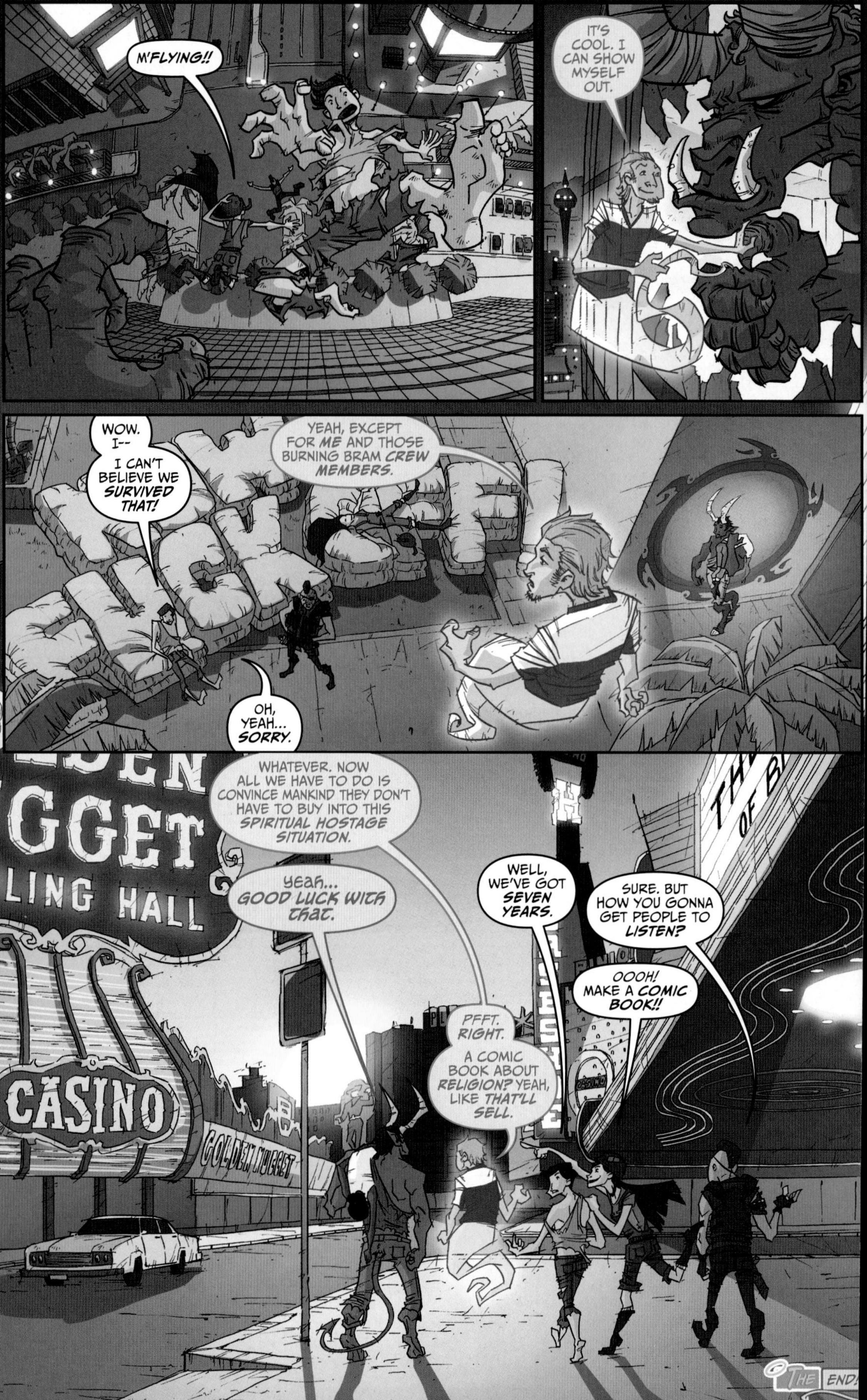
M'FLYING!!
IT'S COOL. I CAN SHOW MYSELF OUT.
WOW. I--
I CAN'T BELIEVE WE SURVIVED THAT!
YEAH, EXCEPT FOR ME AND THOSE BURNING BRAM CREW MEMBERS.
OH, YEAH... SORRY.
WHATEVER. NOW ALL WE HAVE TO DO IS CONVINCE MANKIND THEY DON'T HAVE TO BUY INTO THIS SPIRITUAL HOSTAGE SITUATION.
yeah... GOOD LUCK WITH THAT.
WELL, WE'VE GOT SEVEN YEARS.
SURE. BUT HOW YOU GONNA GET PEOPLE TO LISTEN?
OOOH! MAKE A COMIC BOOK!!
PFFT. RIGHT.
A COMIC BOOK ABOUT RELIGION? YEAH, LIKE THAT'LL SELL.
UGGET
BLING HALL
CASINO
GOLDEN NUGGET
THE END

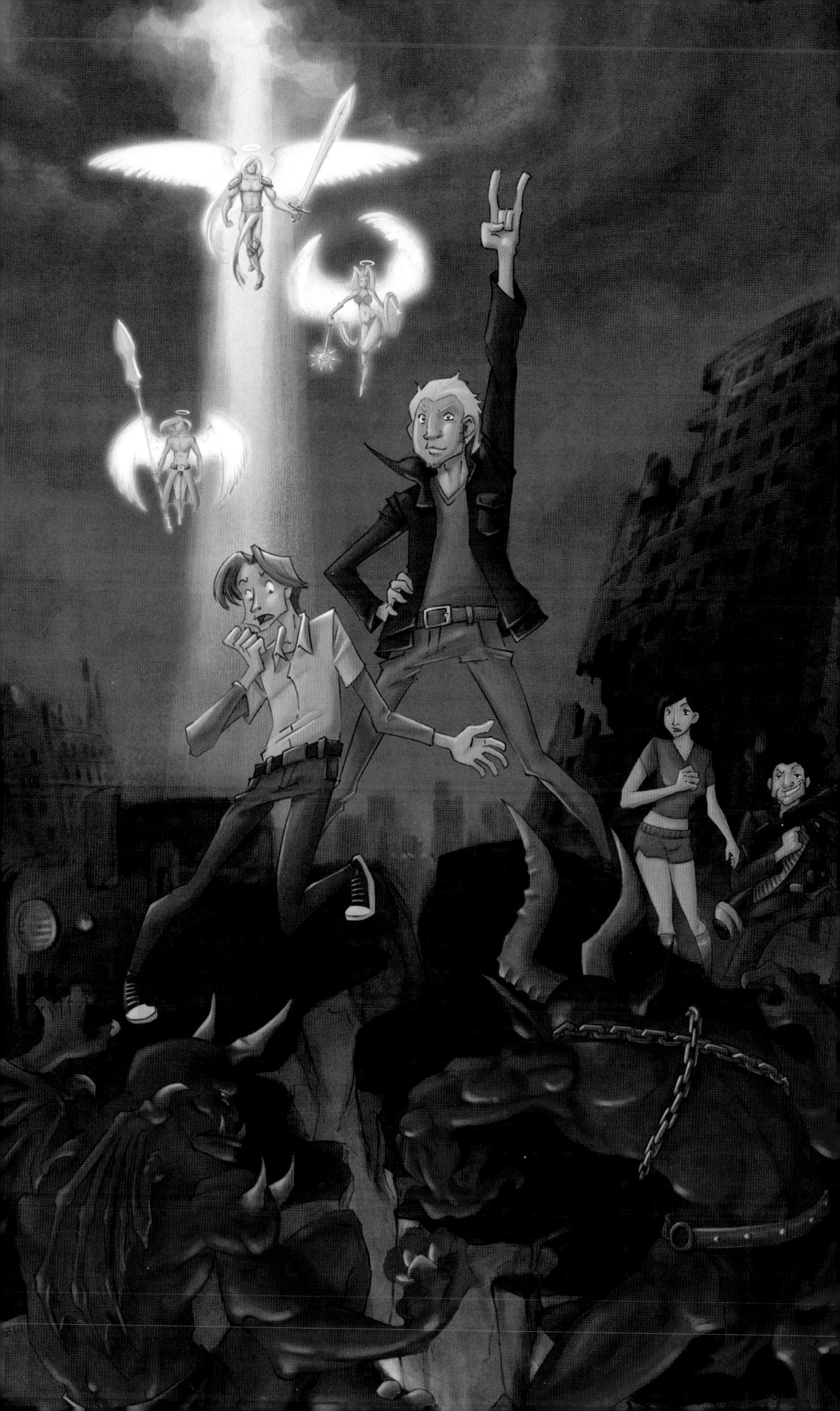

After the series finished, there were a few questions we heard more than once from readers.

"Are you going to do more?"
"What did the kid in Ben's class *do*, anyway?"
and
"So if the angels made a clerical error, what happened to the *other* Bram Carlson?"

We figured we could answer one of those, at least...

WRITTEN BY Jim Festante    PENCILED BY Rem Broo
CO-CREATED BY James Asmus & Jim Festante AND Rem Broo
COLORS BY Jim Festante    LETTERS BY crank!
CONSULTING EDITOR Sebastian Girner

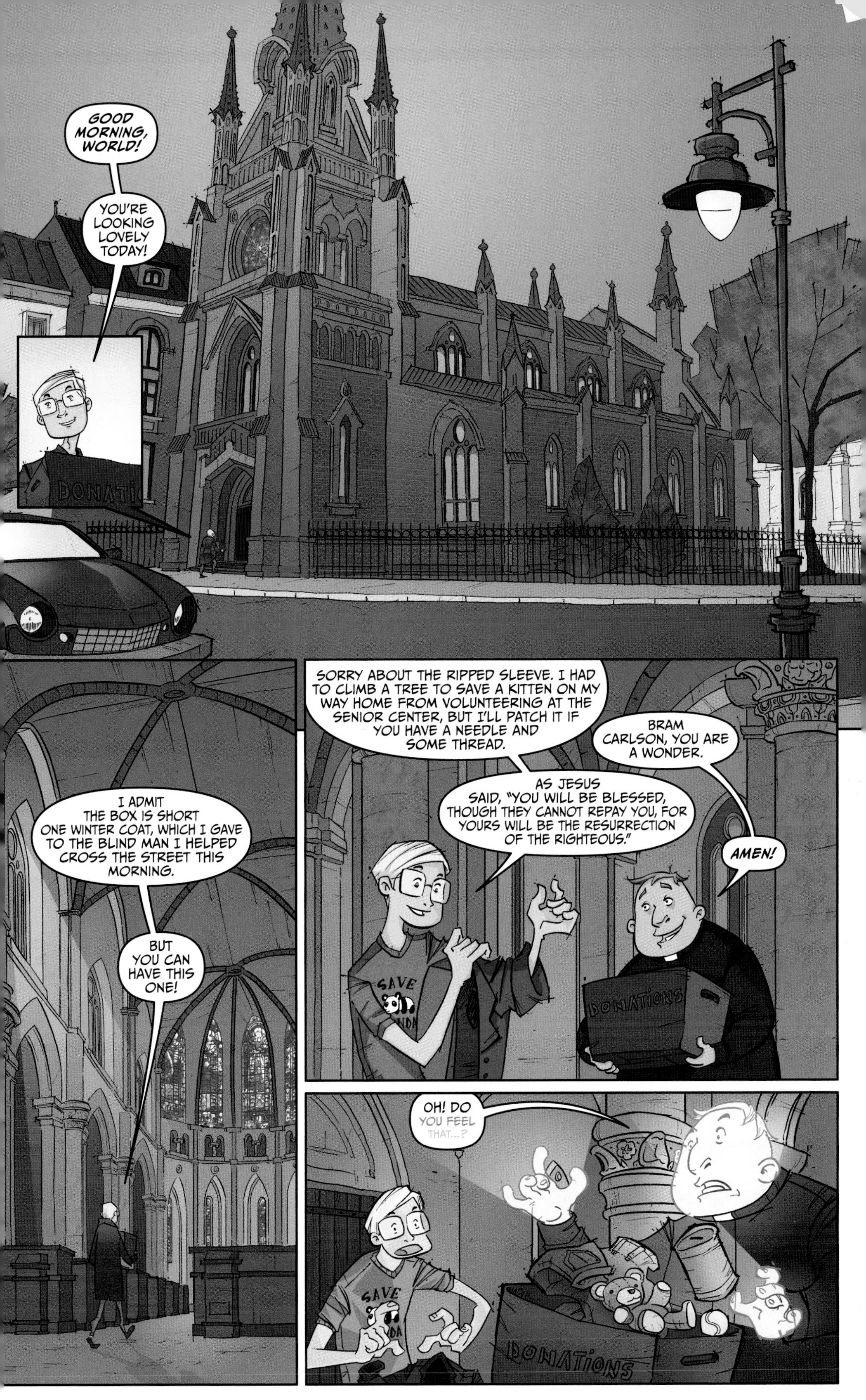
GOOD MORNING, WORLD!
YOU'RE LOOKING LOVELY TODAY!
I ADMIT THE BOX IS SHORT ONE WINTER COAT, WHICH I GAVE TO THE BLIND MAN I HELPED CROSS THE STREET THIS MORNING.
BUT YOU CAN HAVE THIS ONE!
SORRY ABOUT THE RIPPED SLEEVE. I HAD TO CLIMB A TREE TO SAVE A KITTEN ON MY WAY HOME FROM VOLUNTEERING AT THE SENIOR CENTER, BUT I'LL PATCH IT IF YOU HAVE A NEEDLE AND SOME THREAD.
BRAM CARLSON, YOU ARE A WONDER.
AS JESUS SAID, "YOU WILL BE BLESSED, THOUGH THEY CANNOT REPAY YOU, FOR YOURS WILL BE THE RESURRECTION OF THE RIGHTEOUS."
AMEN!
DONATIONS
OH! DO YOU FEEL THAT...?
DONATIONS

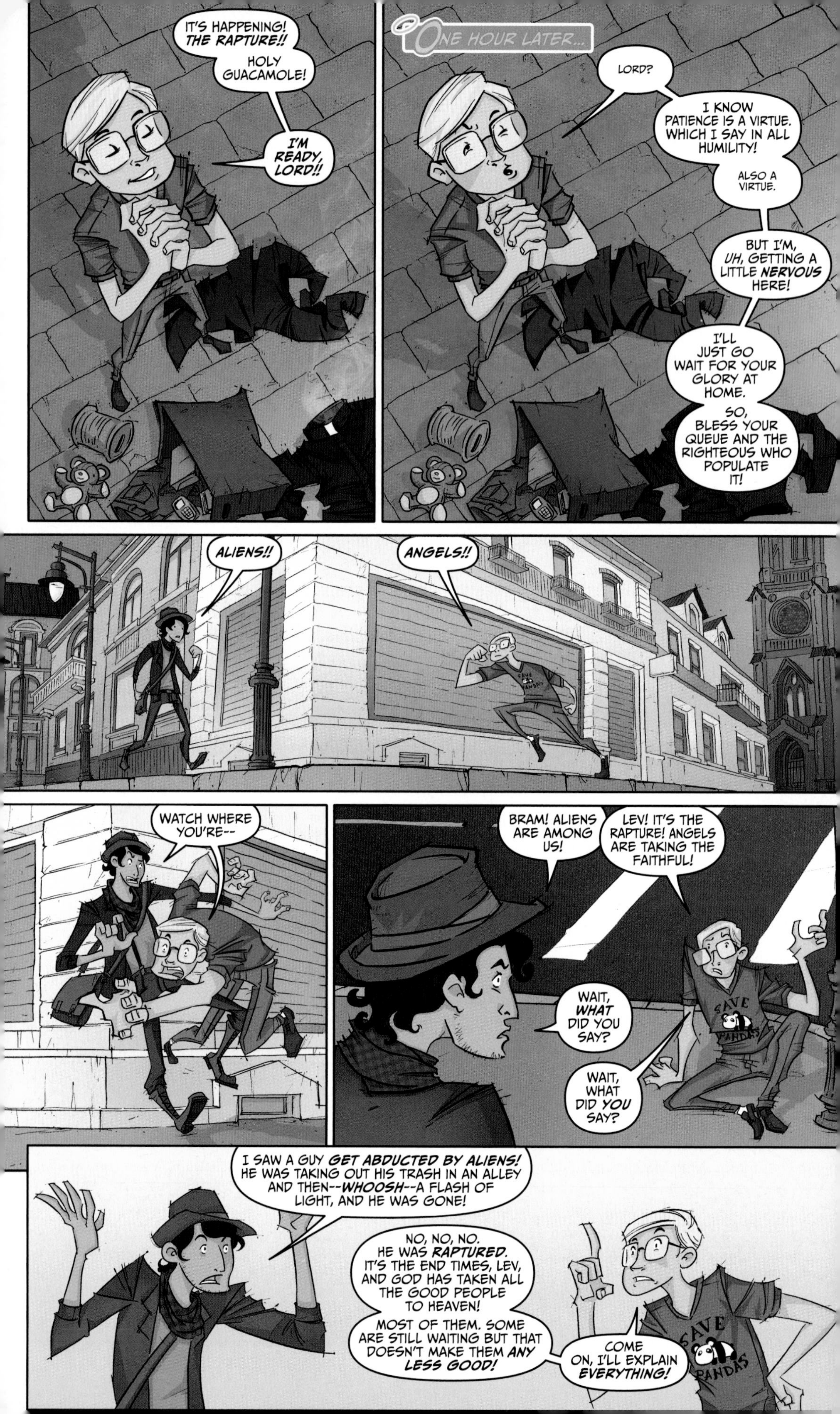
IT'S HAPPENING! THE RAPTURE!!
HOLY GUACAMOLE!
I'M READY, LORD!!
ONE HOUR LATER...
LORD?
I KNOW PATIENCE IS A VIRTUE. WHICH I SAY IN ALL HUMILITY!
ALSO A VIRTUE.
BUT I'M, UH, GETTING A LITTLE NERVOUS HERE!
I'LL JUST GO WAIT FOR YOUR GLORY AT HOME.
SO, BLESS YOUR QUEUE AND THE RIGHTEOUS WHO POPULATE IT!
ALIENS!!
ANGELS!!
WATCH WHERE YOU'RE--
BRAM! ALIENS ARE AMONG US!
LEV! IT'S THE RAPTURE! ANGELS ARE TAKING THE FAITHFUL!
WAIT, WHAT DID YOU SAY?
WAIT, WHAT DID YOU SAY?
I SAW A GUY GET ABDUCTED BY ALIENS! HE WAS TAKING OUT HIS TRASH IN AN ALLEY AND THEN--WHOOSH--A FLASH OF LIGHT, AND HE WAS GONE!
NO, NO, NO. HE WAS RAPTURED. IT'S THE END TIMES, LEV, AND GOD HAS TAKEN ALL THE GOOD PEOPLE TO HEAVEN!
MOST OF THEM. SOME ARE STILL WAITING BUT THAT DOESN'T MAKE THEM ANY LESS GOOD!
COME ON, I'LL EXPLAIN EVERYTHING!

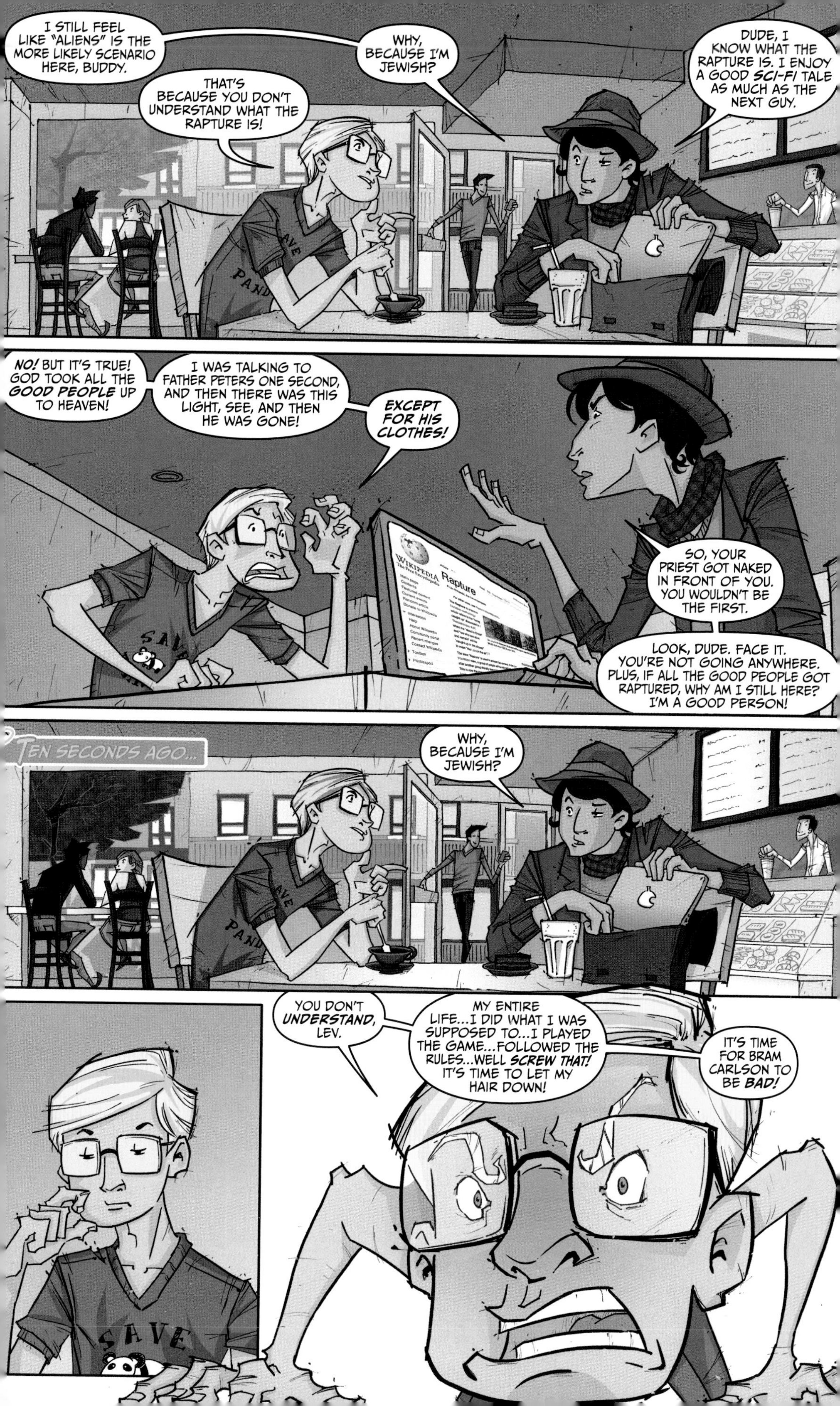
I STILL FEEL LIKE "ALIENS" IS THE MORE LIKELY SCENARIO HERE, BUDDY.
WHY, BECAUSE I'M JEWISH?
THAT'S BECAUSE YOU DON'T UNDERSTAND WHAT THE RAPTURE IS!
DUDE, I KNOW WHAT THE RAPTURE IS. I ENJOY A GOOD SCI-FI TALE AS MUCH AS THE NEXT GUY.
NO! BUT IT'S TRUE! GOD TOOK ALL THE GOOD PEOPLE UP TO HEAVEN!
I WAS TALKING TO FATHER PETERS ONE SECOND, AND THEN THERE WAS THIS LIGHT, SEE, AND THEN HE WAS GONE!
EXCEPT FOR HIS CLOTHES!
SO, YOUR PRIEST GOT NAKED IN FRONT OF YOU. YOU WOULDN'T BE THE FIRST.
LOOK, DUDE. FACE IT. YOU'RE NOT GOING ANYWHERE. PLUS, IF ALL THE GOOD PEOPLE GOT RAPTURED, WHY AM I STILL HERE? I'M A GOOD PERSON!
TEN SECONDS AGO...
WHY, BECAUSE I'M JEWISH?
YOU DON'T UNDERSTAND, LEV.
MY ENTIRE LIFE...I DID WHAT I WAS SUPPOSED TO...I PLAYED THE GAME...FOLLOWED THE RULES...WELL SCREW THAT! IT'S TIME TO LET MY HAIR DOWN!
IT'S TIME FOR BRAM CARLSON TO BE BAD!

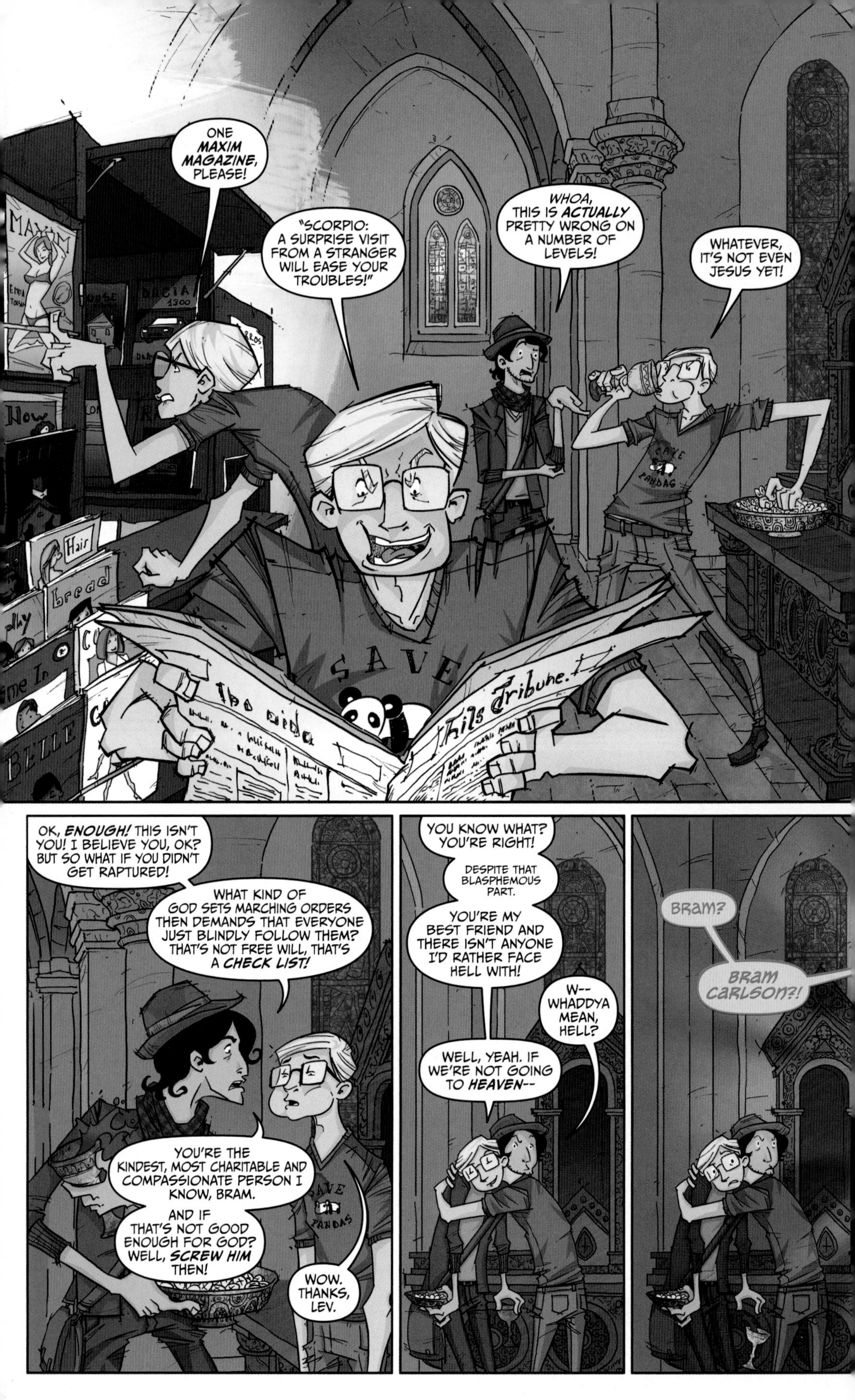
ONE *MAXIM MAGAZINE*, PLEASE!
"SCORPIO: A SURPRISE VISIT FROM A STRANGER WILL EASE YOUR TROUBLES!"
*WHOA*, THIS IS ***ACTUALLY*** PRETTY WRONG ON A NUMBER OF LEVELS!
WHATEVER, IT'S NOT EVEN JESUS YET!
SAVE PANDAS
OK, ***ENOUGH!*** THIS ISN'T YOU! I BELIEVE YOU, OK? BUT SO WHAT IF YOU DIDN'T GET RAPTURED!
WHAT KIND OF GOD SETS MARCHING ORDERS THEN DEMANDS THAT EVERYONE JUST BLINDLY FOLLOW THEM? THAT'S NOT FREE WILL, THAT'S A ***CHECK LIST!***
YOU'RE THE KINDEST, MOST CHARITABLE AND COMPASSIONATE PERSON I KNOW, BRAM.
AND IF THAT'S NOT GOOD ENOUGH FOR GOD? WELL, ***SCREW HIM*** THEN!
WOW. THANKS, LEV.
YOU KNOW WHAT? YOU'RE RIGHT!
DESPITE THAT BLASPHEMOUS PART.
YOU'RE MY BEST FRIEND AND THERE ISN'T ANYONE I'D RATHER FACE HELL WITH!
W-- WHADDYA MEAN, HELL?
WELL, YEAH. IF WE'RE NOT GOING TO ***HEAVEN***--
BRAM?
*BRAM CARLSON?!*

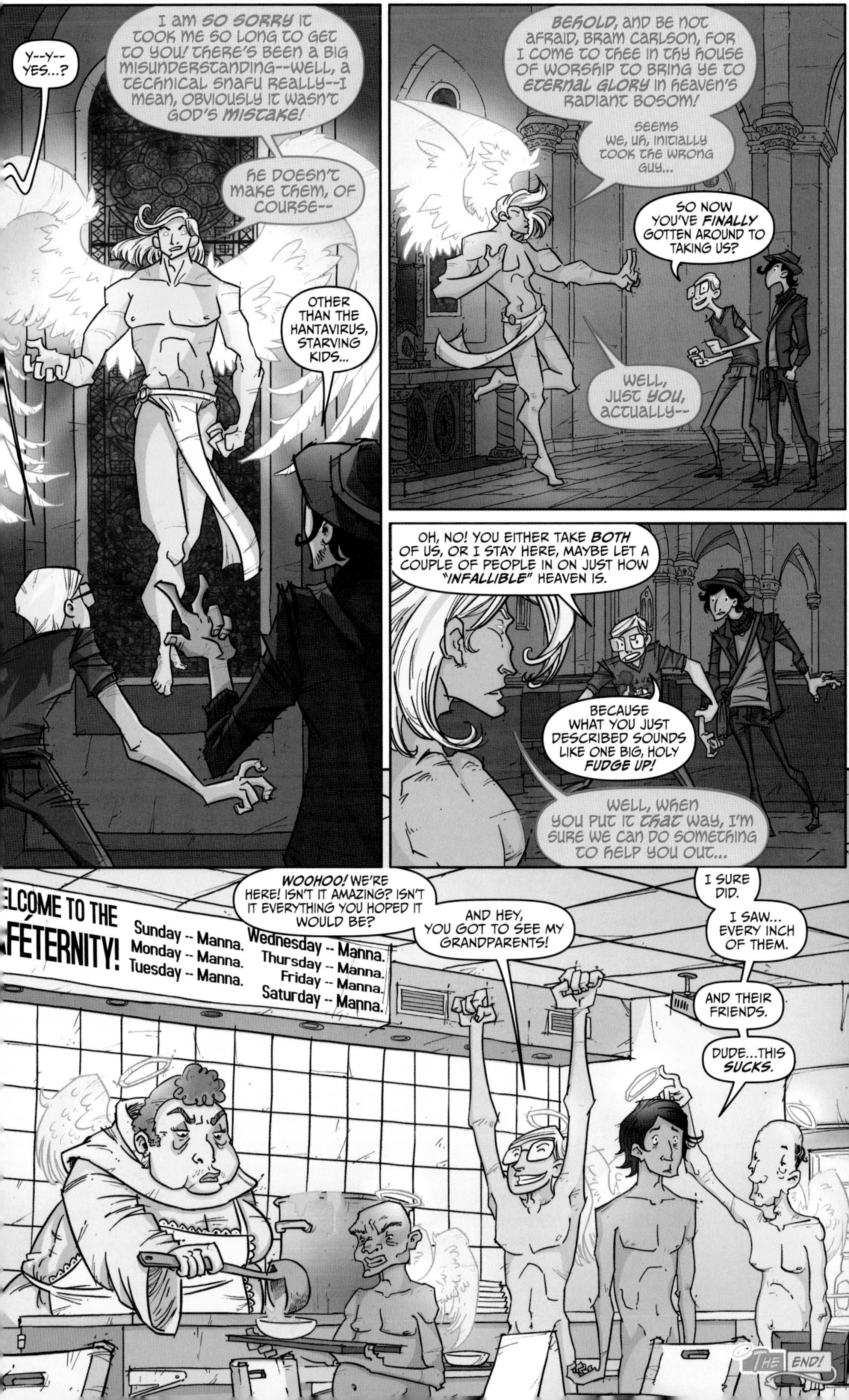
Y--Y--YES...?
I am SO SORRY it took me so long to get to you! There's been a big misunderstanding--well, a technical snafu really--I mean, obviously it wasn't God's MISTAKE!
He doesn't make them, of course--
OTHER THAN THE HANTAVIRUS, STARVING KIDS...
BEHOLD, and be not afraid, Bram Carlson, for I come to thee in thy house of worship to bring ye to ETERNAL GLORY in Heaven's Radiant Bosom!
Seems we, uh, initially took the wrong guy...
SO NOW YOU'VE FINALLY GOTTEN AROUND TO TAKING US?
Well, just YOU, actually--
OH, NO! YOU EITHER TAKE BOTH OF US, OR I STAY HERE, MAYBE LET A COUPLE OF PEOPLE IN ON JUST HOW "INFALLIBLE" HEAVEN IS.
BECAUSE WHAT YOU JUST DESCRIBED SOUNDS LIKE ONE BIG, HOLY FUDGE UP!
Well, when you put it THAT way, I'm sure we can do something to help you out...
ELCOME TO THE
FÉTERNITY!
Sunday -- Manna.
Monday -- Manna.
Tuesday -- Manna.
Wednesday -- Manna.
Thursday -- Manna.
Friday -- Manna.
Saturday -- Manna.
WOOHOO! WE'RE HERE! ISN'T IT AMAZING? ISN'T IT EVERYTHING YOU HOPED IT WOULD BE?
AND HEY, YOU GOT TO SEE MY GRANDPARENTS!
I SURE DID.
I SAW... EVERY INCH OF THEM.
AND THEIR FRIENDS.
DUDE...THIS SUCKS.
THE END!

# FROM THE PAGES OF REM'S DEVELOPMENT SKETCHBOOK

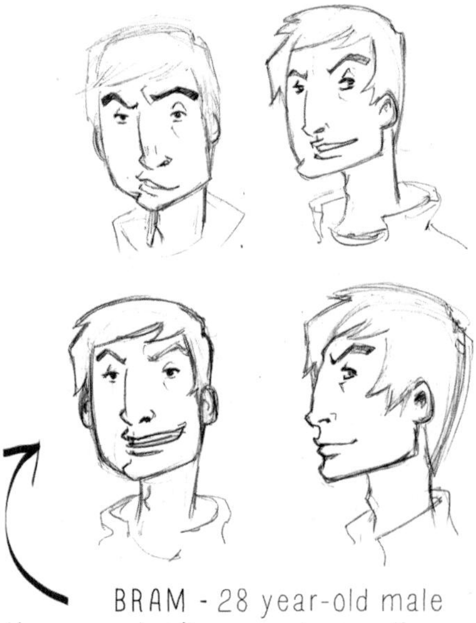

BRAM - 28 year-old male
Self-assured, often condescending guy who's just barely handsome & charming enough to get away with it. A slightly harder-edged style. Medium build, circa 180cm.

BEN - 27 year-old male
Kind, somewhat vulnerable and trusting g who still has a decent bullshit detector. H has a clean-cut, somewhat conservative style, certainly when he teaches. Thinner and a little shorter than Bram, circa 175cm.

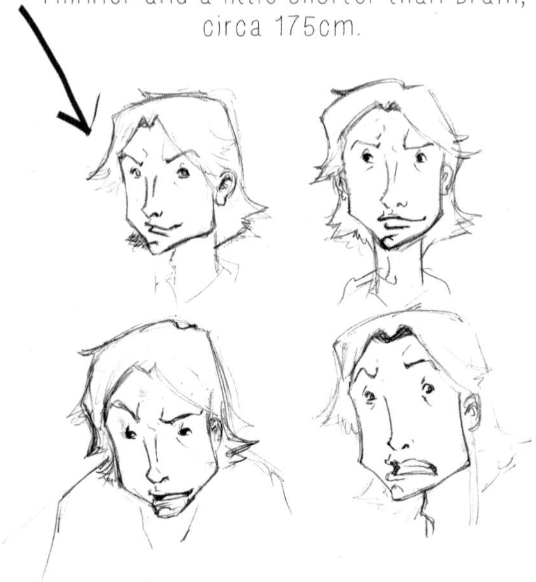

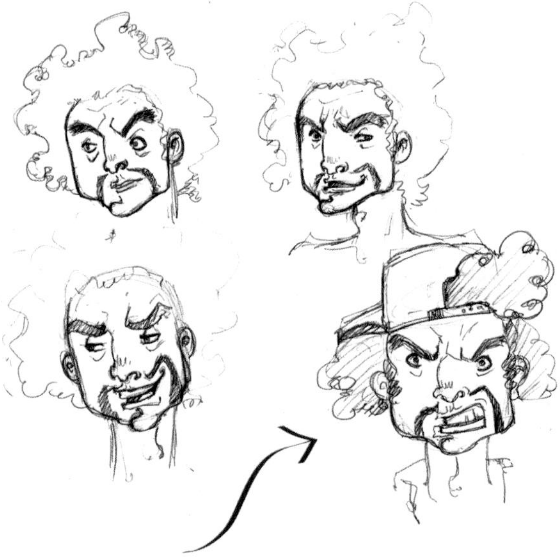

TIPUL - 28 year-old male
Tall & gangly odd-ball who always looks like he's up to something. He's a video game junkie who shops at military surplus stores. Maybe has a beard?
Wiry muscle, circa 186cm.

LAURA - 29 year-old female
Attractive, tough, Jewish woman, she constantly looks like she sees through yo bullshit. She keeps herself sharp & professional at work, but has a much mo laid-back & cute style when off the clock. feel like maybe she's taller than Ben (with whom she's going to get romantically involved).

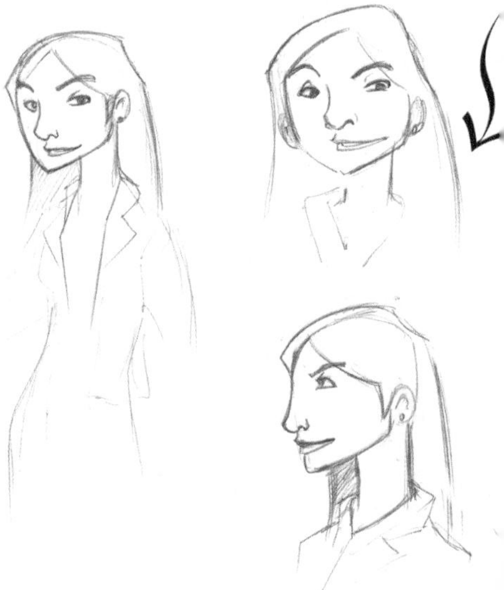

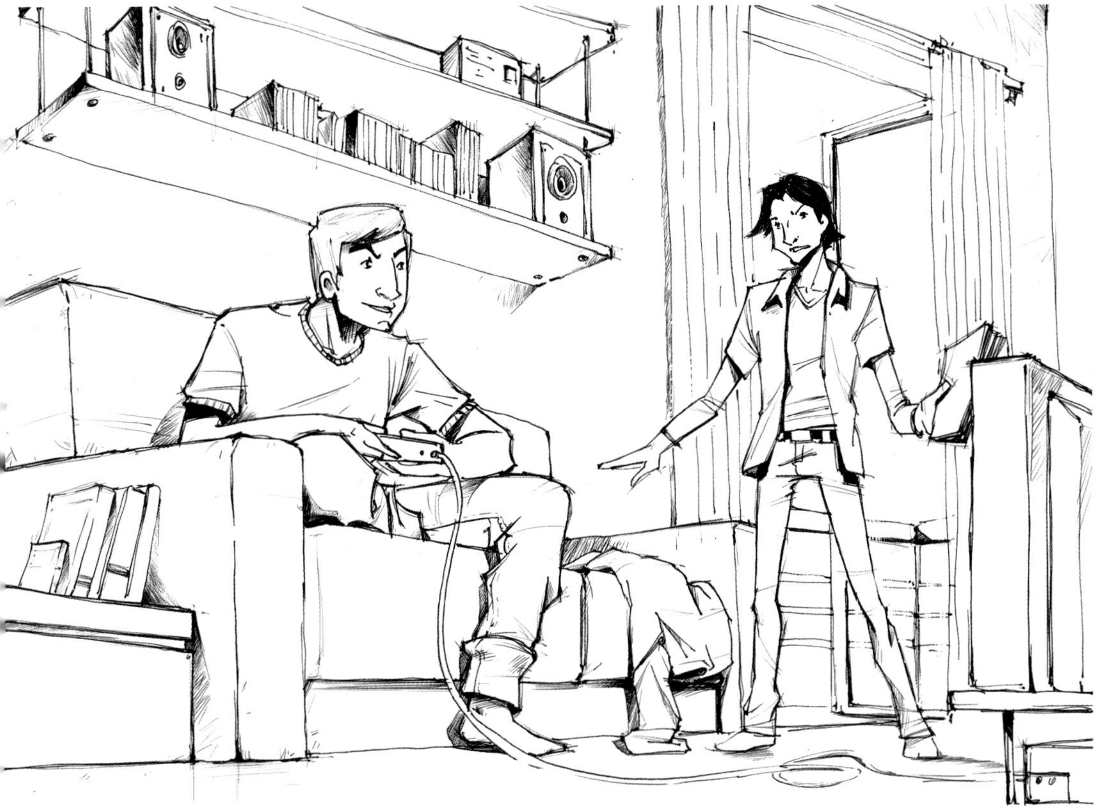

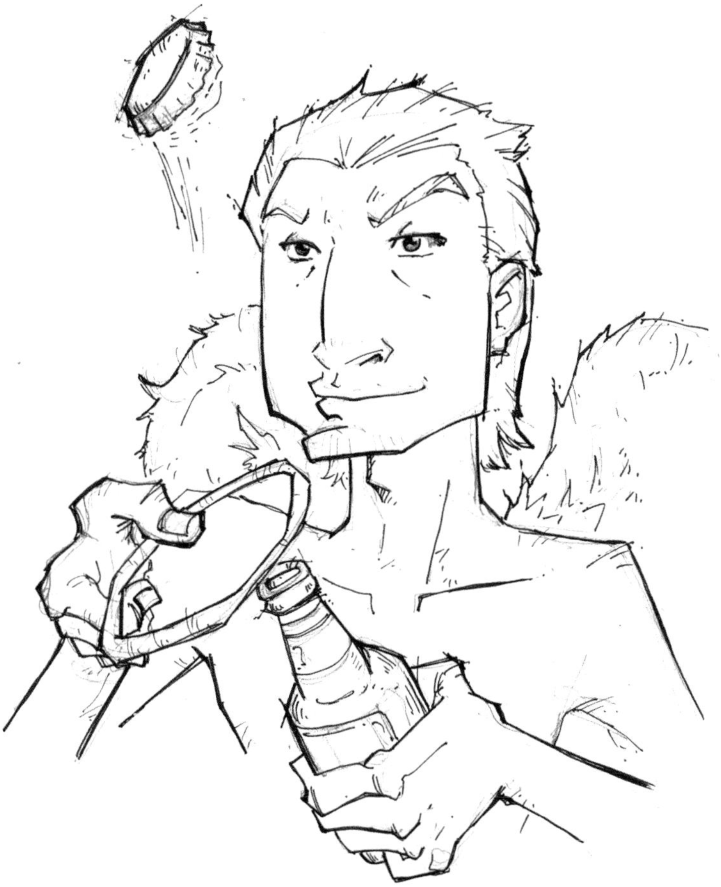

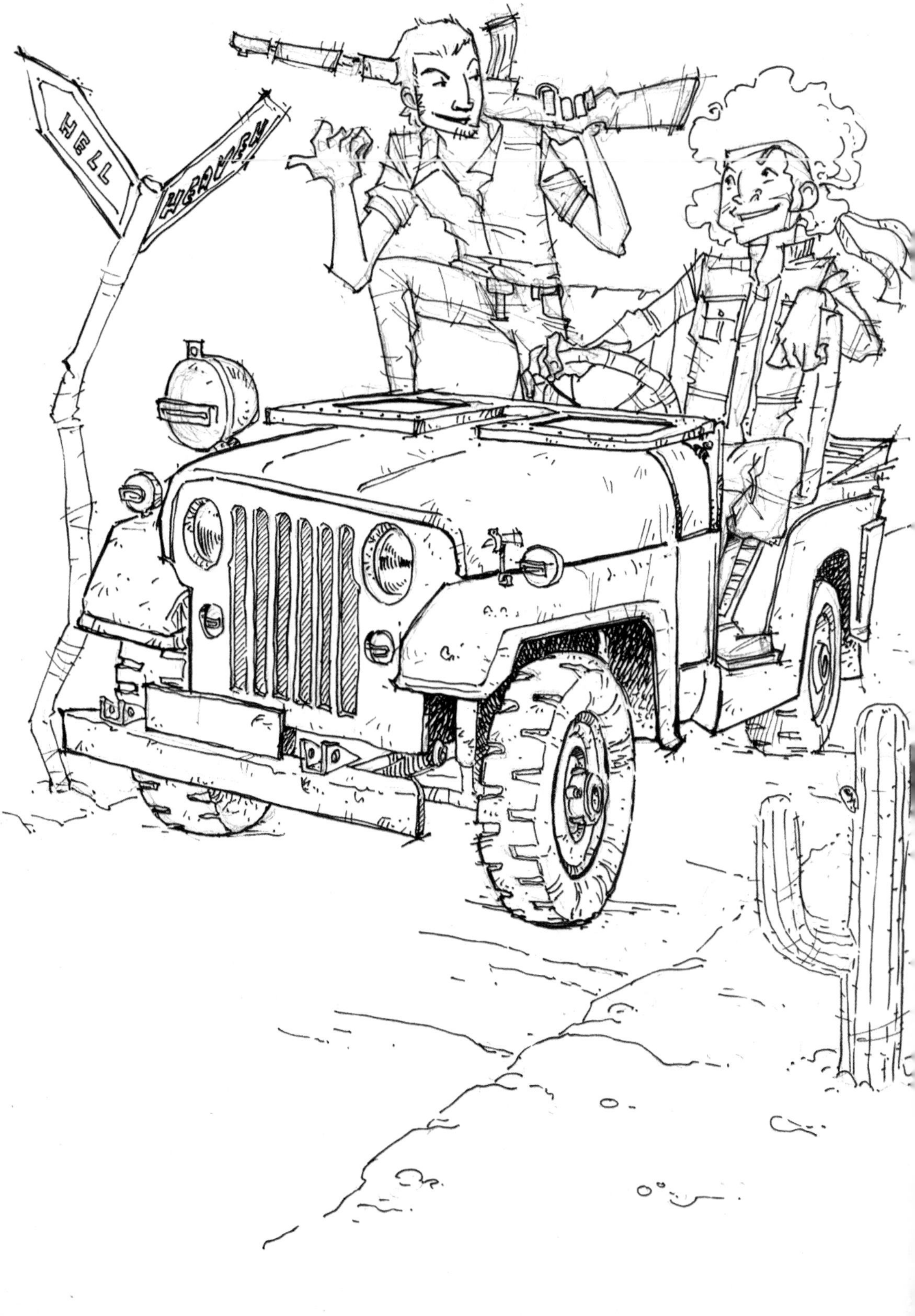
HELL